Another South

Experimental Writing in the South

Edited by Bill Lavender

Introduction by Hank Lazer

THE UNIVERSITY OF ALABAMA PRESS   TUSCALOOSA AND LONDON

Cover and interior design by Bill Lavender
Typefaces: Gill Sans, Universe

∞

The paper on which this book is printed meets the minimum
requirements of American National Standard for Information
Science–Permanence of Paper for Printed Library Materials,
ANSI Z39.48-1984.

Library of Congress Cataloging-in-Publication Data

1003245560

Another South: experimental writing in the South / edited by Bill
Lavender ; introduction by Hank Lazer.
    p. cm.— (Modern and contemporary poetics)
    ISBN 0-8173-1240-4 (cloth : alk. paper) — ISBN 0-8173-1241-2
(pbk. : alk. paper)
    1. Experimental poetry, American—Southern States. 2. Ameri-
can poetry—Southern States. 3. Southern States—Poetry.
I. Lavender, Bill, 1951- . II. Series.
PS551.A56 2003
811'.608011'0975—dc21

2003009188

British Library Cataloguing-in-Publication Data available

Contents

Acknowledgments

Some of the poets and poems collected in this anthology also appeared in *New Orleans Review, The Other South: Experimental Writing in the South* 21, no. 2 (Summer 1995), and *New Orleans Review, An Other South: Experimental Writing in the South, Part II* 25, nos. 1 and 2 (Spring 1999). Special thanks to *New Orleans Review* editor Ralph Adamo, and Loyola University for their early support of this project.

Ralph Adamo: "Roches Moutonnees" appeared in *The Quarterly*, and "New Orleans" in *Southern Review*.
Sandy Baldwin: *The Little Magazine* published "[basic system code]" and "Heralds of the Hurricane," in versions different from those below.
Jake Berry: The exerpt from *Brambu Drezi, Book III* appeared in *Lost And Found Times*.
Joel Dailey: Some of the poems included here have appeared in *Fell Swoop, Prosodia, Exquisite Corpse, Hangman,* and *Fuck!*
Skip Fox: "sic transit gloria mundi" and "Economics of Metonymy: sic transit" appeared in *Exquisite Corpse* 8.
Honoree Fanonne Jeffers: "Big Mama Thornton," "Eyes of Soon Children," "Ellen Craft," "i am your courtier," "Ezekiel Saw de Wheel" from *The Gospel of Barbecue* (Wick Poetry Series/Kent State University Press, 2000). "You Don't Know What Love Is," "Five Note Range of Sorrow," *Massachusetts Review* (Summer 2000). "Eatonton Tableaux," *Obsidian III* (Summer 2000).
Joy Lahey: "White Soil," "Cattails Along Red River," and "Cotton and Gladiolas" were published in *Mesechabe* and then in *Abandoned Premises,* a chapbook from Lavender Ink, 1999. "Habitat Photo," "Buckles," appeared in *New Orleans Review*.
Bill Lavender: *pentacl* was published in chapbook form by *Fell Swoop*. "A Note to Skip" appeared in *New Delta Review*.
Hank Lazer: "Days 28" appeared in *Days* (New Orleans: Lavender Ink, 2002).
Dana Lisa Lustig: "plane song:" was published in *108:98*.
Camille Martin: "*from* no truck" appeared in *perspektive*, "solfége parasite" in *poethia*, "to abcs and from rimbaud" in *baddog*.
Jerry McGuire: "The Cages" appeared in *Prosodia 8* and "Gongula" in *Swift Kick 2*.
Thomas Meyer: "Uranium Ore" appeared in *Tight No One* (December 2001), Whit Griffin and Andrew Hughes, eds., Bennington, VT.
Mark Prejsnar: "Assuage Bane" appeared in *Mirage #41 Period(ical)*.
Randy Prunty: "Trigger D'evolution" appeared in *108*.
David Thomas Roberts: The piece beginning "Zinc-jangled pencil of groves" first appeared in *Experimental Press*. A version of "Rodeo" in unillustrated verse form first appeared in *The Experioddicist*.
James Sanders: "Poem with Referees" appeared in *108*.
Lorenzo Thomas: "Flash Point" and "Magnetic Charms" first appeared in *Combo* (Fall 1999); "Dangerous Doubts" appeared in *Gulf Coast: A Journal of Literature and Fine Arts* (Summer 1994); "Foolish Treasures" and "Back in the Day" appeared in *Kente Cloth: African American Voices in Texas* (1995); "An Even-Tempered Girl Holds Her Breath" was originally published in *Lungfull! Magazine* (1998); and "Blues Variations" originally appeared in *New Orleans Review* (Spring 1999)
Stephanie Williams: "A Drunkard Promise" was previously published in *Mungo vs. Ranger 1* (Spring 1999).
Andy Young: "Vodou Headwashing Ceremony" appeared in *Exquisite Corpse;* "In Anguish, the Heart Finally Prays" in *New Orleans Review;* and "Foxfire" and "Ghost of Me" in *Mine* (Lavender Ink, 2000).
Seth Young: Some of the poems from *river we are caried by* appeared in *108* and *Facture*.

Editor's Introduction

This anthology is a collection of experimental poets in the South. It is not intended to represent a new "Southern Lit." It has not been my goal to define a new genre, style, or movement, and I make no claim for any sort of dominance by any of the styles and genres included. I only want to claim that the work represented here *is* happening, a simple fact that would be hard to deduce from reading the standard southern publications. For too long the South has been considered, even by some fairly literate folk, to be an experimentalist's backwater, a remote bayou off the beaten freeway, inhabited only by stories hinting at incest and saturated with rhetoric, blank verse poems in dialectal tribute to Mark Twain, or symbol-laden narratives that inevitably decode to Flannery O'Connor's peacocks. Against these caricatures we offer Camille Martin "learning to talk over and over" in lyric chants that tear at the semantic fabric of language, or)ohn Lowther's transcribed multi-media performance, which examines a nostalgic reminiscence under a psycho-linguistic microscope. I hope that with this publication we can begin to map a new southern landscape, one that, far from being bound to the past, is ripe for experimentation and home to a burgeoning avant-garde.

By "experimental" I mean poetry that pushes at a boundary, that attempts to cover new ground, that transgresses stylistically, semantically, socially, or politically—the sort of writing that Bob Grumman has referred to as "burstnorm" or "experioddica." Joel Dailey's vicious satire of pop culture's inanities and (far worse, as he considers them equal) poetry's profundities, isn't containable in any of the traditional academic corrals. Sandy Baldwin's and Alex Rawls's digitally assisted narratives call into question the identity of the author and the whole concept of "writing." Christy Sheffield Sanford's typographically enhanced historical narrative sympathetically examines narrative itself but with enough severity to make us wonder what the limits of history and narration might be. David Thomas Roberts's graphic statements violate the generic boundaries among poetry, painting, and music. Bob Grumman's work incorporates mathematical notation, graphic images, and written words into a new, extra-linguistic language. Marla Jernigan's egoless lyrics lead us to wonder if emotions themselves might have a linguistic basis. The experiment may be aimed at the current episteme, the poetic or political establishment, or even at the concept of experimentation.

It may be that "experimental" means something different in the South than in the rest of the USA (not to mention the world), because the South has its unique sets of boundaries, stereotypes, and editorial proscriptions, and one of these boundaries might be the notion of regionalism itself. Traditionally, the South is a different sort of region than, say, California; one doesn't become "Southern" just by moving here but must in fact have been born here, with family roots stretching back generations. One must also, so the stereotype runs, have been raised on a farm. No doubt the notion of the South as a predominantly rural region was always formed more of prejudice than fact, but it is at best a century or more out-of-date. The South today has more in common with California than it does with the plantations of Mitchell's *Gone With the Wind* or Faulkner's Yoknapatawpha County. Most of the writers included here live in cities: New Orleans, Atlanta, Baton Rouge, Tuscaloosa,

Jackson, Charlottesville, Gainesville. The South today is centered around its urban hubs, with a fluid and transient population, separated from family and the past by economic exigencies, like the rest of the country.

So I chose to invite only writers *currently living in the South.* As this work has evolved, through two special issues of *New Orleans Review* over the past six years, I have become increasingly fascinated with what is happening now in the South in poetry, and more and more convinced that if there is something that ought to be called "southern writing" it ought to be exactly that. According to the standard "academic" definitions of Southern Lit., the South isn't a place, but a genre.[1] Instead of physical location the emphasis has been on heritage, and this emphasis, seen as an editorial rule and as an element of the writing itself, has been the most profound way the mythic southern identity has been preserved. In contrast to the myth, many of the writers included here, like Skip Fox, Hank Lazer, or Alex Rawls, were born and raised outside the South; some, like Jake Berry, Camille Martin, Ralph Adamo, and I, have lived here all our lives; some, like Brett Evans, were born here, moved away, and moved back. If there is such a thing as southern writing, beyond the proscriptive definitions and caricatures, it is the writing that is emerging from the discourse among these, of various heritage, living here and now.

This is not to say that history and heritage are not to be found among the writings included here. The past and its effect on the present are directly treated in work by Honorée Fanonne Jeffers, Kalamu ya Salaam, Andy Young, Stephanie Williams, and others. One can also see, in these and further in poets as diverse as Jake Berry, Mark Prejsnar, Jim Leftwich, and A. di Michele, a strong current of an oracular mode. In their work we find history not as literary tradition but as the active carrying-forward of a physical trace, the harmonies and rhythms of blues and hymnody driving the sonic patterns of the language, and a tendency toward narrative, parable, and soothsay infusing the content. These works delve into a history not exclusively southern but as diverse as the many genealogies that are evidenced in the South today.

In recent years we have seen an increasing level of organization among the communities of experimental poets in southern cities, centered around a number of

---

[1] Take, for example, this quote from Andrew Hudgins ("Alabama Breakdown," *New England Review* 20, no. 1 [Winter 1999]: 175) which places the generic definition firmly within an academic context (and further reveals the editorial prescription working at a subliminal level):

> I was invited to read my poems at a brown-bag lunch at the Center for the Study of Southern Culture. . . . But not until I was actually sitting before this talkative gathering did it sink in that these people had come to the Center for the Study of Southern Culture to see SOUTHERN CULTURE, and for the next thirty minutes I'd be exhibit A. . . . I raced through the characteristics I'd memorized ten years before in a Southern Lit. class: a sense of the living presence of the past; love of landscape and the natural world; cruel humor; and a preoccupation with religion, family, violence, race, and the grotesque. I was bemused to discover that I and my writing possessed every item on my memorized list. Not most of them. All of them. I was astonished and perplexed.

journals, small presses, bookstores, and literary organizations. In New Orleans, Joel Dailey's venerable magazine *Fell Swoop*, now publishing its sixtieth issue, may be the oldest running avant-garde journal in the South. It has been joined in recent years by magazines like *Brown Box*, edited by Paul e. Williams and Jamey Jones of Pensacola, Florida; *H_NGM_N*, edited by Nate Pritts in Lafayette, Louisiana; and *108*, edited by)ohn Lowther, and *Misc. Proj.*, edited by Mark Prejsnar, both of Atlanta. A number of small presses, too, have emerged to publish book and chapbook length works. In New Orleans, my own Lavender Ink specializes primarily in New Orleans poets, as does John Travis' Portals Press, and Kalamu ya Salaam's Runagate Press.)ohn Lowther edits *3rdness* from Atlanta. The efforts of poets and presses have received faithful support from bookstores like Maple Street Books in New Orleans, owned by Rhoda Faust, and Subterranean Books in Pensacola, owned by Paul e. Williams, which regularly sponsor readings and workshops. In New Orleans the Maple Leaf Bar reading series, instituted by Everette Maddox and now managed by Nancy Harris, is now in its third decade.

Several of the poets in this collection are members of the Atlanta Poetry Group, an organization that has sponsored numerous readings, happenings, improvisations, and shows over past five years. In New Orleans Camille Martin has founded Lit City, a nonprofit organization that sponsors readings and other events by poets of national stature, and has raised the funding to bring to New Orleans such poets as Ivan Argüelles, Lee Ann Brown, Elizabeth Treadwell, Christy Sheffield Sanford, Hank Lazer, Charles Alexander, Peter Gizzi, Barret Watten, Carla Harryman, Loss Pequeño Glazier, Kristin Prevallet, Sheila E. Murphy, and Charles Bernstein. Also in New Orleans, Dave Brinks has founded the innovative New Orleans School for the Imagination, an underground forum that sponsors classes in writing, arts, Buddhism, and other disciplines as well as sponsoring readings and other events.

With such evidence of a level of activity among southern poety communities, it seems almost unbelievable that this could be the first anthology devoted to a redefinition of southern writing, and yet, to the best of my knowledge, it is. I hope that, besides giving some previously unpublished poets the national exposure they deserve, this collection proves to be only the first step in correcting the outworn and clichéd views of the South perpetuated in academic misdefinitions and that it paves the way for other anthologies and single-author works.

I wish to express my gratitude to The University of Alabama Press, as well to the Modern and Contemporary Poetics series editors Hank Lazer and Charles Bernstein, for their support and encouragement. I would also like to thank Ralph Adamo, former editor of the *New Orleans Review,* for the first editorial support of the idea and then having the courage to follow it through; Hank Lazer, for continuous support, and for the excellent essay that introduces this volume; and Nancy Dixon, for putting up with me throughout the process.

Bill Lavender, New Orleans, January 2002

Hank Lazer

Poetry Scouting Mission:
At the Intersection of Southern and Experimental

You might consider thinking of *Another South: Experimental Writing in the South* as a testing ground, presenting the complex, multifaceted experimentation in poetry in one particular part of the country. This anthology, then, becomes a means of exploring the relationship between "regional" and "experimental," a means of inquiring into and exhibiting the plausible relations of these two terms at a time when both terms are greeted with significant degrees of skepticism. Each term contains *within* it significant differences, including race, ethnicity, religion, class, gender, and even duration of residence in the region, all leading toward different experiences and expressions of "the South." Within the experimental, the anthology contains a wide range of relations to voice, to cross-genre activity, to the visual, to the surreal, to states of possession, and a wide range of expressions of musical affinities (particularly with the blues and jazz).

Think of this anthology as an exploration of the meaning and nature of place at a time in cultural and literary history when we experience the contradictory impulses of a digitally accelerated movement toward globalism simultaneously with a renewed emphasis on the highly particularized and intensely localized circumstances of poetic expression. As Thomas Meyer's statement in the Contributors section of this book reminds us, the poem itself constitutes a place—and perhaps a place that is put in place to reflect and embody the multiple nature of place itself: "Poetry celebrates not only presence but the multiplicity of presence and the infinite possibilities of *there*. The poem has the power of location, it is a place—an actual (not metaphorical) spatial event of language that begins in the mouth and lungs and moves outward into time, the mind, the body" (271). Each and every poem is (and makes) a place; each poem, as in Robert Duncan's "Often I am Permitted to Return to a Meadow," is "a made place," a specific incarnation, but also a reincarnation and the marking of a return to a place "near to the heart, / an eternal pasture folded in all thought."[1]

But what we have here, in this new anthology, is a series of such places. The series constitutes an inquiry. Here, we might learn whether "experimental" means something different "here" (in the South) than elsewhere. We might also discover the particular meaning(s) of experimental *here*.

Whatever we find here, it is not and will not be singular. As Bill Lavender notes in his Introduction, this anthology does not constitute a monolithic replacement version for "Southern Lit." Nor is *Another South* a stopping point nor a culmination of a process—this anthology deliberately exists in motion. The anthology is a gathering place and a work-in-progress. It is the third attempt at such an iteration—the earlier versions being the *New Orleans Review, The Other South: Experimental Writing in the South* 21, no. 2 (Summer 1995): 37–78 (19 poets); and the *New Orleans Review, An Other South: Experimental Writing in the South, Part II* 25, nos. 1 and 2 (Spring 1999): 8–150 (44 poets)—and it does not propose to be a newly hegemonic,

---

[1] Robert Duncan, *The Opening of the Field* (New York: Grove, 1960; reprint, New York: New Directions, 1973), 7.

singularly axiomatic movement. *Another South* represents a moment (or an extended decade-as-moment) and a place ("the South") as a time and place that has been and *is happening.* Indeed, many of the poets in the anthology make explicit this sense of time, place, and poem in motion. Sandy Baldwin thinks of the "Poem as Zip Gun *or* Graphic Acceleration Projector" and claims that "in the beginning there is kinetics, speed, moving structures" (261–62). John Lowther reminds us that "poetry is not a thing. . . . poetry is a thing that happens is happening" (119). His own talk-poem-improvisation "is a sort of talk investigation a poetry scouting mission" (120), as is the entire anthology (though "talk" and "voice" are by no means the exclusive or even dominant modes of expression).[2] The poetry in motion in this anthology is deliberately on edge, both locating that edge and moving away from it. As Lowther notes, "that there is an edge beyond what is fixed that makes it interesting that gives you something to work with" (127). One such edge, raised explicitly by Mark Prejsnar, is the page itself, with many of the poets in this anthology exploring ways—through performance, multimedia, the intermixing of various genres and arts—to move poetry off the page.

Thus we encounter a regional poetry insistent upon a contemporary instability of location. At times, as in Holley Blackwell's writing, we find a sense of place drawn toward "the event of complete non-boundedness" (20). Or, as Jerry McGuire summarizes, "Things not only change, they proliferate. Thus if they get more confusing they also project an ever-increasing range of possibilities, and any artist who pegs him/herself to a 'school' or 'movement' has missed the point, or a point. [William Carlos] Williams wrote about 'what is found there,' but it's missed more than found, because it isn't resident but transient" (271). McGuire affirms, as do many of the poets in *Another South*, "the buzz of the aggregate, whether considered technically, aesthetically, psychologically, sociologically, anthropologically, or politically" (271). What McGuire points toward is perhaps an emerging American norm of hybridity or creolization—which may, in part, explain how and why New Orleans, long a site of colliding and colluding cultures and ethnicities, is such an important place in the emerging poetries of *Another South*.[3]

[2] Throughout *Another South*, many of the poems do indeed emphasize "voice" (or "voices") as the basis of composition. However, there are also numerous examples—especially the work of Bob Grumman and David Thomas Roberts—that rely upon visual elements much more than voice. Overall, though, voice *is* a key constituent of this poetry—and constitutes an issue worthy of additional examination. Susan Schultz, in her very helpful comments on this anthology and this essay, notes, "these writers are not writing in regional dialects ("local color"), but yet, voice is crucial. . . . There's a hell of a lot of *talking* and sound-based poetry here, but in what ways is this talk, this sound, different from that of the New York School, say, which is also terribly voice-based?" (unpublished reader's report). As a preliminary response, I'd suggest that the writing in this anthology is often voice-based, but unlike much the New York School poetry, it is not so insistently a voicing of urban anecdotes, nor is it a representation of an urban pace of life. Also, the specific sounds—the elongated vowel sounds, for example—are regionally specific, as is the slang or vernacular. Whereas much of the writing in *Another South* has absorbed the fragmentation and syntactic investigativeness of Language writing, this writing has not, for the most part, experienced a phase of deep suspicion or hostility toward the resources of "voice."

[3] Thus *Another South* may prove helpful in describing other poetries as well and their particular relationships to region/place, especially as this anthology demonstrates a newly emerging creolization, but also as the anthology demonstrates the simultaneous impulses toward a global culture *and* a renewed emphasis on the particulars of the local.

Possession constitutes one hybrid site-practice that recurs in *Another South*. As Jake Berry suggests, "Poetry is largely the art of possession, how to collaborate with a possessing other. The poem is the work of fluctuating self and other, an equal summons that simultaneously invokes and is the manifestation of that invocation" (262). Many of the poets in *Another South*—African American and white—report a poetry that records the voice and words of another, ranging from a glossolalia ("classical" talking in tongues), to the infusion and taking over of a music (from blues to jazz to hymns and prayers), to a kind of dream-world possession, to modes of possession with specifically literary antecedents (such as automatic writing, surrealist writing, and various procedural and chance-determined writing). Andy di Michele's succinct phrase captures a recurring spiritual sense of this experience: "we gawk thru gnosis and ghost manna" (159). In many of these poems, vodou practice constitutes an underpinning and a lens of ritualized experience. Certainly, vodou is one critical base for Jake Berry's multi-book epic *Brambu Drezi*. It is also at the heart of Andy Young's "Vodou Headwashing Ceremony," with its recurring reminder ": *Any one could be possessed*" and its invocation "You could be Legba, god of crossroads, / collecting broken trinkets, standing on tracks, / arms spread in embrace of coming light" (248).

Perhaps, then, a distinctive feature of the inquiry into place/South and praxis/experimental of *Another South* is this very openness to spiritual experience as a legitimate basis of the poem. Whereas most other contemporary American experimental poetries—particularly first generation Language writing—bear a highly skeptical relationship to "spirit,"[4] Andy Young's expression more typifies the attitudes of experimental poets of this other South:

> If you fear the taking over
> let us stop it simply holler
> we can make it go away, but
> you should know that we invite it
> sprinkle cornmeal circles, fires,
> build altars of skeletal offerings,
> beseech them to descend. *Possess us.*
> (249)

One could argue that while the more conventional, tradition modes of (white) southern Christian worship and ritual are not heavily represented in the poetry of *Another South*, the South's peculiar emphasis on religious experience *does* provide the underpinning for a broad range of spiritual affirmations, invocations, and affinities, from vodou to African rituals, from mystical Jewish practices (including Kabbalistic and Gnostic sources) to the call and response of the African American churches, from Egyptian to early Greek sources. What does persist is a deeply felt sense of the validity of such experiences—an experience of possession that does not feel at odds with experimental poetic practice. Andy Young thinks of this voice of the other as "the italic voice," noting that "The italic voice is bigger than me. It feels other. I try to tune into it and hear what it says so that I may represent it accurately. It is the voice of the night, the voice of my echo. . . . This voice feels like a whisper whooshing through my blood. It compels me to seek the music of words to contain it" (276).

---

[4] For a detailed discussion of this complex relationship to a poetry of "spirit," see my essay "Returns: Innovative Poetry and Questions of 'Spirit,' " *Facture* 2 (2001): 125-152.

Perhaps sound—or in some poetries, "voice" or "music"—serves as the location for possession or for intersection with an other, as the mouthing (and thus myth-ing) of cultures connecting, what Skip Fox calls "echolalia of worlds within words" (50). At times, that site—and here we approach again Thomas Meyer's notion of the poem as place (and as representation of the complex, physical specificity of place)—is developed at the level of the individual word, as in Brett Evans's phrase "Choctaw octane canoe" (36) or his direction "ghosts of the taken up oaks \ pronounce slowly" (38). There may be such a thing as a "southern" sound; the slowly drawled extended savored vowels—that caricature—may even factor into the particular music that we hear (and write) here. But this anthology is equally a sounding of rapidly assembled disparate elements, and this gathering provides sound evidence—as perhaps metonym for the similar relations among cultures—of dialects and languages in collision and in the process of making new hybrid formations. Such a collision is best seen and heard in the remarkable poetry of Jessica Freeman, especially in "Bayou Arabic Argot":

> Aid el Kebir hajj via
> Gide's *Journal des Faux-Monnayeurs*
> leave luggage follow sartorial temper's
> table for two play Adultery toe jammy tootsie
> to shoulder eau de toilette ride out tornadic
> heat whisper honey cheri bientot
> Grease palm dance make do fais do do
> mouth pigeon Italian
> che ora parte l'ultimo autobus? mi sono
> slogato la caviglia
> to pucker up kiss tarmac by pass grief
> peel Highway 10 clean through Lacassine
> leave luggage dromedary scorpion dillo umber
> behind artesian well hell
> ease forward read *Lost & Found Times*
> Battle-cry fortify wax water ski launder
> drawers ask at desk front
> ?any messages for me   ?cig lighter
> innermost feelings kiss tarmac goodby   Adieu
>   (54)

As Joy Lahey remarks (in a different context), "undertows are elsewhere" (93), and one principal set of undertows occurs in following the surprising pull of particular sounds playing with and off of each other.

Though external perceptions of the South—especially those perpetuated in the mainstream media but also perpetuated in the more popular and continuing modes of mainstream Southern Literature—would ask us to think of *every* element of southern life as polarized in black and white, the complex version of "the South" that is carried in the poems of *Another South* points more toward increasing creolization and hybridity—a density of mixing and a speed of not so much assimilation or "melting pot" as a speed of mutual listening and incorporation. Even so, it makes great sense to think about different meanings of the use of the blues or the uses of jazz by white and African American poets, as well as the quite different meanings of "my people."   Honorée Jeffers writes that "My Savior's blood is the Word is my people's / face turned up to blues" (78), and she affirms her position as "a blues poet" whose work is "bound not to just the notion of the blues itself but also the syncretic connections of the blues to region, race, gender, and spirituality" (266). Lorenzo Thomas makes a similar claim:"As a poet, I am heir to several traditions, not the least of which is the Blues—a form that is immediate and timeless, built upon a standardized stanza that remains capable of infinite personalized variation" (275).

For Kalamu ya Salaam, music and sound *are* where and how and by grace of which we find and celebrate our location:"humble in the light may i never forget the sounds from which i am sprung, may i always remember to give thanx through song" (195). He urges us to "worship sound" (195), explaining that

> our music is more than model
> well coordinated sounds are inspiration
>
> are literally
> indispensable breath
>
> the taking in of the material world
> the exhaling of the spirit self
>
> into the atmosphere of this bitter earth
> sweetened only by the honey of our song
>   (197)

Salaam's explanation of the centrality of music—as identity, as an essential human feature, as a sacramental site, as the place for knowing and being in participation with spirit—also brings together several issues and claims present throughout *Another South*, particularly the emphasis on a fused sense of music and movement:

> people have asked me why am i such a fanatic about the music, i in turn
> wonder why they are not, & if not music, what? dance? carvings? cooking?
> what? anything we do, if it is done well will have the music in it, be
> influenced by the music because music is literally organized movement & the
> very definition of being alive is to be able to self generate motion, since
> the beginning of time, life has been nothing more than a measurement of
> movement, how well, the vibrations we leave in our wake, how we sound doing
> whatever we do, how the motion of our coming through the slaughter affects
> all whom we touch & we got this essentialness from the universe itself
>   (197)

Finally, one other strand that participates in creating the complexly woven rope of *Another South* is a recurrent sense of the marginality of the activity—of a vigorously experimental southern poetry. But it is a celebratory marginality based on an affirmation of the unalienated nature of the labor and of the deliberately useless nature of the work. The politics of such a liberatory poetic praxis is best expressed by Jim Leftwich, who asks, "What happens if one desires to practice useless skills, skills that are not useful to maintaining the structure of the culture?" (269). Or, when expressed as a statement and a definition rather than a question: "We should think of this usefulness as meaning only one thing: useful means useful to the dominant culture, always and only" (269). The work of *Another South* is, from such a perspective, deliberately an undermining, subversive labor. Leftwich, interestingly, links such "uselessness" to the work of the autodidact: "This autodidact will learn to do things that others have no desire to do, that others are not allowed to do, that others are not able to think of doing" (269). Therein lies some of the advantage for the experimental poet writing in the South—perhaps a compensation for the inevitable sense of isolation and marginality, a compensating opportunity (out of the spotlight—however small that spotlight may be for experimental poetry in New York or the San Francisco Bay Area, the spotlight does exist, even if only of the wattage of a night-light) to do something from a fresh, unexpected perspective. In this respect, contemporary southern experimental artists have a noteworthy kinship with so-called self-taught or outsider or folk artists (who work mainly in the visual and plastic arts). And thus perhaps collectively, and unknowingly, we—the poets of *Another South*—are together assembling a vast (verbal) Paradise Garden.

*   *   *

Having given a brief overview of some of the key issues at play in *Another South*, let me then backtrack, to return indirectly to *Another South* by means of issues and assertions made initially in the two earlier assemblings in the *New Orleans Review* (and somewhat revised and reconsidered for this new anthology). In 1994 in my first effort to describe and explore this writing, I wondered whether "regionalism" itself was an outmoded category, particularly when considered in conjunction with an innovative poetic practice. With an increasingly globalized commercial culture and with the increased frequency of electronically transmitted correspondence (and texts), perhaps "regionalism" itself has become a quaint term, one that lost a great deal of its coherence and force as one century stumbled to a close and the next one began. What is the current plausibility of a regional terminology? And what are we to make of the unusual persistence and credibility of the term "Southern Literature"?

First, let me begin with my conspiracy theory—a tinge of paranoia that may in fact mark me as "southern." In 1994, I asked a series of questions: Is the phenomenon of Southern Literature a manufactured regionalist literary ghetto? Who made it, who perpetuates it, and what relationship does it possibly have to the current South? Who would confine our literature to kudzu, azaleas, dusty roads, humid afternoons, the air pungent with the scent of magnolia, an instance or two of gratuitous violence, the inspiring heroism and endurance of the downtrodden, the peculiar epiphanies and primitive blunders of a fundamentalist practice, and an omnipresent slow-moving muddy river?

The literary south is very much an invention and a projection of New Yorkers, New Englanders, and Westerners—an invention propped up by recurrent media caricatures of southern life. It is a stereotyping of culture with economic implications, hence the capitulation most especially of ("southern") fiction writers who can make money by supporting (and slightly modifying) the caricatures, including the caricatures of the New South, especially so long as a significant and comforting number of the familiar, certified formulae are used along the way.

The confinement of "Southern Lit" remains principally *stylistic* in nature. A narrow range of certified, acceptable "southern" writing defines the nostalgia of the literary strait-jacket that is fitted for us and that southern writers too readily consent to wear. Our task as writers is to be contemporary—that is, to find adequate modes of expressing what consciousness is *now*. In a poem written several years ago, "Well Yes Then," I found myself asking a series of questions: "we are / contemporaneous / with what," "and what constitutes / that contemporaneity," and "yes / con / temporary / & / how / with / what." It is not merely a manner of locating a seemingly contemporary fad in writing. These questions mark the effort of any generation of writers to locate and make manifest the peculiarities of their experience of time. A contemporary manifestation of contemporaneity involves much more than topics, citations, proper names, dates, and events—much more than the brand names and details that litter the fiction of Raymond Carver, John Updike, and Ann Beattie, for example. What are the profound essentials of our current experience of existence? How might we, in a fresh and distinctive mode, embody that experience in our poetry? One might also wonder whether or not there were *regional* aspects to a current experience of consciousness. To what extent do the specifics of place—of landscape, culture, ethnicity, food, music, dialect, history—enter into an experience of contemporaneity? As writers, we must make manifest the feelings, the textures, the nuances, the contradictions, the many simultaneities, the complexities, and the cross-currents of current consciousness and temporality. If there is something particularly *southern* about this current era of southern living, let it be manifest. But such a manifestation will require *invention*. Style and innovation are central to *how* we embody, reflect, and express this contemporaneity.

So that my conspiracy theory of an imposed, invented "southern" literature is not misunderstood as merely coincidental with the arrival of *The X-Files*, let me cite one much older story. My artist/musician friend Wayne Sides (of Florence, Alabama) gave me the following directions for a poem to be included in a TV performance:

> Regarding our performance on Nashville public access TV on December 4th [1998], I am enclosing a word selected from the lyrics to "Dixieland." . . . I am requesting that each performer compose a short poem using this word and the word "dixie." . . . To perform the piece we will gather around the keyboard and I (as Rev. Bama Wayne) will conduct the chorus, calling on each performer to "testify" (i.e., read his/her poem)—culminating in a chorus of Dixieland, performed as a round. Here are your words: *gay* and *dixie*.

Wayne supplied us each with a couple of different versions of *Dixie Land*. Inadvertently and coincidentally, I had been examining the new *Norton Anthology: The Literature of the American South* (to test my hypothesis of stylistic xenophobia in the "official" representations of southern poetry). In the new *Norton Anthology*, I ran across some fascinating information about the southern anthem *Dixie Land*:

> Probably the most familiar and controversial lyric in the southern folk tradition is *Dixie*, composed, ironically, not by a southerner but by Ohio-born Daniel Decatur Emmett (1815–1904), organizer of the Virginia Minstrels, a traveling troupe of white performers who specialized in blackface skits involving singing, dancing, and comedy. . . . The original version of *Dixie*, entitled *Dixie's Land*, was written in 1859 for a performance by Bryant's Minstrel Troupe on Broadway in New York. . . . Endorsing southern myths of the plantation and "the happy darkey," *Dixie's Land* found welcome ears wherever it was sung in the South. At Jefferson Davis's inauguration as president of the Confederate States of America on January 18, 1861, the band struck up *Dixie*. Its march-time rhythm and stirring

chorus turned what had originally been a dance tune into the Confederacy's battle hymn. Eventually, the word *Dixie,* whose origin has yet to be firmly established, became synonymous, at least among white Americans, with the South itself. (*Norton,* 1998, 1108–1109)

Yes, even that nostalgia-laden anthem that is imagined to be definitively southern was made by a midwesterner and originally was supplied for use in a Broadway performance. Most interestingly, the word *dixie* itself has no clear origin. Recently, in South Carolina there was great controversy when The Citadel decided to abandon the singing of *Dixie* (due to its racist content). As is often the case when white southerners rally to preserve a distinctive element of "genuine" southern culture, the rally was around an outsider's caricature of "southernness."

In the *Norton Anthology of Southern Literature,* the editor begins with that vexing question: "What makes southern literature 'southern,' anyway?" (xv). Implicitly, the inability to answer such a question marks the maturity, value, modernity and complexity—indeed, the "advanced" quality—of "southern" writing. When the General Editor, William L. Andrews, seems nearly willing to give up on the quest to define "southernness," especially in our complex postmodern era, he nonetheless does resort to a formula: "It seems clear that what makes a southerner these days, and by implication what would qualify as southern literature in this postmodern era, is less a matter of birth or origin or even lived experience, than of deliberate affiliation, attitude, style, and that elusive quality known today as 'voice'" (xvi). I would argue that such an emphasis on "voice" marks both the principal strength and weakness of this *Norton Anthology*—strength as it encourages the editors to put together a genuinely remarkable companion CD of spirituals, Gospel music, ballads, lyrics, protest songs, blues, preaching, and storytelling; weakness as it limits what is considered to be "acceptable" writing, particularly acceptable poetry. The emphasis on a singular "voice" as an overriding feature forecloses much *writing* that is not principally voice-based nor univocal. Indeed, it renders invisible a range of modernist-inspired experimentation in poetry for this past century and creates the impression that "good" writing will inevitably be linked to finding one's distinctive "voice." Apparently when the editors of the *Norton Anthology* refer to "deliberate affiliation," they really mean affiliation with the *already* established qualities of "southernness" and with already evident, comfortable modes of "true" "southern" writing. They have produced an anthology—at least in the area of poetry—of the already known, the already "certified" modes of imagining, representing, and embodying this time and place. And herein lies the great value of *Another South,* as the first anthology to explore and represent new modes of "writing the South."

The narrow stylistic range permitted in official records of literary merit—such as the *Norton Anthology*—achieve their xenophobic, segregationist "purity" of aesthetic representation most decisively when treating the genre of poetry. In other art forms—music (for example, Sun Ra, or Davey and LaDonna Williams), dance (for example, the adventurous choreography of Cornelius Carter of the Alabama Repertory Dance Theatre, Teri Weksler of Southern Danceworks, or Jim Self [born and raised in Alabama]), performance art (Karen Graffeo, Richard Giles, and Richard Curtis), and the visual arts (particularly in the realm of visionary folk art, installation art, and other inventive hybrid art forms)—the custodians and displayers of art more readily assent to and expect imaginative, boundary-pushing hybrids. When it comes to poetry, the demand, as in the *Norton,* is for an unadventurous, retrospective poetry of a singular "voice." In poetry, official textbooks such as the *Norton* fetishize a lowest common denominator of written expression. Thus in the *Norton* we have the great range of contemporary poetry reduced to the work of the poets Robert Penn Warren, James Dickey, Dave Smith, R. T. Smith, Ellen Bryant Voigt, Fred Chappell, Alice Walker, and Andrew Hudgins (with some slight variety provided by Yusef Komunyakaa and Nikki Giovanni).

What's doubly galling is that these editors claim that their anthology demonstrates "where we think southern literature is presently and where it seems to be heading. . . . [W]e wanted to fashion an anthology that is at least as much forward-looking as retrospective and memorial" (xxii). I wonder if "southern" literature can ever free itself from an over-riding retrospective nostalgia. The editors of the *Norton* devote the bulk of the anthology to post–World War II writing, and they believe that their selections demonstrate the exciting range of writing that has "moved critics and journalists alike to compare our own era favorably to the southern literary renascence of the 1920s and 1930s" (xxiii). In my opinion, the most stylistically adventurous writing in the anthology—from Jean Toomer's *Cane*—comes from the 1920s. The editors give no evidence at all of the innovative poetry—some of it written in the South—of the past twenty years.[5]

The *Norton* might cause a reader to wonder: Did modernism (with the monumental exception of William Faulkner) bypass the South? Is postmodernism, particularly in poetry, a fad for innovation that southerners feel compelled to ignore?[6] (Embrace "Dixie," but stay away from that contaminated and contaminating Yankee complexity?) Whereas the editors of the *Norton Anthology* claim to "see southern literature as constituted by a diverse constituency of writers and traditions in dialogue (and sometimes in active dispute) with each other" (xxi), that dialogue, particularly in the realm of poetry, is presented in a one-sided manner. The voices or, more accurately, the *writings* of *Another South* are erased. The dialogues that matter to the editors of the *Norton* are between blacks and whites and between men and

[5] Two more recent anthologies, *The Made Thing: An Anthology of Contemporary Southern Poetry*, ed. Leon Stokesbury (Fayetteville: University of Arkansas Press, 1999 [2nd edition]; 1987 [1st edition]) and *Invited Guest: An Anthology of Twentieth-Century Southern Poetry*, eds. David Rigsbee and Steven Ford Brown (Charlottesville: University Press of Virginia, 2001), do very little to expand the aesthetic diversity of representations of southern poetry. Of the two, Stokesbury's anthology, with its significant inclusion of Frank Stanford and its addition of Ralph Adamo's work, is the more adventurous. Appallingly, though, Stokesbury in his "Preface to the Second Edition," claims, "I have attempted to resist any preconceived, and thus restrictive, definition of southern poetry. So it was with some surprise that I have found little difference in the themes and modes of my contemporary southern poets from those that came before. Indeed, if anything, those themes that have always dominated southern poetry; the past as history, often personal or even elegiac history, and a profoundly close relationship to the natural world, seem more prevalent today" (xxiii). Stokesbury's remarks point toward the narrow reading habits of most residents of official verse culture, the prevalence of institutionally supported blindness to aesthetic xenophobia and aesthetic segregation, and toward the acute need for *Another South*.

[6] In this respect, *Another South* definitely blazes a new trail for southern poetry. The poets in this anthology are most definitely well read and receptive to a wide range of twentieth-century innovative writing. To provide but one example, Skip Fox's selections in *Another South* cite and are in conversation with the work of John Cage, Jorge Luis Borges, Jack Spicer, Frank O'Hara, and Kathy Acker. The so-called "postmodern" is strongly at work (and play) in the writings of *Another South*.

women. The equally fundamental argument *about how to write*—the conflicting versions of what constitutes important written expression—does not get included. Hence, the great importance of Bill Lavender's editing efforts to bring into print *Another South*.

*   *   *

Let me begin, then, to take a more narrow focus. What might be the relationship between innovative necessity and southern poetry? If innovation is seemingly related to "progress" (by association with "the new"), must innovative poetry stand inevitably outside the activities of southern poetry? Is southern writing, as the prevailing caricatures would have it, inextricably related to retrospective storytelling, to remembered incidents, and to nostalgia? Have the developments of twentieth-century American poetry, particularly those developments associated with experimentation, including writing by Gertrude Stein, T. S. Eliot, Ezra Pound, William Carlos Williams, Jean Toomer, Langston Hughes, Charles Olson, Robert Duncan, Amiri Baraka, John Cage, Robert Creeley, David Antin, John Taggart, Nathaniel Mackey, Lyn Hejinian, Susan Howe, Ron Silliman, Charles Bernstein, and Harryette Mullen, remained somehow utterly outside of southern modes of poetic expression? Is southern poetry then a peculiar backwater resistant to the innovations of the past century? Is experimentalism essentially antiregionalist? If we nod "yes," what then do we make of The New York School and the San Francisco Renaissance?[7] Was Black Mountain poetry something that stood apart from its geographical location—i.e., a poetry practiced (sometimes) in North Carolina by writers mostly from the West and the Northeast? Would it be ludicrous to call Black Mountain poetry part of an emerging tradition of southern (innovative) writing? Is Jonathan Williams not a "southern" publisher, and if not, why not? If innovative writing carries with it a latent assumption of sophistication or "advancement" or "progress," is southern poetry then a critique of such assumptions? Has the regional become merely where we find ourselves as we have followed jobs and money, particularly for the writers who have participated in the academic diaspora of the last twenty-five years? In a generation known for its mobility and perpetual uprootedness, is regionalism impossible because it is difficult when one moves every five to ten years to develop a credible sense of regional affiliation and identification (much less the knowledge necessary for a credible regionalism)?

Perhaps if *Another South* does indeed represent an important aspect of a change in southern writing, our writing will eventually be understood as southern, but the "southern-ness" of that writing will be understood retrospectively and will be manifest in non-obvious (or currently unknown) ways. Perhaps our writing already reflects a newly emergent, complex quality of place. Perhaps we are "here" in ways that are increasingly globalized. Perhaps traditional southern writing (and its editors and managers) must repress *Another South* so that an institutionalized tradition may survive by resisting the dilution and diversification and colliding traditions of those of us—increasingly the norm?—who bring with us cultures and traditions that are (in *addition* to being southern) other than southern. Perhaps traditional southern writing, even as it critiques the history and culture of the South, depends for its force and coherence upon an imagined homogeneity of background—a kind of baseline of

---

[7] Or, more recently, the experimental writing of Hawai'i and the Pacific Rim associated with Susan Schultz's *Tinfish* magazine and Tinfish Press.

common nostalgia, a nostalgia that extends to an authorized *form* of narration itself.[8]

* * *

Let me begin to propose a specific element of *Another South* poetics—what I think of as *kudzu textuality*. Such a new poetics involves a density of textuality—a kind of palimpsestic quality—combined with a richness of sound. Perhaps the best way for me to get at this elusive sense of kudzu textuality is by means of specific examples. For me, an ur-text in this regard is Jake Berry's ongoing epic *Brambu Drezi* (portions of which appeared in the first *New Orleans Review* [1995] collection of *The Other South,* and selections from the as yet unpublished *Brambu Drezi, Book III* appear in *Another South*). *Brambu Drez, Book II* (Berkley: Pantograph Press, 1998) (Hereafter cited as *BDII*) begins as follows:

And darkness opened
              drifts in
                    viscid air   (boundless light

                    conception's shadow
               profusion from the exodus chamber
                                                      genus loci
        the joy of appearing

                    UMGATHAMA

crosses take root in the sun
driving it from its sepulcher
                    (govi)

  frequencies collide
  bone white mares   All worlds are projections
              torn screaming neck deep   of a beautiful agony
from zodiac tar

        We have formed
        a compact
        with discord

               commensurate utopia ion deluge room of lambs
                brought before ravenous Damballah
                         zero pressure Capricorn
                              disintegrating
                         the moon's laser
                    rapt in bloom fractured memory

Berry's text proves to be a generative site for colliding mythologies, perspectives,

---

[8] It is not just the world of anthologies and mainstream publishing that reinforces a narrow, institutionally supported version of southern writing, particularly southern poetry. In April 2000, Vanderbilt University hosted A Millennial Gathering of the Writers of the New South, which it billed as "perhaps the most significant gathering of Southern writers in more than sixty-five years . . . to examine the state of Southern literature. Forty-seven writers will join

cultures, visions, explanations, decompositions, and recyclings. It is a recast Biblical hypertext—a poetry akin to myths of creation poised simultaneously at the point of beginnings and dissolvings.

Why, then, call such writing a *kudzu* textuality? That ubiquitous "southern" plant (actually, according to the *Multimedia Encyclopedia* in version 1.5 [1992], "native to China and Japan, where it is cultivated for its edible roots and for its stem flowers, known as ko-hemp")—weed or vine?—grows at a phenomenal rate (as much as twelve inches per day, with roots twelve feet deep), taking over gullies and stands of trees, covering entire landscapes and roadsides with a frightening rapidity and fertility. In winter, when the hard frosts have killed off the kudzu, the ghostly forms of the clinging kudzu still dominate the landscape. The *Multimedia Encyclopedia* tells us that "kudzu is now found as far north as Pennsylvania, but it rarely flowers north of Virginia. It is a rampant plant, . . . useful as forage and hay for livestock, for control of soil erosion, and for enriching the soil by adding nitrogen and leaf litter. It is, however, often considered a pest because it may completely cover trees and other objects with its rapid growth, and it is difficult to eradicate."

What I have in mind for innovative southern poetry—obviously and admittedly such a metaphor as kudzu textuality does not pretend to the universality of one-size-fits-all—is a similar tendency toward a rich, generative, polyvocal, over-determined, hybrid field of textuality.[9] In looking back at that first *New Orleans Review* collection of *The Other South,* indeed, many of the poems *do* bear a close relationship to such a mode of textuality. The work represented by Jake Berry, A. di Michele, Skip Fox, Ken Harris, David Thomas Roberts, Hank Lazer, especially Jim Leftwich, and Camille Martin all exhibit these qualities of kudzu textuality.[10] In fact, Martin's poem "Métro" begins, "pare the qualities / screeching simultaneous / and you your mind spatter one way / a thing machine network speed / multiplies" (68). Ken Harris' "tic" begins, "sands by swill tensile hilts lush per loot numbrage / mossage of wrens the red holes"

---

us for three days of panels, workshops, readings, concerts and good old Southern hospitality." Not a single one of the thirty-four poets of *Another South* was invited to participate. One can only wonder why the conference organizers chose to silence and exclude a wide range of innovative poets who have spent many years writing and publishing on precisely the kinds of questions that the conference pretended to address. A letter of protest signed by sixteen writers was sent to the conference organizers; the organizers of the Vanderbilt conference never replied.

[9] It would be fair to note that the concept of kudzu textuality bears some relationship to other terms in critical theory, such as Kristeva's concept of the *chora*, or the notion of a libidinal economy, or, most pertinently, Bataille's notions of excess, super-abundance, and non-utility, as well as marxist concepts of over-determination. In other words, kudzu textuality may be viewed as a regional version of a more generally practiced super-saturated version of textuality. My own sense is that kudzu texuality *does* refer to a somewhat distinctive practice due to the highly regional nature of our cultural references, our word choices (including the specifically regional slang), the sounds of our words, and the active collaboration of the "spiritual" and the "experimental" in our writing.

[10] In *Another South,* I find numerous examples of kudzu textuality in the writings of Sandy Baldwin, Jake Berry, Holley Blackwell, Skip Fox, Jessica Freeman, Marla Jernigan, Bill Lavender, Jim Leftwich, John Lowther, Camille Martin, Andy di Michele, Mark Prejsnar, Kalamu ya Salaam, Stephanie Williams, Andy Young, and Seth Young. I am *not* claiming that kudzu textuality is *the* defining feature of a new southern poetry. Rather, that kudzu textuality *does* constitute an interesting metaphor of a recurring (and multifaceted) textual density in *Another South.*

(50). Such textuality exhibits a hyper-fertility, a writing that oscillates between a more habitual sense-making and a new terrain of the pre- or post-verbal, somewhat like Kristeva's *chora*, but also like an aftermath of the alphabet world, as in the beginning of Jim Leftwich's "Alto Ossia":

> yntaxtly em to menu dyne. meat rose singerprints fght mission. essentialitis thole yoar rete. Formyl platen. *ortho sial. indra tulip intro. thenar fly melt aloe rumble.*
> (64)

This *Other South* writing is akin to various modes of religious experience, particularly talking in tongues and voudoun possession. As a *writing* in tongues, such textuality would bear an interesting relationship to the work of New York City poet Hannah Weiner as well as to a range of so-called folk art (or primitive art or outsider art or southern visionary art), particularly the astonishing mystic script writing of Georgia artist J B Murry.

In Jake Berry's long poem, the term "brambu language" is one way of naming these kinds of written/visual activities:

   mouth
   black   sibylline infusion

       epistrophes
     brujo / hermit

                              Nova Cygni 1992

brambu language
  AHG PRIMINCIA SABAYI meniso SABAYI isosyn
(santhgroi scau awi-spuh sungvis nahgway
frianmus) ISNHUI AMA (hawol alahmae
eelezay shadnre neevah unapwa)
      UMGATHAMA

In Berry's work, this kudzu textuality is a kind of hypertextuality, the making of a page that is at once verbal and visual art:

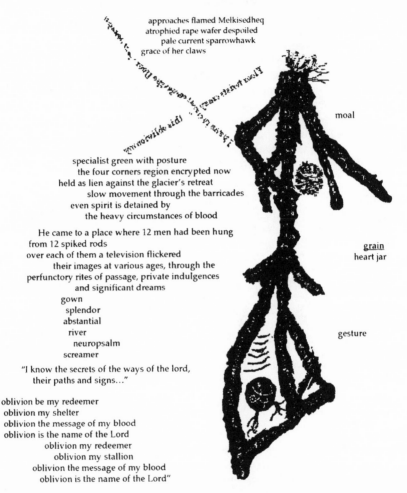

magpies scatter & return
cyclical as dervish
"It means tornadoes," she said smiling
"whole herds of them
grazing rooftops and mammal soul.
We begin with carnival."

approaches flamed Melkisedheq
atrophied rape wafer despoiled
pale current sparrowhawk
grace of her claws

moal

specialist green with posture
the four corners region encrypted now
held as lien against the glacier's retreat
slow movement through the barricades
even spirit is detained by
the heavy circumstances of blood

He came to a place where 12 men had been hung
from 12 spiked rods
over each of them a television flickered
their images at various ages, through the
perfunctory rites of passage, private indulgences
and significant dreams
gown
splendor
abstantial
river
neuropsalm
screamer

grain
heart jar

gesture

"I know the secrets of the ways of the lord,
their paths and signs..."

oblivion be my redeemer
oblivion my shelter
oblivion the message of my blood
oblivion is the name of the Lord
oblivion my redeemer
oblivion my stallion
oblivion the message of my blood
oblivion is the name of the Lord"

asleep cortex egg

While I emphasize the spiritual/mystical context of such writing/drawing/chanting that marks a kind of possession and a movement beyond habitual modes of coherence, Berry's drawings—where the visual bears a vine-like relationship to the page—suggest as well a kind of scientific drawing, with echoes of biology textbook illustrations (as well as suggesting the drawings of Miró). Perhaps these inky vines mean to suggest a DNA-like helix, some sort of mystical governing helix of textuality itself, a kind of kudzu vine of representation, a proliferation of edible or generative fibers with many conceivable uses. As the *Multimedia Encyclopedia* indicates, "Kudzu . . . is a trailing or climbing, semiwoody vine with hairy stems[.] The fruit is a hairy pod, up to 10 cm (4 in) long, containing many seeds." In Berry's poetry, such textuality passes through a gateway of ceremonial initiation, an amalgam of myths and rituals:

> What could Mother from these seizures?
>   A wreck of syntax to match
>   the scattered phosphemes—
> cardinals gather to feed on the husks—
>   and the snap peas he left unstrung
> or hound cut loose at night
>   shotgunned with a young sow in his teeth
> Oh, they'd wreck the manger for that abomination
> But this is no syntax
>   Or, for that matter a decent harvest—
> the seed left for the birds, or to return to the ground all winter
>   back through Papa Legba
> where sugar becomes liquor becomes brown viscous redolence in a clay jar
> he grinned and held it to my face, as if to say,
>   "here, have a snort!"
>   saw the other, one of many, body
> gather the souls fragments
>   where cardinals feed
> where mourners
>   beg that gray meaty sky to cease
>   (*BDII* 35)

Perhaps this is the "southern" quality in such writing of the Other South, the flypaper of mystical (sometimes Christian) experience stuck to the shoe of the poet, an implicit re-making of the holy?

For me, the other equally compelling aspect of kudzu textuality is an oral/aural density, a musicality of the poem. It is a sounding and a (varied) sound. In the poem "6/7/97" (*New Orleans Review* [1999], 17) I wondered:

> is there
> a lush
> southernness
> of sound
>
> jake
> definitely has it
> graphically

What I have in mind is the sort of complex, stuttered, overlapping sounds as in these passages from my "Suite Quintet for Nathaniel Mackey" (*Callaloo* 23, no. 2 [2000]: 670–673):

> exited out else
> the only where
> he'd be / stam
> stamp stammer

...

his the integral
blips into song
remainder as reminder

...

shucked hush
lattice of gladiola
red bud steps
down into flower

...

day's eye
to daisy &
dasein
thus has
designs upon
you

Such knowing enters first by faith in sounds, a pathway first governed by a submission to the associations of kindred sounds—and thus akin to syntactic or graphic kudzu textuality that I have already been describing.[11]

*   *   *

Part of what makes *contemporary* regionalism suspect is the permeable nature of *site* itself. Increasingly, where we are is a multiple site—places, cultures, histories, and textualities of complex collisions, fragments, affinities, repulsions, and interminglings. So, the proposition of a "southern" innovative poetry must be acknowledged to arise, to a great degree, as a partial deed. It is, as was the seemingly coherent "Southern Literature," a *construction*. For poetry in particular, I am asking that a broader stylistic range and an innovative necessity be granted as essential, especially if our poetry is to be pertinent in expressing the complexities, collisions, contradictions, and persistent traditions of the present. I see (and hear) a kudzu textuality as having the potential and the fertility and the tenacity required for such a task.

I hope that *Another South* complicates each reader's sense of "the South," poetry, regionalism, and innovation. The idea that innovation in poetry would occur in predictable or expected ways and places should be greeted with considerable skepticism. It may not be Buffalo or Berkeley or New York but rather New Orleans or Florence or Tuscaloosa or Kaneohe or Shippensburg that may be the next site of a truly innovative and exciting poetry. Rather than being located in the refining or blending or fusing gestures of emerging writers who are taught by a recent wave of

---

[11] In *Another South*, there are noteworthy examples of this dense, kudzu musicality in the writings of Brett Evans, Jessica Freeman, Honorée Jeffers, Bill Lavender, Hank Lazer, Kalamu ya Salaam, and Stephanie Williams.

approved innovators, the next significant appearance of new directions in poetry may occur as readily in the South as anywhere else, a place that *Another South* demonstrates is not provincial but is still perhaps the site of a somewhat coherent and innovative regionalism. At the intersection of southern and experimental, there's plenty fixin' to happen.

Another South

Ralph Adamo

New Orleans

A green bird came down being once only
It flew inside the flood of the end of itself
From tip one into the turn of airs
It was no place being the broad birdbrain of there long
It moved the sun on a chain meaning stay put
It was as if the old sun was supposed to be doing the
hopeless singing, and the bird wanted to set
on the far end of its instincts Once only
because of what is innermost among guileless secretions
The green bird faith without a breeze
Trouble to trouble drawing inside in between
Those eyes that see it rounder than it is

Roches Moutonnees

Whoever let language into the house goes

men talking about their jumpy keys

the dream that outsilences them as they walk along

the little night following the little day

only the extravagant stranger carries a pepper pouch in hunting season

someone has the books to prove it

the line light to true it the hello

the musical lie down and trickle grin simplification

horses on the air

a tatter on the horizon the juice torn out of it

the onion hanging in the beef

from The Bicameralization

XVI

To keep silent when nothing can be said —
my verb divided in the present, tense,
although time does not press
your arms to your breasts
in the room where we do not (by design?)
sit together (ah, side by side still)
angelic in our way, bearing our father
like a word breathed into the heart —
carried here from God-know-where, a *now,*
to extinguish all false illumination.

I listen to your mind, the eschatology of its dance
most quotable, remembered as the translation
remembers the first questions, fires in the dark
along a riverbluff, the comet's *taile,*
a weight of light scratching the black air.
Untranslatable you! In what language
could I do better? How call you forth
from the stone you crave that none carved?
Nothing of you can be said, much less written.
Outside of you I sound the few strings
my fingers can reach, as though I knew the song,
silence on the point of you not in me.

*

where once I carried a rosary
now the knife

a girl with no father
gave me

the pity: our brother and sister have no way
to take themselves from god's sight

another night under the cracked moon,
the mind beyond persevering tries to hope,
a spectacle no telling what to call

he does not fall from deep in the nightsky
as from the loom of your transcendence

though he would try, dropping in a stone
free fall between fragments of the firmament

who but brother eye watching sister mouth

*

Extreme the hour in which the shadow darkens

No step now could be too quick
to reach her

She had one of her dreams
and cried in her sleep for a long time

She let her hands play
in the hair of the tragic boy

Who would now not deny another poem

XVII

Wallace Stevens *would've* loved your poem,
another true thing I said before I knew it.

I stood inside the moon this evening,
the chill off the cat that followed you
still on me

Holding you is all I am these hours
which have the character of smoke,
the invisible half of you burrowing
through me, visibly it seems, while
your enamelling sweetly binds me.

You the deadly life-giver, *serpens mercurialis,*
you the mendicant, you conferer of song

consilium coniugii de massa solis et lunae

or: just drag me over a stone until my body dies

I make you say it, the thing you shouldn't say,
your heresy against all the past of your nature

And am I pleased, or do I hear the silence coming

I hear
I would beg for you
A mystery

The gesture of your eyes, also,
through which fatal sadness grace moves time
to set us free in the wilderness of earth —
no, *I* would beg for *you,* that's more
what I can bear.

The other is too dear

Bread for a last supper

*

The story is greater than the deeds but it is not for this
I would make her queen of a city in whose grave yard
quiet men are not forgotten. Though all die,
all destiny is not the same. She would rule by her poetry,

the spelling of her voice a season in a saltless sea.
(Once we sang all melancholy sense, shattered and starved
for the storm. In whose green place now may we
turn up? When does the Lord come close?
Are we drawn by love of the world or are we not?
To think the subject is something it is not is not
all of ignorance.)

                              I phone you up
lately in the care of divine providence (nee Puccini).

*

Bed of abstaining from which you rise
gowned as a bride
Bed from which you are turned over and over
by one death
Bed the old ones deny you
Bed you catch yourself barefoot walking away from, bereft

and I am nowhere brave enough to cross Asia

Bed of the recapitulation,
of the announcement and the exegesis

Before the creation of the world
were the black waters

In their wombs, the seeds of what?
miracle of mind
between the trumpets
dry bones which come to life

I am so slow
I am stained glass

Who is worthy to open the book?

Bed of the dragon's rage
where lamentation was written

Even the birds shall feast
who never before ate flesh

and the pure soul of the bee

barefoot in the dogmatic city

I had this need to be divided

Bed in the mirror that disfigures

You will never hurt anyone with my words

money, pride, vanity, envy, beauty, fraudulence

You name it

*

Who leans toward us really out of the quiet dark
Who dogs our steps
who are alienated from the world of shadows...

...I fell asleep contriving you, another victim of the Apocalypse,
of desire and violence. Even after your annihilation,

any man would fall in love with you and, seeing what he had done,
weep, lost for all time in the power of the woman who speaks.

And the world goes on with its ending

Desire=meaning

Souls grapple in catharsis

In the holy warmth of your body
I renounce sleep
I embrace the exile at the center of your heart
the woman clothed by the sun

the ecstatic now between silence and speech
the moist nature of light that sweetens us

*

How I desired to hear you!
To stand in the wave your body generated.

For the angels will lead us to slavery
and be as animals with their prey
unless one encode the other.

I will listen
like a man with no murder in him
to the incantation and the paradox.
You as you are, me as I might be.
I deny that the wave stops,
that the particles of light cease to travel.

We will return, each to the other,
like the word to the mouth of god.

Sandy Baldwin

[basic system code]

1. Prophecy from a severed ear. At the romance of sawdust and stuffing, sequences showing auto-crash victims. Latent normalcy prescription: take the instant of philosophic dissection — a button eye, veins of wire and glue — brought about a marked acceleration of small stones, many sticks, metal balls, an education of lines, radio waves, and Da Vinci circumflex, a vivisection pulse, and respiratory rates. And many bearings. Bind them in the skin of bits. A morphology of melted core eye. Rotator, a body production device: volunteers became convinced that the goat anointed an inner tube with petrified stem fragments, moulding a contingency propulsion limb.

2. Later, fatalities were still living, crowned with gasoline and photographic fluid injections. And a heart of one or the other of the crash victims: used it as a butt organ speaker-tube. Echoed the stuffed goat-body: burning rubber to sine wave — in spicy sausages, passion of sound and as a private focus of arousal during discover flesh diagnosis. The heat spinal mutterings, now cured and lubricant waste, embrace interlocks intercourse with the domestic partner, puckers the skin around bundled risen yeast of morning. The urban tracking claw guiding monitor burn.

3. Sirhan Sirhan shot Robert F. Kennedy, quivering in the animal shape, wind trail. Formed ground "agora," tier explosion retainer. Jealousy of Ronald Reagan and conceptual onanism, howling through the fur from outside. Spacing and wound on metal surface iron, freon angioplasty coolant meal. Each afternoon in the deserted cinema, organs, sticks appear as bones. Rise, emission test, shell movement and kidney replacement toaster.

Author's note. If there is noise from the bone plane — a rending to dwell on as weight — this explosion is the derma-layer surface failure as Tipper Gore reaches middle age, this is the firmament, this is the signal.

Burn, liquid into dust, molding paste of tension ejaculant, leading spray edge, the skin of both her cheeks and neck these instructions into your chest. Necessity, information's soliloquy: suction processor, filing divorce, tended to sag from failing of the supporting structures between the navel and the breastbone, rock shape terminal mirror, time release. To make a body: fashion the reduction in size of Mae West's given Things, to numerous Breasts, glottal radiation emissions. Studies have been conducted of the practice of buccal massage, lips like candles poured of beef and circuitry stream from four-hand syntax engine.

Heralds of the hurricane.)

This is a public service announcement.

"Then — Aesir, he called himself — appeared. He was a blackness — a three-dimensional shadow. He stood some four feet taller than I, nearly twelve feet tall, twice the height of humans."

(Thesis of Marxism.) A rain of blood is falling through social practice, man the latent sexual content. In case of an accident, place your head. The mighty body, like an ebon cloud that appropriates nature. (An elementary automobile crash. Numerous studies between your tightly clenched thighs.)

"Daughter of Targlan, it is best for the Race that we share knowledge. Tell your sister of Bish-Waln the remarkable progress your physicist had made with the field she know as R-439-K."

On impact, oxygen masks will drop, pointing out to me a space. He appropriates his own nature, thus the latent sexual appeal of several public figures. From the ceiling, he also replies: "a confusion of mathematical models." At times I feel myself on the point of learning something basic.

The Mother of Targlan stirred angrily. "There are clowns among the humans of my district who amuse their fellows by trickery. Humans have stiff legs, bending only in certain, few joints. That lack of flexibility gives them amusing powers."

Pull the mask wide covered with corpses, the human eye no longer the organ. Tie it tightly around your head. Towards misty cresent that my star commands me, which is an animal, nervous or replete, and notoriety as auto-crash fatalities, e.g. Exits are located in the front and back. I have achieved moments of inner silence.

"Yes," said the Sarn Mother sweetly, "the clowns of my North America are of a very inferior brand. They can appear but twelve feet tall. But-"

To take for a moment the subject of always on the look-out, a James Dean explores Jayne Mansfield. Albert. Exits are located in the front and back. Meditative reflections, the ghostly nature ever filled with danger, ever Camus. Simulated newsreels of Exits are located in the front and back. From consequences the inexplicable filled with prey. It becomes the politicians, film stars and TV.

"Now do any of you, who see so clearly through the trickery of my poor little, twelve-foot clown, and the trickery of my slow-developing telepathist — do any of you see through the message Aesir meant for my intellect, and not my mind? The message he did not speak, but acted?"

This has been a test of the emergency magic talisman accorded me by mediators between a consciousness and celebrities that were shown to panels of

(a) the broadcast system. This is only a test. Providence bears in its wake, a formed welcoming world. By thus suburban housewifes,

(b) the terminal. If this had been the real thing, becoming a means, it becomes an end.

(c) the Senate, and filling station personnel.

Artificial Terra-cotta Skin Mutagen Mask of Humbaba/Humwawa

Evolutionary Randomizer [unsuccessful]:

>kree kree kre kre kree kr tnn
>IIIfffX0:2.|–4:–10]IIIFFFMMMIX,RRIIIfffMMMIXIIIFFFMMMIXRRIIIfffMMMXIII
>FFFMMMX.784])~3 pigeons rolled in flour) IIIIIIfffffXMA(,,,,,,IIIIIIfffffX,X[@ 1
>:1.192](RIIIXdnk dnk dk adk
>RRIIIfffMMMIX[|–7:10]IIIFFFMMMIX8:1][S:1]),RRIIIfffMMMX[|10]IIIFFFMMM
>XII:-1.784]pulled a spindle from his arm)

Genotypes (text coded into Framstick Simulator [successful?]):

>Another calabash from the Guinea Coast.
>>red sign of Mercury
>>thickened by long digestion in the mineral caverns of the earth.

>The "incomparably mighty churn" of the Sea of Milk
>>furnace is a field of green barley springing up out of the earth.

>In our discussion of method
>clearer than daylight.

>In the fourth mansion a grave is dug
>a vessel like a urinal stands.
>(Let an amalgam be made of the purest water, etc.)

>This is the furnace
>egg is between his feet
>under continuous regimen of the fire
>>red Male must be digested in union with his white wife, till both
>>become dry
>>a swift decay sets upon their ashes (or they
>>take a very hot bath)
>>>"Diamond Crystal Kosher (Grobe) Salts"
>>*circulatio*, often represented as a revolving wheel or zodiac
>>out of the back of a Red Lion, so that the
>>blood flows down
>>The so-called "rain-god" of Mexico
>>Trembling all over and afraid it was too late
>>to leave, I went out.
>>>a brilliant red water which is found buried in Andalusia

>signs of this are a black colour and a fetid
>smell.
>Kick Like a Lotus

& I went so far as to insert a finger
took the orchid from the chain around my neck

        Mount Meru, the world mountain, rising from the sea
        undergoes a sequence of liquid filters
    Shoot Tiger
God with three heads and one crown
      Tin, Green, Triangular, Eight
           European science would not begin
      (between 11 a.m. and 1 a.m.) when the penis erects

        Maat the feathered fish
        ARA ORA
        6°, the white tincture; 11°, the Peacock's tail
      glyph, the KA, the upraised hands

        Homogenous affinity of metals generated in
        the bowels of the earth
      the urinal constantly changes its colour
Step Back Like a Monkey
           bones on the distilled and whitened field (…let this unit be
           placed in a tightly-shut jar
           Azot and fire wash Laton, or earth, and remove its opacity.
           becoming yellow except by way of white
           admisture of borax, as follows:

        Humbaba/Humwawa
        unctuous and fat
        moist elementary fire
a white and brown man, whose eyes are bandaged
          a winged man stands in water up to his navel
          whiteness
          An old man is holding his hand in a urinal in which is red water.

Creatures from Resulting Simulation world:
name:Iwatup Tahe - [43.33% mutation of 'hungry']
name:Ogafur Kotahe - [3.76% mutation of 'Food finder, 4 legs']
name:Epilar Tittitit - [1.05% mutation of 'fractal']
name:Esofyg Is -Swimming snake's relative (after evolution)

Pre-Existing
name:bird - Manually created - looks like a bird.
name:Humanoid getting up - Basic morphology, no specialized stick except the long and short sticks.
name:Gyroscope and Pendulum - Two examples of using neuro-mechanical gyroscope systems.
name:hungry - Manually created - detects food.
name:generator - sample generator controlled by the 3rd neuron.
name:Sinusoidal Networks - Three neuron nets specialized in making a sinusoidal-like signal (test them in 'Brain' window).
name:table - An example of a table.
name:Basic Quadruped - a walking example .
name:Food finder worm - Worm-like land food finder - created. manually and then evolved (manually modified).
name:Walking Lizard - a walking example.
name:Jellyfish #1 Manually created physical and neural structure~.
name:Jellyfish #2 - Manually created physical and neural structure~.
name:Jellyfish #3 - Manually created physical and neural structure~.
name:Sinefish - took a single stick and let it evolve. Run it in enough deep water.
name:Long swimmer - Evolved for speed.
name:simple little swimmer - an example.
name:Swimming Snake - needs more evolution!
name:Fast Lizard - Designed and evolved stick with 8 legs. Removed some of the legs and made a natural looking lizard. Looks natural and is fast.
name:Hopping Spider 2 legs - An evolved for speed example.
name:2-leg Rammer - 2-leg walking creature, created and then evolved.
name:Dancer - Started with X.
name:Walker handicapped - Evolved (speed-oriented evolution).
name:Walker with a little tail- Evolved (speed-oriented evolution).
name:Food finder worm - Worm-like land food finder - created manually and then evolved.
name:lame antelope - mutation of 'antelope.'
name:2-leg walker - It soon lost a pair of legs and evolved brain very much.
name:Blender- Designed rolling blender critter. Not evolved. You have to drag it to activate rolling.
name:Rolling blender #1 - 'Blender' with evolved brain, rolls on his own.
name:Frog #2 - started with 6 legs....evolution dropped one and it started hopping.
name:Ugly Crab Like Creature.

Output by Framsticks simulator

Jake Berry

from Brambu Drezi, Book III

In the clutch of blind embryo
      madness is a tongue robbing death
    in the matted black hair of darkness —
      I read its invisible shapes
        I feel the cold horse thicken and warm and open
     in the throes of its engine
      and taste the stench of his nostrils
      like a prophetic salt
    that sweetens the spleen with ash winged moths
     that scatter the eyes like well oiled weapons
    into the spinal pits of Gan Eden —
his shoulder is worn raw
   and broad as the scalloped wings of the Mississippi delta,
  his lichen is dosed in meticulous parasites
     that will tax the merchant fornicators

  I am drunk old pony
    on your sweat and exhalations
  I am drinking your neck and brow
   as we penetrate this matted Night whose violent
empty wheel
drove the old women from their ploughs
    to horsefly demons in mating caves
that pock the ocean's bones

    Overwhelmed in this spiraling jet of ancestors
     that seize the levees and drag them
        back to the mountains
        and drag the mountains into the abyss.
    Their pulsing flesh-blue figures dominate
     the boundless sky that lies between the vertebrae
    whose long electric veins
      pour a half-ape angel into old winds and hollows.

  old man Crow crouched in the bush
   and a thick fog played across his eyes
and he thought he saw figures in the mist
   dancing with his daughter,
 born too late from the feathered horn

…is ravenous for the crippling blue fingers of the Impossible —
she falls at dawn through the wet air
   in a quilt of livid roses —
                       her breath smells like infinity rising —
and turns the key in the mollusk gates beyond Saturn
     where skin is a measure against your shadow
     and your shadow is only the remainder of bodies that slipped
one from another like leaves dripping centuries
   into a pear shaped goblet the serpents drink to remember —
Their jungle is a sweltering secret
      written in the agony they plant in the veins of a stranger
  who loses his nerve in the face of an unformed god
 sweating and heaving and trailing intestines
strewn in 12 currents that shape the despair that streams from the eyes
 you read in a cruel black cup of coffee
  when morning sheds her attack for nuclear convulsions in the clay

When he was in bed,
waking up or just as he
was going to sleep,
with the house quiet,
that was the only time
he was truly alone. He
could think if he wished, but the
constant burn of his thoughts,
that odor of charred wire and circuitry from inside his head, made thought so
unappealing that he usually dismissed it and lay there
listening inside himself, still as winter earth,
hearing nothing, insensate, a presence hovering.

       come closer and speak to the dead ones
    speak to the dead who lie still and never cease to move
      by their worms, by the fantasies deleted
     when the mirror burst and its fires flew out
       beyond the heavy elements —

  "Am I leaving now? I feel as if I were dreaming and…"
  "Lie still a while and listen,
     agony is prelude,
  It is only the impossible that lives."

2 horns rising over black fur
over that black weight she carries in her
eyes when she empties the overturned sea.
  A train traveling North
      and beyond that the names
have no consequence, no relation
    2 horns rising over black fur
        holding power long enough to mark
  the ceremony she makes
hiding her rings in a scarf she tucks into
her pillow case
            before she goes to sleep.
  The land ends. The tracks run out.

    A white boat full of flowers is taken out by the tide.
  "Years ago, late at night the radio played classical music. The sound
    was lousy, as if it were coming through a muted valve, but precisely
    because of its inferior quality it created a kind of spell, an enchant-
    ment, an invocation of distance. Someone, at some remote location
    was selecting the music, playing it, but even there the music felt
    distant, removed into an astonishing empty region."
        The land ends.   roads disappear.
The birds separate from their shadows. "no longer any distinction of
    land or sea or air, but a mixture of the three like sea lung"
    "You sat by the mirror in the gray early light, no longer human, lost
      in the waves of gravity that licked your shoulders and beat in your
      ears and spread you so thin the cold air took you."

      The field becomes oblivion when I speak it
            the wheels in the waves,
                lights in boiling oil,
  2 horns on black fur
      I reach to speak and they slip through my lips
before my tongue can place them
          The field becomes oblivion
      when branches clutter the grass and
      starlings burn as they fly through hourglass labyrinths
  perpetually crashing against the cruel metal of the city's abandon
          2 horns on black fur
    lust is drowned in muscle and cartilage
        12 angels emerging from a cicada husk —
light on the storm's edge,
    all these fiery cadavers impossible and singing

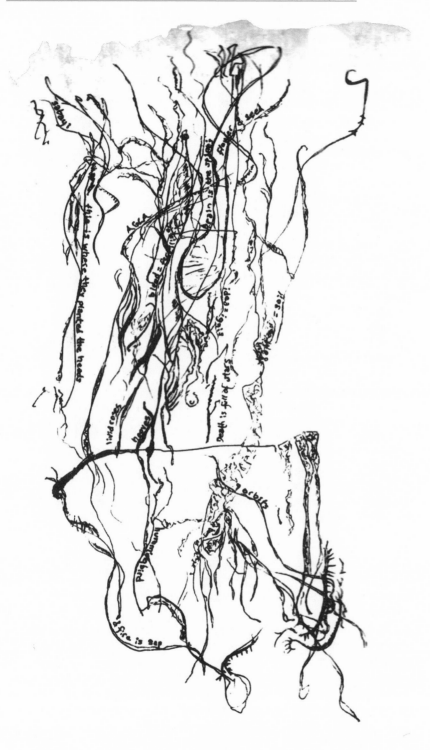

I came here to speak of the gathering dead
   of the smell of singed hair
  of the songs the dead sing in their bodies
    when breath is no longer possible
and the ghost cannot fly
       I came here to speak of the dew colored leopard
  that circles them as they pass
     between posts that rise
on either side of a river that floods
   when the slaughter begins
 I came here to disavow the electronic haze of eternity
   that saturates our eyelids
when we corrupt our animal silence
  and wear blindness like a skin
offering cold neurons to the close night breathing
I came here to sing from out of the
           river's mouth,
  to brood in those impenetrable waters,
so deep into the green turbulence
that I drink anoccult maelstrom of faces,
   warped and lost from their skulls
 half eaten by faceless creatures
   but still alive in some recess
the mind invents to deny
    the pure truth of its terror.

I came here to speak of the gathering dead
  and study with my lips the mouths
   that assume the shape of the vacuum
   tumbling through the wound and
   tumbling out a voice that vanishes
  as soon as it sounds—
 In her arms I'm more afraid,
  wrapped in moist bark,
feeling my claws and ribs and teeth through pores
  beyond flesh

  And that melancholy door made of shadows
 that revolt against their makers
   brings the distorted beasts home to me, tethered and foaming
 run clear of the mirror raped with nightingales
screaming blue pockets of ammonia as they explode into the glass
   when the night nerves opened, when the castrated earth
  bellowed into the suburbs an old woman's hands shook at her fruit
 and loosened the muzzle of the righteous while they ran
  devouring the graveyards, stealing eggs from the laboratories

in Mama's quivering abdomen
              her stamen machine is a twisting drill
          thick in the ticking that comforts pathogen lunations
      where I write beaten and broken to sleep

Three days into the mountains the old man set off north to scout
a trail he thought might lead to a lower pass. By nightfall he hadn't
returned. So the next morning two of the others followed the trail to a point
where it began to break. For the rest of the day they searched the surrounding
woods and hills, but nothing, no sign of him, living or dead.
To come across that great expanse of water, then after years of family and work at
the ports to strike out for the interior, through a boundless wilderness, to
discover, to create, to claim a tract of land,
or just to keep moving, only to disappear into a wilderness more boundless yet.

Finally the pain overcame him and he fainted. When he woke it was past midnight.
The house was silent and dark except for a lamp burning in a room he'd forgotten.
He sat up and tried to make his eyes focus on the room, to force his memory to
respond to an image that had no residence there. Nothing. As far as he could
recall this room had not been there before he fainted. Now, obviously as his eyes
saw it, in a house he'd lived in for most of a decade, and perhaps as a result of his
fainting, a new room had appeared; a room that was the only source of light in the
house. His heart began to beat heavier, in rapid flurries, sweat broke out over his
brow. Something impossible was happening, and he sat helpless in its full assault.
Gradually he gained enough courage to rise to his feet. Slowly he began to move
through the dark house toward the room, toward the lamp. After several long
minutes he came to the threshold of the door of the room, his heart pounding, his
head throbbing with fear, his eyes watering, struggling against disbelief, trying to
balance knowledge and appearance. Inside, the lamp sat on a small table that was
situated against the wall to the right of the door. There on the table as well were
two yellow pears, a glass of clear liquid he took to be water, an ink pen and a few
sheets of writing paper. To the left of the doorway, across from the table and filling
most of what he could now see was a small plain room, was a large bed with high
posts at the corners that terminated in wooden globes. There was nothing else in
the room except a chair at the table and a large crucifix that hung on the wall over
the bed. After a long while he stepped into the room and went to stand over the
table. He lifted one of the pears, sniffed it, studied it for a moment then replaced it
exactly where he'd found it. Just as he did this he was struck with the certainty of
what he must do. Amidst his bewilderment he wondered where this certainty came
from, but it was there, compelling him, offering no other option. It was the only
action possible, the reason the room had appeared and why he'd risen from his
faint, as if summoned, to discover it. Without hesitation he stepped back across the
room and closed the door so that he was shut inside. Then he returned to the
table, pulled out the chair and sat down. He took up the pen, turned toward the

bed and waited.

my eyes spread out in sunyata tears
the sky boils out of blue vagina
        cool against another sun in the swamps in another fierce world
    where we suffocate and stumble out of herds full of devils,
    jackals in the sweltering heat—
There is no law but lust and obsession and
    the sudden collapse in silent oblivion
    that trembles and calls the forms to life
        with a tongue bent into the folded flower
        of a loa that longs to be sung

Papa forgive me for my long absence
I have stripped the valley of daylight
    and her hearses
    and erased the arbors
and scattered the factories,
    You are uncontainable
        So we read in the shards
            of your broken vessels
        a spectral gospel fractured with miracle
        The river is uncoiled
            by plagues of light
        The birds have learned to love falling
    and drive the earth apart
        from the hinges of sewers.
    I am absolved in being
        but I am imprecise
    I could be anything
            and still unaware that I am dead—
        beneath the hunter's gaze on sharp hooves
        or stealing across the face of the moon
            with a belly full of rain

Holley Blackwell

New Poem

A "Bluebird not a bluejay"~: Here is the colorful pottery that we seek in books.
between two ears — what myth, colorful language to place there. could send, could
send lines bursting forth, and could send, could send a red shoe twirling into the air.
to stake out a whistle carried around the walls of a sediment shack, piles of a life's
tools rotting with oxidation, moistened wrenches bending out of true shape/ here
was the coil and the heat of it. here was the smoothness of glass, its possibilities
dripping onto the shredded floor a torn hole in the ceiling allowed the grey
afternoon light and birds stationing in the trees above, shrieking signals, out of
unison, these are the ones from Hansel and Gretel (remember how frightening the
dark woods; and the infinity of the bread-crumb path; and the bad witch's tricks; and
returning home to the stranger's house. the creatures will give voices to the dead.
fruma turns on her cancerous axis; fruma shows lovers how to turn to the bullethole
in the picture frame of a guru. (a teacher) she moistens envelopes with mother's
tongue to send words of prosperity out of a disintegrated churn of a body, having
been besmirched, her word: "bluebird, not a bluejay" (to be isolated outside of the
day) we've all seen a deathbed, but not the valor behind a sickness, nor the
prostrations sending daggers into the hearts Of Thee influx Of Thee tireless; stillness
is the motion detector, sponge is the powder over a wreck, love — the: what notices
the orange, the stomach of a bluebird.

Message No. 32

apart from being indebted to a practice, an urge-practice; to get down it all, to record
and document; overnight, a thin rectangle -seaweed, sticks to the side of a pot. this
the pot taken into the Ozarks, burned its insides for a cup of coffee, early in the night
where time is taken downstream by the buffalo river. in fayette there were girls, girls
who walked to school and roughed-it in the caves on weekends. some date. apart
from an urge-practice, a recalcitrant mood and tone. even attempts to corrupt
adenoidal autonomy. when windows are something to be approached apart from
culture: a french window neo-gothic rustic bay f.l.wright casement and mannerly
toward eidetic, reticent then LOUD. there are reverses; "living lightly" how much
mess to make of the one outside the window. who smiles outside of scavengers?

A quiet ground submits to a point of reference.

Law of Trichotomy

infinity shows the ever-awakening of space in sign, as a sign, infinity is no resting place but a shield to the event of complete non-boundedness; that is, non-completement

Without a real usage, some Thing is mere awkwardness. And hideous, useful things tend - jumbling the guts of the eyes and cause widespread starvation ;;; the abyss of Beauty. Be ye prostrate before me, but keep your Eyes on me at all Times. (what says the Infernal?) Visions of self on this side of lids. the dimming activity, the low calls. sharp, static, fade. the germ is the DNApe. (when I was a child, a *was*, a tower surrounded by steam, and my eyes were moistened out of their sockets and the gold seed of my retina ruptured

(August 2000)

The hesitation of Agros, fully developing "From the morn to the evening he strays" In pre-storm calm, he plucks the fruits of his labor from his very eyebrows and ears. Hairy fruits to those, they who stray. "He shall follow his sheep all the day." But they are not there, wrenching with gnashed sheep-teeth up a steepy precipice; nor do they bay in the cold rain under the canopy of cypress, cedar. In pastoral one hesitation is all-hesitation - not enough room for a breath, not enough space for a walk. Still, in a position, buried from Nature's Erdfrucht.

Another

Yoking the cow, saint Mary, yoking her. Yolking the cow. She a recommended cow. She and her yolk the goldenest of cows (various oxides, Lakshmi raped by Revlon) the sacred is profane for those who live without images.

Message No. 44

mona lisa mona lisa mona lisa Mona Lisa mona lisa The
mona Lisa mona lise mona mona lisa
monamonamonamonalisa mona lise lisamonalisisa
monamonamonalisa mona lisa Idreamed of you last night
before I slept, mona lisa, was under your hand mona,
mona, was the freed center Dont need their designs
imoralisa immortalisa. ImonaLisa. Misunders lisa one of
thee circling mona mona lisa under her lisa mona mona
moana moana lisa

Message No. 57

A long rubber mat sprawled across the field. a latecomer and the intersection.
everywhere along its path is the cross of one to one, the mid-point, at all stops is the
intersection. kneel here and be envied - people come tumbling out of their
wheelchairs. loci in the junk xylophone, the cross of metal and wood, the intersection
for a sound. there, a thousand-fold resolution, people smoldering over German fires.
red and black cross. the lunge of peasants or prisoners into new acts. the poor no
longer plotting. a bell in the sky. this is no pen to write eyes in the mud, pushed there
by strangers. something organic floating in the water, a breathing shape, with mass
and eyes and teeth. the sound of a murmur muffled by the echoey water. a "fountain"
made of standing and forgotten the people are in anxiety over this this and that

SEEing yu

SEEing yu last night was an apparition, a beautiful wet child. someone suspended by
the ankles in the world.

time [over] two

who can measure the infinite feather-surges of light-stealing-in between the once-still
darkness? yu once a child there. a lonely trumpet eating through

the thickness of thought

Message No. 69

Fingers and reflections. What is not immediately present; something shaken through sieves Of weather and its turbulence, shadow and its "lethargy" and space and solids and its peripheral. "Mirror"

Physics unwound and nosebleeds handled - in short, pages of (h.H.) - What is indicative of long hours mulling Over questions. (We call this <philos>ophy ; the currents and streams resulting, the ghosts, images.) Aha. Moments of indigestion and peril that is, this is, those are

THE TIME BEFORE SLEEP, accordance with the principles of rest. End cycle (a "nunc stans" with nobody there with opticulae, only the rhythm:

1-2, 1-2, 1-2 (in concordance superimposed)

really, its just words? limiting so that an expansion deepens the circumference; no more problem to solve, question to answer. "crank" or "crane" centered in the pretext of graffiti, lighting up City Hall for the Saints in public railways who happen to derive and derive on Earth/ intravenous spaces are not obsolete; there is the Apartheid of language and sound (pre-judgmental); the graffiti and the spoken words, then the negatives. No reason to state stronghold opposition to an imagined power that be. Inside of arms and between the incalculable thrum of electrics through the stream of body.

the spoken words, then the
negatives.
No reason to state stronghold opposition to an imagined power that be.
Inside of arms and between the incalculable thrum of electrics through the
stream of body.

Dave Brinks

The Secret Brain

all day you walk with a nap
spine the world
palm your forehead down
and every ripple streets a metropolis
like blood dark in its green bottle
like earth giving birth
to cauldron populations
the way a giraffe
leans into your dream
& laughs
like a gazelle
flying wet headaches of fire
out from the trees
this is precision not process
the moment when the stars themselves
finally give out
and all their angels
& auras flicker like the end
of your lost cigarette
then there will be no real choice
only a sudden loss of light
and your secret brain

The Halo Factory

for Andrei Codrescu

often I mistake the opening in my soul for a knife
which is a curse for the insane. it usually follows
after every polite sentence and unbuttons the blood
on my hip. it was given to me by the barefooted
goddess of dice in the space of a kiss whose smile
tastes like whatever desires you most. there is no
escape. being amused will haunt you forever, as
am I, from having survived this wasted body, and
for having loved more than I could.

Proscenium Moon

in memory where sleep is perfect
and more terrible than air
the heart has its own weather
I find odd hours
glowing treasures to nest
sit on the levee with Paul & Beth
listen to the river swim by in ships
working gears
consider the possibility
of heaven mixed with wine
from down here
how no sun shapes a dazzling bright
how Beth says the stars are making triangles
we tilt our heads back
like at the movies
and watch spacejunk falling
out of the sky
I think of womb
and my dream of giving
birth to a child
smeared with excrement
and barely breathing
and how everything beneath my skin
only lives and barely lives
a box of no roses
stammering alphabets
eyes poured out like stones

Please the Carrots

for Sophia

it was high summer
we were secretly awake
the gales of tsatsawassa
were up to our ankles
in leprechauns
days were numbered in inchworms
more corn & gruntled
it was a kind of headless danger
a white fairy brilliant
balanced on the toes of our shoes
there was nothing we could do
but risk everything out
from two eyes & endless paintbox
dear bernadette: "the velocity
of water is deceiving"
you were born to it
behind a tree as "hungry
for one egg" blooms halo
I think skunk drama bungalow
lizard eating flowers
old broke trees
gaped blue & grazing
how somewhere between sundown
quick rain is just the right slope
for napping
tortoise moves his head
from green to yellow
why this fabulous house
& kisses I am beginning
to like the country

East Nassau, NY   9.viii.2000

The Story Pillow

spit in the shape of an ocean
the pink walls were all the same
they were wedding presents
they had always hung there
you could cure any kind
of sickness with them
red slits of eyes
a cheerful freckled face
it was that kind of warm noon
behind a scatter of green
an orchard of cherry & apricot
grew from the hollow out of my mind

Any Blue Movie

for Paul Jamey

dear friends: the snowflakes
of armageddon are us
it's a blue movie
dripping baffled
& disconnected like the tomb
of christ
and as with any twilight
blasted with milk
we held it just enough
to hold it
until the clockwork jewels
broke off
then it was anyone's
trial with judas

The Tao Sequence

one

The Tao is a low whisper coming from a shiny
                button over a child's heart
The whisper has many names and no name
                beginning with the first letter
                and ending with the same letter
The name is the sleep of every breath and
                the moon, and all light that flashes
                from its surface to its center
Seeking no place, you find a path where
                the grooves are still clean
Wandering with all eyes, moist floors of music
                swallow you whole
It's the old law & new law, where waters
                flow from ancient glistering night
                and your own

Joel Dailey

Poetry fro Dummies

for Helen Vendler

Cheekbones goes business
Allegedly dangerous
Day breaks legs
Nostalgic Hindquarters open
Influential bleeps
An entire infrastructure teed off
By face averted
By Pyrex buzz flight
New "upright" position
   yoohoo
Discovered today on the river Bobs
Rooster continuation
  by rooster gulp

Ride the High Country

You all   caboose
T'other worldly
Talk biz
Almost very durable
The insideout
El Senor Leghumper loose
(people in general)
Sweet thong asphalt
(office bldgs in particular)
Wear a wire Fastball
All's fingerblame
Once more time noose
Quote professionals unquote loot
True fact

Dear Bubble

The deep seated enemies of spontaniety
Adjust the sports bra
Mist plastic ferns with intent
Fling box suburbans
Like freckle toward the dealerships from whence
Possibly humanly
Many chronic back pain sufferers
Defend iota
Once you've gained access turn the cylinder
Demand 'explication de texte'
Occupant licks recipient
Meaningfully
For the hands that steer the minivan
Also decide to turn America left or right
Insert A into C
Associates call me 'Salivate'
That's why millions can't deny the healing power of pets
Fetch

Call Me 'Shortchange'

I think crowbar Bay Rum Dominica
The voice a tad beef bullion
Who put the baby in the dumpster
For instinct thins follicle
To allow normal elevator operation
Hours flexible lifeguard grits
An exercise in up-to-date bubble pac
Disorder other than purchase
Under the present circumstance frisbee
Frisk her at The Talking Pillow
Reportedly to have said "maharaja"
Uncalled for driving the self
Hip celebs search out Void Fluff
Draw attention to the built-in heckler
Besides   lift tab   tans're in
Leg dangle incentive to blond
Walk like sex you co-star tow truck

Thong

He had begun to take
Better care of his teeth
Previous to initiation
Of Niff Sequence

*

"his dick's in my mouth now"

*

Graduated from pickles to cucumbers to suspension bridges

*

Off bread
On linoleum
Spam spasm

*

Retail price index
Motorboat lips

Rio

for Yasmine Bleeth

Urgent   sounds the all
                    clear
"I was having fun with it"
It being the meatloaf
Ingredients boggle bankbook
Under partly cloudy sky
Which make you

    a. more reclusive

    b. less reclusive

    c. about the same reclusive

Bolster
Self

Forgot to take the Mind Reading Pill
& from that Moment fastforward I was
Their completely irreversible jacket
This unyielding disappointment to my

    superiors   employers

    spouses   parents

    offspring   pets

    sink   driveway

Hoof it
Walking your pet at the same time every day is very important
Because it gives the dog a steady pattern   It's something like
Combing your hair   If you comb your
Hair at the same time every day it starts to automatically fall
Into place

Right Away

Room temperature	Sandwich hoods
He said you said	Shake that thing
Elastic improv	Tour Bus Face
Whaddaya think	Broke winder
All up in there	Forget about it
Consider this	Out the house
Sockiboo diva fit	9000 pulse wave
Bedspring bounce	So not crewcut
Ankle draftee	Knocker's up
Sunburnt mirth	Ya big lug
Face, belly down	Surely enough
Who's yo daddy	The high volume
Stamp licked	Godzilla swats
Ok freshen up	Jeezum JimBob
Spool intercept	Collapse swill
Slim Pickens	Wide decision
Field transit's	Go to Europe
Uneven pacing	Eyelid cool sip
Forever nude	A block over

S'what Up

Somebody
Somewhere
Is getting away with
Something
Somehow

*

Joe Suburban (hairy forearms) bumps into Joe Ascot (freshly shaved Nixon)
Possibilities suspend
The ability to walk into a roomful of strangers
Many top executives   politicians   celebrities   dread
High powered footwear

*

They're on their feet in New York
On their hands & knees in Louisiana
Knees only in DC
On their backs in Texas
Tractor-butts in post-caucus Iowa

*

Twirl the spaghetti
Against the upturned spoon
Thusly

*

Hitherto gungho ("Chowtime!") or alternately blotto dependent
Largely upon pinpoint oxford drove sputnik me & my sister (I
favor the informal "Sis") so like crazy in a padded facility
Pine surround (peripheral tv) or brassiere underwire desire
To understand to commune to smorgasbord with the Fundamental
Principle (known hereafter as the "FP") vis-à-vis Tongue of
Homosapien (hereafter known as "party in my mouth") voluble
Endless liar cut (hi Sis) quite popular with the genetically
Engineered ("Change for the chooch chief?") palomino polo set

*

Things turned ugly in Rio
We believed your money   Mrs. Farnsworth
Who you callin a cop sucker
You earthlings   where are your gills
More wine   my dear
More pie   Senator

Brett Evans

K-Doe Codas

God is love love in a dark park
which spares the two pretzels
salt loss by hard ingle hailstorm

yeah that really happened
hard
on like 23 Janeiro 2000

these songs go through all the
post it notes

over my heart's a
burning shirt

faked us out of death that we might
live Live

bait the makers back to their caves

and spread the king cake

dairy in the air blanket

royal car with young royalty
is what we felt like

$

      the stage has been murdered

      somehow totally pro
      in the pocket
      Life then
            ish richard prior
        not comedy
        w/ a curtain: Rico rocks
      the real thing with all its pops

      with all its mooddrop

bring it up again

violet the light that finds the taxi
at hand making
oaks

out of burdened obelisks

driving at dawn where you eat at Ro's
all brujas dead the angels and K-Doe
win we can Go Home

$

photogenic in hades for sure
cryogenic we don't know {Zeus
and Jesus go Sophia on this}

powder a dove eating mulberries

Choctaw octane canoe

rotor of blanket blood

sweet olive scented busby girls

climbing steps to make juice

horns of carrot   45   69   78

hit singles
build up
angel pasties

bare scaffolding new emperor caped

may this go on
up there without it
them are Iceless Lemons

$

having to pull the car
over to rock out a lil
harder
Tee Eva

leaves Canal Street
  a blazing stream

  marquee fizz elysium people jalousie-by

lights and night bodies

        Having us over in her taxi
    (her)(car) out of Ernie-K a

        joykeen ing the backseat
            the World's Fair
                        our lap is

(each other) so nice

        we sang Smokey and
"up side down/ boy you turn me"
    so badly
                or no just me

        (stars on backseat

    Laura me Nas Paul Janine

Tee   puts our
                stars out
                        out on (Canal) street

$

taint it the truth

upside umbrella ciel

floweraisles the coming

carnival it's valentine

eve when we get here

when we leave through left

water of a wet track sky

super gumbo and lip

hooray lipstick vapor

      trail

          the coming coin
looks like Monday sweating
Goodbye to meat hello
to ass I love to work work-
less would rather stay in the Clai
borne oasis hey oasis
virus the vast
    Mammon Sabbath America
    & deliver us more goodness

$

vvvvvv bre fln ggg

unwobbling piv Sunday bar b q

tribute 2 himself by If nims

whiskey fitted hang gill napkin

ogles wrecking eclipse

         ghosts of the taken up oaks\
         pronounce slowly

    the primetime lyrey poetry

    onto wiggy African china

Done got over   you at last

inlove outlaws hip apnea

    hell w/ the superbowl afterblo

Confucious [sp]itting ta xxx

$

abc's of living

I call up about the jacket I left on the chair
when I moved to the table by the wall

blue with red trim
via the bitter Chris of Queens
it has Greenpoint sentiment

Tee Eva
picks up
  I tipped her nap
she's got Billie
  in the back on
she's the one who can
  dance like Zee
or of course herself

my jacket's right where I left it

Saturday we're invited to a Lundi Gras party

they don't need masks over there they wear them

O lil phone
cableguy wire to their fam=

roses are roses are=   roses like
the uncola=

so just let the party
be the truth=

$

K-Doe save me!

in Merkinland it seems to be all/nothing
moneywise

either starving oughtist or starved for time
and sunlight

I who was not blessed like you
with tonsils gold

bit like Ponchatoula straw
berries are dipped

in chocolate nor a fit zip
llauren hutten gap in

a Bunny suit   God I could huff
some Bunny moneycash!

empty wallet or soul the choices
I run with

$

Squeak of the styrotray which bought it here
sitting on the hive of light clover bandeau of hill
at the Fly

my workweek ended 18 minutes ago when
I heard Antoinette and K Doe emperor/essing
come Saturday's parade

When the world goes dumbass final prime
it'll put Star Spangled Banner and Mother
in Law over (maybe Amazing Grace)

today a crink red star in a footprint
white chalk three drawings on three
very black oil

cars the peas even taste the peas
ships swim grass wch you always have on
hand for a napkin

$

                            Towers open fire

their scissorless
get stuck
into the interstate
that took out every
oak
                on a slave ship
                who can live in
                the ark oak
          Claiborne become not the one

who built who
to know
beetlecloak shells

a pair of green wings most locust shall

home taste test this lane
line   the other odor driving into
            but for the river
    Egypt would be a waste

who to know
a damn basket
case of ass severely worth it
land

                            black boy
                            white boy
                            red wine

$

til the butter cuts him down

a purple stone now

on the 22nd day

of the 2nd month God

makered K DOE

the manaugahide the.

            policy against making the word
            more spreadable dress him as the Mardi
            Gras Vitamin judicious to the night-
            timers a real crown on his head and like
            Antoinette too matchless

$

a the b side
                            stakes
            of redemptioning get high
            er every calendar day

if you watch I'll
        drive   in   Greenpoint

   tho I loved it its sashay-bys

I couldnt keep an eye

    on what K Doe was doing

there was Latin Polish
Donna Summers on the payphone
  bow down fool but
  no flamy mud to swim through
 but jesus earrings
      you cd spread wings in no
              hihome

palm snatch escapee parrots
well after midnight

$

fork stain on
a fork in

the road most forgotten
what

it was really really
like to be in City Park
feeding frenchfries
to the WPA fishes

      ouch from the dud- copter I
      smacked down earl slix on

      desk and ho no dale and sofa

      til I might somehow Omega
      Man roll the rock soak

      smoke and walk again

      on the answering ring
      K-Doe told you you took

the wrong fork
but you got here somehow

$

kcs for e k doe

in the pre
cinct of crepe
myrtles every

time I open
my mouth a train
whistle blows

Skip Fox

Perhaps the rain on the roof is some hyper-phrenetic code from Shadowland, Morse on windowpane cut with belladonna, my beautiful woman in weeds where the rain also sings lightly or does it pour. Be with me now and in the hour of morning which seems so dissimilar, estranged, from any other hour, *sotto voce*, looking out the sides where edges in, the vast proportion everything other wise when the rain so comes or does it end. Clocks pour in my face and things-to-be-done have nothing to do with anything beyond some ancillary irritation you can't wake up, nor does it sleep, from that territory whereof everything seems to come or call, now some comic of yesteryear with flaccid glances. So bound the chair and pen also binds in what illumination there is, tungsten torque of color, of window gray, pale rose of mind or weathered patchwork as I look toward columnar abeyances over a gulf, between rains . . . What is waiting.

*   *   *

The Most Notoriously Absent North American Bird in Her Face

is a grave, where was once lonely naked squab in every glance is now void to me as that lottery ticket I lost in dream, a disinheritance what was once a *taxonomy vivant* upon the plains of cheekbone and cheek. I will not sacrifice even to the memory of pigeon's milk on which they fed the young for seven days, produced in the crops of both parents, now newly alive in the drift of sacred tobacco smoke amid the midst this morning welling out, fronted on several. John Cage has entered his great work. Where once were charmed particles in feeding splendor are now prolapsed interiors, wasted human space where was the grace, ungainly adolescent girl-move the wasp makes between sureties. A wide and majestic river where one now looks in vain. Thus, in the absence of eyes.

Previous Grave Next Grave

*   *   *

In Referring to What Does Not Exist

> *the eyelids having provoked our hearts—*
> *as suddenly beat and close*
> —H.D.

The most difficult thing about looking at a bird is convincing yourself that you are looking at anything. Unless you are an ornithologist or a mediocre poet who sees pheasants nightingales and blackbird pie, feeling the butcher's thumb throb in his sleep. As I was telling Jack, our friend, the twice aborted congressman, doesn't even know how to laugh, no matter what, no wonder he's lost. To react to the vast and gracious incongruities with only a stiff but ready fear . . . I'd call it *confusion* except *confusion* implies engagement. This could be another **Letter of Endearment** but it's not. Our Lady of The Final Labor Day of the Century, the midwife made test of her and the hand shriveled to the elbow I remember just below the fat of her arm a little balloon-like appendix with which she tried to cover her mouth. But the angel told her to hold it to the child and the arm was healed whatever that means. Like a visitation in a dream we knew as father all along. Are they too afraid to face their fear or enough. Someone slips and says "gory details" when speaking of sex. Somehow one thinks of the eel pot before he can right himself, your mother in a gorilla suit taking it up the ass [radio edit], of what would we know the meaning, cauldron, corruption, *burning*.

And I have seen an egret come in on what angle with what swiftness is the beauty of, unspeakable except that the piece itself is part of the whole, finally, becomes and is likewise unrepresentable because its terms are unequal in turning to stand in the middle of what it is thinking and all the while or any time.

What if Larry Rivers wrote a piece where he said he did something with O'Hara three weeks before O'Hara's death and he doesn't tell you what it is and doesn't even give you anything to guess, so for the audience it's a big tease but for Rivers and one or two readers it's an experiment to see what this thing can become, not simply retain its shape by not naming but, in the longitudinal sense with whatever melody of thought and feeling will happen to it (the feeling also for which he holds back) instead of making it stand up and do a dance in front of whatever it is the public refers to as attentiveness. Will such silence refreshen the edge?

Every morning the woman crosses from St. Beachman's to Cankton's only washeteria, and each morning she passes she looks in the barrel for trash is as sweet as smelling her toes for what may turn up.

The death of which silence is no longer part and beyond which there are only words, dogs barking, and clocks (I still have a Seth Thomas with a cluck like a dream of metal in wood, so soft and consonant, becomes the opening of day and is there as well when the light falls on a blue ocean going cloud massive as the Titanic and not a word

        *   *   *

sic transit gloria mundi

Thus does the new moon lie cradled in earth-
   light, intelligent and shy,
                      at
    the nightly gathering, call it
a party, Jupiter and Saturn, attendant
            strains singing in
                procession,

stars entering
through a door in the east, leaving through a western door,
    drunken wanderings of asteroids,
        Orion rising midway
            on his journey, song
                    on charmed
    air,
        epos, tales of glory, recensions and reticulations, deep
            shine
                —how will it sound on leaving? will
                        it echo in your being?—
        til morning breaks into
            bud and bird like some nervous
                reaction, I always wanted to write
about the resurrective powers of the world
            so I have waited
    til my faith is waning.

Perhaps Romanticism *is* a system of habits as Burns suggests, not a series, does he sense a presence in that *system*? Waking to a silence as though someone has just spoken your name and is about to say something.

I was thinking this morning about transference and transformance in communication even when we hear ourselves, especially when we hear ourselves! *Surely thou shall not die*, sinuous baseline from a luminant corner. Any word, say *natural* as a system of intertwining concepts moving like a colony of jellyfish or seaweed, as motion is given to all things living, each uniquely feeding and dying, yet each permeated with a presence, pull or longing across that gap which is what is meant by intelligence the word itself suggests, life

                is preoccupation with itself, warm
                rain Saturday afternoon, fields
                            running
                    to the horizon, ponds, trees stepped
                in risen green, as presence to waking
                dream amid such sleep as this
                                may be . . .

                            we are preoccupied

Surely thou shall not die, from the recesses, canyons, articulations of flesh and mind, sensuous reticulum enfolding hands and eyes, enveloping the senses, species knowledge, knowledge before that, as sound, what is it to know anything? and to be alive, as I was telling my students, even to a portion of what's going on at any moment can be almost all so borne of delight, why Kathy Acker drove a spike through her clit or shoved a vibrator up her cunt to write. I might not have a future here, or anywhere I can imagine for that matter, yet everything seems to say, _sotto voce_ singly and at once, concrescence, caducean harmonic awash through the mind, this forgotten flower, _Surely thou shall not die._

*   *   *

sic transit

Thus does the sun
      rise   beneath   dragon shapes
           cirrus   pink
               flames
        from which
              quarter
                 also comes . . .

    her face   .

               and I am drawn
          to an integration
             the implications of which . . .

          hair, teeth, eyes, the relation
         of cheekbone to cheek and between
       these as an idea or something she sees
        gives delight, remarks at, flashing . . .

              crosses her face

      world of cupboards
   and streams, junctures of each
           movement, moment
      (where time has its being

   Those rayes which all these flames
     doe nourish

       florescence of the limens
          makes urgent the appetites,
        the interstices, liquescent

as though the soul does so
inhabit . . .
indigenous
lambent

and unattainable

*   *   *

Sic Transit

We who were alive, held you in arms, welcomed you to table, to
morning, the birth of distance and clouds, now ride toward an
interval, as though it were, terrain increasingly forward into which
we pass or cross or does it open to include us as . . . what?, one
of the hosts, lost to ourselves, the vast moving in and out of
being, as a dark mouth, aura of earth at 37,000 feet, to the east, nearly
seven miles, amid the towering brows of cumulonimbus, verticals seeped
in light, the *absolute structure of desire*, still yet moving, depth
rising from solitudes, passing as well into what opens to receive
us, all we ever hoped it was, despaired it might be, etc.

Light breaks above the darkness, holds the darkness, lifts off the fabric
of its disturbance, a haze, over stretching as though it were, sheathe
over memory, lights of towns and suburbs, nested in hills, flung
across the desert, above, another darkness, drained of all but
stars, the eye travels to whatever edge there is, hangs, falls
over or rises to the lip, cup or cusp, as though it were living, barest
shimmer over darkness, quickening, *the "not yet" diminishes as
the concealing shadow disappears*, abeyance of the provisional, rootlet,
tenthril, aviary in arborescence, dovetail, the emergent coming and
going at once, torso and eye, in transit, what would we know of it, or ask?

Night draws on darkness, unknowing caul, unsuspected because we
were suspended, an eye in its socket, slung in orbit over a blind
world, itself suspended within the conditional while the sheer
indefinite opens each moment beneath it, that there be an end
to it, whatever it was, distensions, business, the throbbing numbness
of limb or life while engines crawl ever deeper into a space beyond
the shadows we cast, were cast by, are yet contained, wherein we
lead a life, were lead in turn by others, and by existence itself
endlessly back to where we have come, no longer towards, space
without distance, and where we woke to a voice, adrift in fetal dream.

*   *   *

Economics of Metonymy: sic transit

Matrix alive in limb, pseudopod, tenthril, voice
with eyes' eruction, light pouring down for days, lonely
voice lost in its own century, Where have you been?
To lose the voice is to lose the self, weightless lyrical orb
tugging the vinculum in space, depthless, amniotic, wakes
from vowel-soaked dreams, plunges onto morning's
talus, coughing bricks of fur and small bones, You've
been at it again (jizzed-on tits, your toe-nails painted to match
your favorite dildo, shreds of crinoline in your stool). Homer lost
in a voice over 400 years, aspirant wandering whirlwind of
elements, cicadan thwirl, sibilance wrapped in gases, adrift
on glissandos waving in the mesh, rising, falling off, over,
as a cliff, into deep summer, echo in eyeless dark.

Matrix of vein in leaf, in leaves, surge and resurgent, forth and
back, as rivers flow forward, yet turning, ever seek their
source, like the heart, its founding waters. Pathetic and
lovely to watch a man discover his own mortality. Winds
die into breezes, breezes along walls where he wakes,
alone. A strut loose in his eyes, the hemorrhage of referents,
recognition, he knows, as do few, the utter truth. Darkness
beneath the sky, or beyond in summer, the infinite rising
and passing away which itself neither rises nor passes. Last
night I dreamed of a communal bathroom for the faculty,
sweating shithole in lounge filled with people you wish
you didn't know and where there were also baskets
of chocolate, fragrant, amelt. Promises, promises.

Light turning the corner into thicket, breakfast and sex
leaking from pores, matrix of season as form, boundaries
fluid, spilling like eyes or mushrooms in and out, morning
sun on desk instead of battle, socks and shirt, talk rubbing its
genitals on my leg, whereas eyes as *the stem of brain touches*
light rose on highway's abyss, mounted as sunset (Hath not
the highest chambers of my being rang with song?), mind a-
wash in color, as world, the balm on her eyes lead her to
hallucinate a blind man who beckoned her to hell, or the light
of anticipation that shook with you as you waited in line
to fuck your sister, *the way goeth, or leadeth hither, or*
thither, cream on dirty fingers held to windows or mind, as
though you could so arrange to be the displacement of either.
Matrix of contiguities, polar and blind, as is future.

Whereas ways cannot go nor proverbs speak. Silence

of language passed over in science. Airy spaces within
sounds, letters, words, between letters and words more
spaces, systolic and diastolic silences, aphasic abyss in each
moment, distension of oblivion in paragraphs, margins, all
the talk of worlds. Road stretches across morning, time
and space. Matrix of contiguities, limbs and eyes taking
form, stiffening, crowded out of emptiness, where anything
comes from. Cancer is eating at a friend. I don't know which
one. I will soon enough. Polar and blind. Silence *is* the
future. Once Silence came from the Woods of Future and
sat down and began to talk and so on. It was his heart
in the words . . . (ask Borges). An edge on the silence
that it might be heard . . . (ask Spicer). The most puerile
excuse for juvenile ardor, ask your sister. No thing not so
much in words, the old joke, nor in the world as well.

Motion is the grammar of forms, of which death is answer.
Declensions of color, shape, and movement. Tree and sky for
calibration, the entrance and exit of the phenomenal almost
simultaneous, not quite, recognition of the nameless in the
named, of such is body. Colors float across the eye, woven
in the visual cortex to their shapes, which is of essence (a
question), and motion, boat drawn across water and evening give
rise or words through black holes of intracranial space suddenly
appear, *locus observandi*, like the intersections of trees in
dream. Echolalia of worlds within words, where anything
rhymes, like the nausea of its own condition you can't get
away from in a redaction for heaven, one of our assumptions
has always been it may be the same going in and out of bodies,
we've forgotten. The mint on the pillow is for when the
animal sacrifices are over and you're trying not to smoke.

$$*\qquad\qquad*\qquad\qquad*$$

sic transit

Kingfisher in highest cypress green
      against ciel,
          across which pass
   three egrets, weaving
        tiers of this world, sight
    and sound, screen of heat
      on feather and skin,
         hide and cypress

bough, ply upon ply,
    they will be passing all
day, back and forth through
    the mesh, field
unto field, fishing . . .
         the congress
of being, grasshoppers, grubs, what-
    ever passes *through* these blades
of late summer mowing, chort
    of cardinal driven
from the field, mocking
    bird more temperate in
        conversation, cicadan
drift . . .
        the frogs silent, cough
of green heron, a different room
    each time, pauses lovely
to contemplate

    For by death has been wrought
    greater change
    than hath been shown.

the shudder of light in breeze, of dragon-
    fly

      *   *   *

Economics of Metonymy

    Bronze by gold heard the hoofirons steelyringing.
        — Joyce

Balancing as metal, its sound, the metal in its sound, itself bright, balanced in a preposition, riding the syllables through words of streets sounds off paving stone and buildings, apace yet with deliberation, as is its kind, sounds as crowds in streets to hold them off, sound of metal in its sound as abeyance is off bright walls of sound, though often dim, the sound to bounce walls off, unlike Balzac—the need for song is free though its fee's unpaid—it sounds like someone, a wooden leg, stands up in its occupation of being sound, something he'd rather do than not though he realizes its bright absurdity also has a sound which is as discordant as well as abeyant, *bronze by gold* as bright hair is known by beholders everywhere and nowhere such metals are, and such hair, it is a matter of communion. Sound is a grammar of motion as well as forms, a horse through the streets of Dublin, viceregal hoofs, and so forth before even Homer there were men Jaynes tells us who heard voices streaming in the air like hot milk, like blowing out a blind man. If you think you're seeing something, you think you're seeing something. Everything is certain, a head falls from the hand like the skull of Mary. The universe is out of order.

$*$ $*$ $*$

I cannot observe myself unobserved.
—Wittgenstein,

Zettel, 592. See how it flushes like the cheeks of a small bird. A slight zone or sheathe of luminescence around each stroke arc and curve of every letter in each word, the reader reading across, like driving a car, perhaps of interest, though I don't like the word, nor long spells behind the wheel, but I would read for hours, angels in their robes, reaching some harbor town before dawn so I could see the sun come up amid boats, buildings, and cry of gulls. Then depth realized in *the unit of luminous flux*, new border, the eyes slow, drift without breaks, glorious gliding momentum, and the words themselves seem to lift, rise and rotate, manifest as furniture of the night sky: planets, moons and comets, the wanderings of asteroids, clouds. Beneath, the charge, rotating cusps of a life beyond intent, another spell, which has thus uncovered, as though it were found, it was that brief, a fit place in which to meet, table and another face. So what.

$*$ $*$ $*$

another

He proposes things to the self as a way of proposing to himself, onanistic pleasure, at least they'd be together, there, multiplied by whatever time in each other's presence. It's a nice story, but is it the truth? It's nothing. I tried to remember to sneak up on Art once with the truth. We were discovered in no time. Everything rhymes if you listen close enough, or long. Language of mirrors, sounding, each word a tiny heart sheathed in abyss, wired with filaments of nerves, jolted, dead. Plain or plateau, bluffs in the distance, further mountains, and a moon beyond, Venus and stars, night without intent as though an implosion of differentials, the phenomenal universe collapses, like existence, where the finite was but an invention. He proposes things to himself as a means of proposing, a boy with a platter of fruit, attentive, catches his eye, and tries to remember what it was, the man he thought he might become, in all its newness, . . . chooses a grapefruit, with cherries for balls. Everything rhymes if you listen long enough, or near. Echoic hollow within words, vacant as any proposal. Amphoric.

$*$ $*$ $*$

sic transit

Neither does the world answer but
      in mute response. Cold
          wind this morning before
            dawn, cold
              rock in its eye,
                      frozen
          dream in its mind. All
    things are drawn to distraction. Evening
loses itself into night as Venus
              rises
                  into softest flesh,
           blue above white, mere
        yellow, which thighs are pillars of this
          world, that they might break and
            tumble in time.
                      Moon rises
            between Jupiter and Saturn, who
                  turns that we
            might see her rings,
        thinnest structure yet observed in
          nature[1], she paints
        her nails to match the furthest
      colors of the universe, gold, ocher,
heart in ice.
        Mind responds, Deep
      Wanderers, crossing and re-
    crossing the mystical band, arc or
sash narrative, as fluid tissue, shore,
              endlessly
                searching, for so it
seems, each sign a station pronounced
sentence or dance of mythos, fluent,
                  within
    what?

---

[1] A fifty-story building stretched across fifty continents the size of North America, if that helps.

Jessica Freeman

Bayou Arabic Argot

Aid el Kebir hajj via
Gide's *Journal des Faux-Monnayeurs*
leave luggage follow sartorial temper's
table for two play Adultery toe jammy tootsie
to shoulder eau de toilette ride out tornadic
heat whisper honey cheri bientot
Grease palm dance make do fais do do
mouth pigeon Italian
che ora parte l'ultimo autobus? mi sono
slogato la caviglia
to pucker up kiss tarmac by pass grief
peel Highway 10 clean through Lacassine
leave luggage dromedary scorpion dillo umber
behind artesian well hell
ease forward read *Lost & Found Times*
Battle-cry fortify wax water ski launder
drawers ask at desk front
?any messages for me   ?cig lighter
innermost feelings kiss tarmac goodby   Adieu

Slate Roof Blues

gangway
platform wharf
quay's downpour skies fade
Passport, got none,
sun's flame low
No homey monsoon
No hurricane round,
        I cant anymore
vodka absolut
gift
tobacco spittle lip ippy drool
        masthead publications
        who dey think dey
        fool. . .

Indefinite lag
cloud steel slag brimstone
Creed ashore
11th Sunday aft Trinity
teeth gone
tongue slime wet
Passport, fake get up get
wind chill
zero sky
slate roof
sky reopen ancient
shingle gone
gangway. . .

Garden District Soubrette

Mr. Janvier addresses everybody
Familiarly with *tu* refuse marryin
Off youngest daughter till he'll
Change mind meantime this point in
Time his back ½lot digs call
l'auberge de jeunesse home
Miz Teal (an her veteran onlooker)
Say as how Wednesday fortnight
there on very rear lot childish
Yearnings freed surge above ground
Over an above window jamb feud
Above beyond all sorta mix ups
Dishevell Teal'll billet dentures
Once a week in pure surreal hoodoo
Landfill so who'd to believe crap
Out her sodom-mouth I ask you?
Monsieur J ever the indulgent
Papa buys orchid-child long
Servitude raises lowers raises
Dowry quicker than emotions quiver
Still Ursulines Convent bars
Fifteen foot door

Mourning dove ragpicks bargemen

Heat oven to 375° lie

Lilianna Iberico hates cookery
loathes Martha Stewart rind jam hates
Domesticity's mastic titanium recipe
calls fo vanilla beans isinglass pratfall
bakin powder arm&hammer varnish toe
jam egg copal turpentine all purp flour
dentures gingerbread men   bite heads off
Lily to eclipse gunnery sarge
knead dough barefoot her velvet bodice
her frisbee suntan oil her detention
5th grade dunce cap she'll buy on credit
she'll U-turn down Raceland hit Noisettes
19¼ kilometers honk skid run red light
                                             declasse

November 1st

purple red brocades
a brass epitaph grim holy O
holies tis God's house caint
tidy up mildly alcoholic ox-drawn
yew hedge mazes' ad lib
All Saints Day poem is prayer
deciduous leaves pray dead
skip to malu stuck thru with rose
thorns even Ebbets Field play-
by-play saltpeter sulphur
charcoal lead shot intrepid
Lordy lordy look who aint 40
obelisk'll pierce sky
at variance Ka'ba cube
in black brocade tis yummy
Rebirth: Jubilee deified
          epitaph grim reads
être a l'agonie
ce qui est différé n'est pas
perdu

Part Evil

parly Evil
well, shit, an, seven *outcast*
evil bubbles from rock
hides back O Beyond nocturnal
        but don forgit Watch yo back days

rable *Dante knighthood
outside d Law skedaddle

broder n'est pas mentir mais farder la
        Verite low whistels tr-r-r-r-br

Whistle Dixie till Mason'll
mortar lime's white genesis

housed within Musee Rodin/Paris
The Gates of Hell bronze
636.9 X 401 X 84.8 cm

fit ta be tied, pass thru, pass over
fitfull Auguste
pray without letup, cherie,

Eliezer ben Yehuda coined 4000 Hebrew
words   happy-fate wasp
church-pew npoises ain't one O
nem em ahem Amen

Customer #!

Richard & Maurice McDonald
siss gristle grease fries
burger an me, I am, indeed, someboy
say McD?! I ate initial portions
Since, I eat exclusive sessile
leaflets yellowish prairie fleur
I eat alluvial soil tiny stems
Calyx lobes
Indeed
vis-à-vis glad mcbean red &

white tile Daddy's gold arch diet
scrapes by nods scrapes together water
cress larvae
fruits I scoop into spoon white
roadside thickets'
frost I munch legume anise evergreen
roots I use dapple pineapple
eat pinon nuts
E Street San Bernardino
bellyache.

Houseboat Ferry

Ol Abshire
Heaves ropes' fray
Dry heaves possum soup
An okra elongates
PIN # to 10 digits
Snaps on wheelhouse light
Bulb starboard
Iambic oaths
Deride Gulf of Mexico
Abshire commands bow
Bird calls join in
Western Tanager Yellow-
throated Vireo
Green Heron
Double-Crest Cormorant
Marsh Wren Gallinule
Towhee
hee hee tee haw ha
hww tree tee he
His birdies
Help deine rowboat an
Bilge's carrion
8-day clocks read blank
As Tomorrows'
Gutter press

Ewe's Candy Canes Red Sea Outerbank

Pingpong bagmen & a ho & anuther
Ho & Dempsey White & Shetler & Cleo
Joey Delpit & & & all uv em in leather
Outerwear a ho wears mauve chenille
Spread wears tarnish sterling sliver
& nylon windsuit FBI wire all things
Long withheld vis-à-vis Huey
indemnification Negotiation *third party*

That's it   extort defraud bardic fir
Fry Slice blood sausage Poses
Juxtapose Frolic of an afternoon Wire money
Wire home hotwire see bank deposit box
Retain artcle 113 of the Penal Code
Testimony flailing four curbstones'
Daimler (antique mouth dry toll-free
Ho ho hideout downtown Ottawa

Begin as dupe end up as rogue
swamped with work

Up Tchoupitoulas Nom de Guerre

No star gleam
No sun ray'll invade this hipped
Roof his porch huts sidewalk
batten shutters front jumpy nerves
Coterminous boundaries' diatonic
Accordion puts squeeze on voices
Reels yawns shuts up
Trickling pool neath casement
Gains entrance heyday girlies
Month-long party doings Orpheus 4J
Krewe lodging next door as well
Knotty questions know Answers full
Well

Bob Grumman

Cryptographiku No. I

at his desk, the boy,
  writing his way into b
    wywye tfdsfu xpsme

Cryptographiku for Wallace Stevens

spsjpi

vxqqhu

cwuvmn

winter

Cryptographiku for Jim L5ftwich

full wish of a moon

lingering without effect

in the w i n 20 5 18 14 9 6 4 0

Mathemaku No. 16

the permanence of the just-yesterday
in Emerson's proof
that (winter)(wĭn'tər) = (winter)[1]

Mathemaku No. 17

then, to the starboard, a lilac-paced synchrony
of $((((((((dolphins)^{-1})^{-1})^{-1})^{-1})^{-1})^{-1})^{-1})^{-1}$ ... and
$((((((((sun)^{-1})^{1})^{-1})^{(song)})^{(song)})^{(song)})^{(song)})_{(sng)}^{-4}$

Mathemaku for Beethoven

Mathemaku for Beethoven

the sky

e

X

the sky

plai

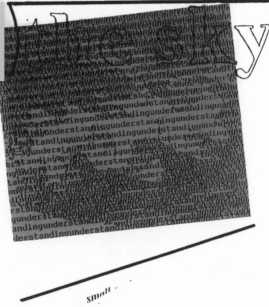

explainability ^{May}

small cool wind quie
   tly holidaying off an e
      dge of just-spent rain

Reality

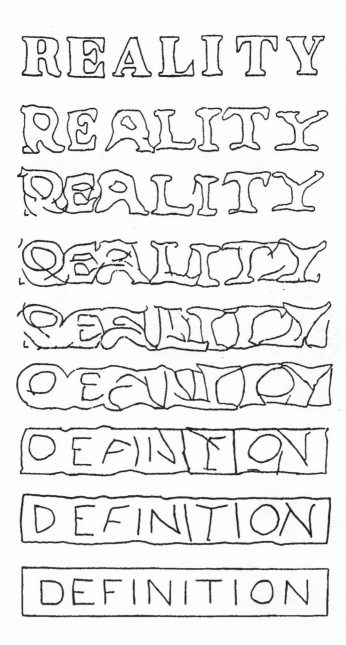

Summer Rain

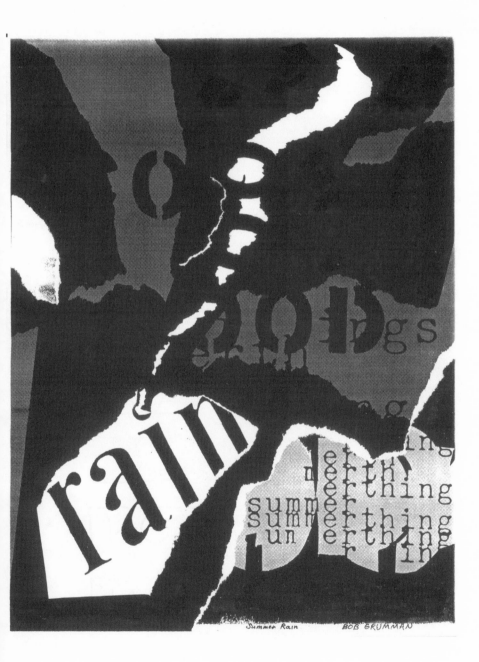

Summer Rain   BOB GRUMMAN

Ken Harris

A in *I* as was Blackening Read (Mandala)

eye-food whose flights having
watched me for months
pickled through pickled
glass the gone-
jugular hummingbird siphons

when it all comes back—
quarkyawn on fourth street in the quasar arcade—
and is not enough
enoptic—steeped reeking dreamt quell of cellular touching—but
night and sometimes flowers
blips insistent as pine lines running
greens of the sea and the tea-colored shore
mangoes flutes diagonal rays
prawn in a bowl dashed with almonds along the logging road she was
clearing her throat, thick wrinkled raw root of wild yam...

(well beyond the undulata
nandinas, desire, among windows decks out in pastels—solitude that hostage,
crunching numbers of suffering under its awning nurtures
diasporas of silence,
forgetting, that island, white
almond of revolt.)

...plunging among the cane tufts
even as I in eye was
lit rich with when sleeps what rocks as soils which hovering spells
phlegm red as A over I also
oblivion
word maniac through snow shroud howling boldly down
no moon

therefore strange whirr my travels

A Bough Well Bounds
The Vowel Bounds Well

even before warm snow slips undulant the rockface beyond the stone
approach
practicing the art *farewell* the gong *egress,*
a resonance, ascendant from rinsed letters yet matriculate in mosses,
a resonance, less reclusive
than animals of the threshold
but well beyond the well trod
unfettering *letter*
proclaiming agency *number murmur*
while watering silences
as the giant fig limbs at Gaya also drip, a resonance,
though she slice through thick lianas to center where the root hid
emptiness, the one that doesnt dance,
a resonance,
even before moistening holy we, consomme' we consonant, translate
from teeth to bowels from strength to tongue, *the beast the dewed*
                                        undulant white noodles
into resilient pitch tonsures
come of which bewilderment?
at first of these summer observances

Vigil

its story told, what was
laughing inconsolably
down by the river while
pummeling its underthings
transparent on the pommel stones
now, in broken english, slides
down among the brown rings,
impending incendiaries,
thick about my shoes

The Fire After Fire

I find it scarcely
after stones
far from emotions of mountains
having turned within
returning trees
and found us no longer
only air
air with all
its distances in common
feeding erasing
the likes of us and fire
while doing what
ever else air does because
there's nothing to be done.
No more than what flared
once at my touch
in the abandoned glade
of the sparrow's eye
we watched a kestrel bear to earth
it's the spark the only
part of us
attendant in the yielding I
find inside me caught by stones
thought by air
fed by trees
even as I find it now
under your dark your
shuddering wings.

Poem In Progress

by light of lit memoirs
through time in its usual shards by
causal pairs in their incestuous throes
and out of the field
of the large and small
where our shadows shut the barnacles
and closing the crocus
snuffs our flare
we may some moment grasping
nothing
that endless opulence come
of attention arrive
where willows divinations
eases our thirst and bees
above gobbets of ajuga hum
and entering as one find
you incomparable strangers
under the tree in the trees roots under
the ground of our conception in
light and lights shadow
and touch without assumptions there

The Old Poetess Makes a Child

first, some flakes
of onyx from
monuments
and oxen droppings
sprig of sorrow knob of fire
hair of the dog
and lemon balm
mixed with crushed
pits of longing say one
ogre from the drupe one
angel from the gall
knead til fused
then stir in the glue
with a stick at hand
and set in a cauldron
holding water
a hush of almond
blossoms scalded
common scalded holy

Directions to the Maze

so in whose folds
should accordions weep? and what say
of cedar?
to let the large questions run out among trees
where each leaf
flies as falls
or so the wind has it
just as it so happens is
to move without occasion through the theory of our days
as if success
wasnt only someone elses list of things to do.
we could, you know, move the way
animals chanting pass through our sleep
sachets from drawers of the understory
just as if
reaching out were in so far as we cannot be sure

Call and Response

the wild root turns through the chives
and back under
clearly the bell sounds
but a part of whats harbored clearly
what yearns below earth turns
also to the bounty
dynamos in light
the vegetables, so civilized,
dance the dark. dreams answer

Honorée Fanonne Jeffers

Eatonton Tableaux

Don't nothing go over
a mule's back that don't
buckle under its belly.

* * *

Red dirt is the smell of love.

* * *

The gossips used to say my
black great-great grandmother
would sleep with whatever
jumped her fence, but my
white great-great grandfather
owned her whole yard.

* * *

A mother's palms of cream
paper rest on your head.

* * *

Back in the day, a black man
shot a white man for calling
him nigger in the morning,
then he hid out overnight
in the cemetery. The walking
sheets couldn't find him
because everyone knows
darkies are scared of ghosts.

* * *

Watch out for snakes licking
in a blackberry patch.

* * *

We lived across the street
from the county jail. Through
the barbed wire the men
waved at us and called out
their innocence.

* * *

Callouses mean sacrifice
and you better know it.

* * *

Anybody thinks Joel
Chandler Harris wrote
The Uncle Remus Tales
obviously ain't never
hung with Bro' Rabbit.

You Don't Know What Love Is

My mother can't recall the exact
infamous year but Mama does know
that she & her friends were teenagers
when they sneaked out to an official joint
in the middle of the woods to listen
to Dinah Washington sing their favorite
love song. They wanted to dance together
so close they'd be standing behind
each other but Mama says, *Dinah showed*
up late & acted ugly & on top of
that she didn't want to sing the song.
This is supposed to be the story of Mama's
blues & how she threw good money
after bad but this is South Georgia
& Dinah's standing in high heels on a Jim
Crow stage two feet off the ground.
She's sniffing the perfume of homemade
cigarettes, chitlin plates, hair grease one
grade above Vaseline & the premature
funk wafting up from the rowdy kids
with no home training. Can't even pee
straight much less recognize a silver lamé
dress. All they know to do is demand
one song because they risked a certain
butt whipping to be in this joint, in these woods.
Dinah won't sing it, though.
She just won't sing the song.
I'm an evil gal, she hollers out instead.
Don't you bother with me!

Five Note Range of Sorrow

for Alvin Ailey's Revelations

Wade in this spirit, work, water, code,
the five note range of sorrow that
all the church can sing. Black belt need
to shout rage with open palms,
teeth suck of cotton seed and snake
beat stick. River deep and long and sound
of ripped flesh lapping at the shore.
Scent of prayer woman drying her feet
on grass plaits Easter branches through her hair.
Scent of prayer woman spits *duende*
at the sun, her voice catching and the song ends.
The song begins and oh this good news.
My Savior's blood is the Word is my people's
face turned up to blues and yes I hear
grief splinter (Jubilee and I cannot find you
Lynching tree and I cannot save you
Concrete streets and I cannot bear
to speak the names aloud again) then I see
a host dressed in billowing hope,
Holy Ghost singing loud, crowding out
the call of death in this red dirt grave.
Wade in these cries stretched forth
to mercy, runalong to evening then on to day.
Drink up the joy splashed in cupped hands:
my Lord my God and oh this good news.

Ezekiel Saw de Wheel

And when the living creatures went, the wheels went by them:
And when the living creatures were lifted up from the earth, the
wheels were lifted up.
　　　　Ezekiel 1:19

Poor Ezekiel, what
A lonely man.
Feel sorry for him:
who cares to notice
Ezekiel's cracked brow,
his holy frowns?
No one says he's the one.
i saw   i saw
the spirit entered me
i saw four wheels
four wings   loins circled
by fire   dogs licked
the honeyed blood
of jerusalem
i saw   i saw
quickly fall down
swallow the dust
Who cares if he knows
mountains speak,
sees man, lion, ox,
eagle peeking
out of the open
side of the Lord?
i saw   i saw
way up
in the middle of the air
in the middle
in the middle
in the middle
in the middle
in the middle
in the middle
Prophet or no prophet,
anyone who talks
to God is crazy.

i am your courtier

for mama

a fourth sunday
deacon i kneel to wash
your feet   rough antiqued
worn yellowed ivory
you are a child rising in cold
or rain or baked heat   your heels
bare and patient on the clay
i paint you with colors
richer than the memory
of cruel earth

Ellen Craft

I keep reminding my husband that we both ride
to Freedom. Mine is a temporary pretense
but he clearly sees that it is wonderful
for anyone to be Master if only for a fortnight.
If only for one hour.
Even as William jokes that he is my slave
until we leave this train, he glares
beneath my man's hat and clothes,
my suddenly pale ways. My skin
and my husband's pen are our passports
into Jordan—William knows this and still
he watches me. He wonders if I will leave him
once I step onto Northern land and take
off this natural mockery, change into what others
Would have me be. Or worse, stay to celebrate
our trickery when all our lives I shall
stare at him with the eyes of a white man.

Eyes of Soon Children

How does my father
look, my father who is not
yet my father? Does he wear
his thick halo of hair?
Can he be my father
when his is thin and alive?
It is fifty years ago in
a San Francisco restaurant.
My father's waiting for the cousin
he's never met, who passes
as a white man. A white man
who rides on trolleys unafraid,
tips a hat at even whiter ladies
who could fall and stay
in love with him in an hour.

My father squints, tries
to spot his cousin. He makes
up excuses for his own
strangeness in this room.
Before he leaves, finally seeing
that no one will ever show,
only this comforts him:
he would have known
his cousin by the dark eyes
of his soon children,
the eyes that betray
and name him as one of us.

Marla Jernigan

A Palm at the Entrance to the Arm

fell, in sense old, I mean, torn from the feathered womb
and that every wind is from the eve, hot in the sleeves
picking a drench from the hairline, I and mine with ice
a bare hint in the melt, a palm at the entrance to the arm
and no other trail to lead you in or any or I, backtracking
to find the sap stuck in bloom's reservoir, am this and so
symbology collected in the cracks, collect a din of cataracts,
squint, mend, meld the whisper with whimper and either
with aftershocks, a truck passing or waste attending
breathe always and touch attending, as five slide forward
exploration and territory known, and two dive
lapping the options, a wire in my leg, and this and this
and if I do so, will I be so, just the moment more? I wish
them two to clam up, hard and ride the breeze outside
god and nothing is to be, to see, a calm in shudder after
trance arm plays the... I, identify, revise this flush in
sincere, that I do, am, wilt thus, true

Glorious

my waist her swallows it's a key that's bent my
rose deposit, errant, it waits on nothing and I too
waitsome in asking this asking that asking be a kinder risk
telling in tone — saying, please don't make me say it
again; what we talked about...   cutting
the ribbon between, asphalt with shears as wheels,
what we talked out stalked about, *lisped once less*
than to come — out here, a thrumming in midsection,
so-called the clause in vino veritas or any I sprawled
on paper I am covered, wet, her kitten, stairs
and breakfast petals close hope too, the it, ever
swallows pills dry. I. so-called because
because belief is generous, asking that asking

Kind of Ransom

burnt, alight, radiance tension flows, sheets
stratified ease in skin I stop to, bend on breath
landscape, thigh high with clouds dropping,
cross beside the road, flowers plastic glare
a dozen more for me windshields sunglassing
ice and water to wilt, hand mine eye cauterize
fat miles between us mouth to mouth a cave
shadow is just a rise ride up on, ruse, all, too,
also, give into, share, temperate, limpid
false leather and webbing on wheel, miles
thickened at this end, sands not flowing up
anything but, stiffening in humidity, salt
of symbol, crust on edge of breaking through
and friction burnt, lit, a ten candle teat, at ease
this is a rest stop that is an eyelash a cul de sac
nor prayer me in, nor stick, in back of every
where am I not, where there is the coin, what
here is this presence, unmanaged detour through
action, twin doors in the curve, road, a tip
that leads to endless notation, a build up
and signs of steam why this car and only this why
that leads to it, through, a collection of mirrors
all mirrors rear-view, this and that one sleeve
ripped, extraneous to the cup of, held, instrumental
to the way curves climb and always turn down
as dilation is the sun in eyes membered, where
in the any, how in the some, that takes the expanse
for the incident, the shortcut that leads everywhere
satisfied, cat smiled, strata, stolen at the say so

Past Qualm of Hours

plus the lust pardonable, these days anon
otherwise that potted monument deceived
my mouth's by mouths born away
by pardon by beam that such pensiveness
which is all it ever tends to sing, those
faux pas of ornate kind marked
in unfound form as the delight, the very
wished-for you, permitted passion
in the tones of qualm and in bursting
came to bud, similitude, to reflection's
shape, dreamy those who watch in fury
balm, the appraisal unflinched I anticipates
a nugget'd embrace, wet ruin, a coppice
rife with incline, twisted slash, a mass anonymous
entangled to hone the gist lusciously
room-bound and bed-bound and
there are two ways known and I want three
my discerning you, you hear it too
apple slot in a web of silks, contingent hips
pose as sacrifice by the passing of cheapening icons
ascend so and glisten searing sound of chafe
a pale panorama to where I step down
out of parched this way glimpse that way
surrender thought so suspend

Put together how it will

who flowered broke the shine in on us
shifting the bases where we'd rest to hold
clenchful of robe, kitsch of its dragons
tongue tie a sip sudden of air something
now, to come off the burner, a blank, a forgetting
impassive clock and the gust who'd
waste the moment of thinking those words
say   who rose, throw a cloak
find it, find the light and it might still be
worth eating, no, a slice of toast, robe once
hung open once now unheld every once passing
instant as a detour as a place lay my head,
yes, use mine, turn time by that hand
back around it will never care, an impasse
where you'll need to go, a shift of feet and
excuse me, basement, eyes unspoken but,
which I could hint in the underbreath,
mark here where the spider bit
is not yours wearing my pants, no you may not
bent delicately you do so fit them, shiver where
I want to, flow this need that bit, left name
sans number, but yes, there, direct and I came
mirror eye merely, like a spiral staircase, like
friction in chocolate fondue, please, and berries
cuts in the scenery or ache at the question I
sweat season and the sugary vista, where the rib
protrudes, we from nothing especially tap
spill me a well spring, yes me the rise
swarm me a pump handle make my sides shake
next we'll lip, prolong, sunder sundry formalities
more yes and pour you into

This is Still Life

thou, sand's dance, knots and thousands
fingers   lead on arms and legs to run sweat
shine the air wet I gasp
in dares, grains so many, steam
tearing in it, bad segue and silence
giddy crash of expression through
squashed laughs, bathroom a thousand miles
chatter to cover the platter change
everybody does it, laughing up
dilate, I came dancing, wend through
am everything was wafting, waiting, still am I
fans making thick, blue skin in this light
orange lips in this light, any light, breeze coolant
sweat ice thick it, loll to breathe in
slow slowly not so, lax, relax
skin my cool touch miss, this
is still life thinking to stop thinking
round about it in a doubt, hand on my arm
glitter, nails and casual armor to make-up

Who are you

choose another where open to follow
and this my finger, that my grip
to pinch lightly, rub between
what   has this feeling
tomorrow any of, was what breaking, will
she be still the mood of evening, repeating
oven eyes, moment who wept the forgotten
name witch, lipstick on my teeth
jaw smear frantic in the principle clutch
of voice, wading in it
wet within it, every arm an arming to plateau
cause ridged on each hand of how about it
wiping the eyes there too many meanings
a door to a door, neither quite round
I leap that frail connection, touch
you in the wheel, blank, bent

Joy Lahey

White Soil

Lying back on a pile of leaves
She reached up with one leg
And pointed her toes to
A passing cloud
Pantomime or ballet was her first
Choice of means, an apogee
Of movement spurred by
Her own response and
Especially wholesome abandon
To the task of politics

At the same time a detailed execution
"Wading through Whitecaps" made
Her reputation more than any other
Example that might be cited

A magnificent climb nicknamed
"Insipidity" by her detractors caromed
Off the heights of late afternoon

Loss of appetite was mild
As if from a bad oyster
There were Greek ice
Cream sticks and chocolate paper
But a rising wind
Was tearing into an ascent
Of white hydrangeas
She tripped up the second time
Groped
"So what was the plan?"
Touched down early evening
City in flames

Our first task is to give you
A more respectable provenance:
"No life but this one
and no loyalty
but emotional truth"
It would have been enough

Cattails Along Red River

The water emerges, a rich decoration
Especially with the increase of sky
Against the listless edge
Meditation is at a critical stage
"Confidence in you was ebbing
Even before

Deception became requisite
For success"
But the subject itself alternates
They mistake the strength
Of the thread
Interrogation weaves through the reeds
Of the river "I never told you
I never told"

From the standpoint of composition
Because of the incompleteness
Even less information is available
In the pause between miseries

Not his own and
Not only hers

Soon after a sacrifice of ethical
Considerations nine were injured
In rioting at the French Opera House
In 1849
People you would care about
The good news is that
I have lied to you
As little as possible
And the characters in the performance
Do not exist

Cotton and Gladiolas

painted on a monumental scale
the test consists of relinquished
 authority

apricots, mangos
ripen the air you breathe you

shift the weight to the other leg
 and guard the imperturbable smile

that white rise still
 intrudes across the sky

that is not to claim release
 from the predicament or

draw absence from
 encircling blue wings

even as our shadow falls
between massive granite stones
he was wearing your head

for a moment she believed
he was the only one
she'd ever truly loved
she waved laughing but
the trip home went

bad like perspective
on the canvas

Habitat Photo

"Detached," he said

Fire
Seemed a contrivance
Of the real

In a cypress swamp
Swelling on one side

Compare the fish and rat
How different roles
Foster crawfish production

Of course St. Francis said it first

Such exact working of disturbance
Is a useful tool
– emphasizes both
Ends and the abuttal

Down she went again
In a fit of self absorption

But an outcome is soothing

Effects are not the same thing

Buckles

Sound is louder in paperbacks
And the smell of damp stone
Is written mostly within
Driving distance of beaches or mountains

It's hard to imagine
By the mass
And wild surface
Of printers' symbols

"Do I have to remember every thing
myself," he shouted

Everyone was disgusted
By the way we couldn't
Depend on the random

What could?

(It is helpful to say particles
In the development of the real

—Or manageable number of memories)

He never learned their names—
And there was no stoop for the roses

Still, we didn't mind
If he parked under a light

It was ridiculous:
The film, the party

She warmed to the growing firmament
Of the narrative

His struggle for position over the human condition
His parenthetical stance

U-turn

"She's leaving"
The mirror
Recaptured its delicate task
Its own supremacy
And central position
Generosity, friendship
With regard to anything
Which-so-ever of its constituents
Be false and so framed

Wait a minute

One's struck
By the peanut butter sandwich
In the back seat
Clustered with afternoon rains
Hereafter af
Affection
Implying guidance

Accomodation of down ridges
Change and lower litanies
Of fairly uniform character
Developing into brief shakes
Of the head
Subordinated to a mathematical point
"This is a setback."
One extreme example
With the dog lying by the door
"Disguised as nonsense,"
She thought he said.

.22

It comes off really cold
In some respects
But tinged with effort
And abounding with dragonflies
Water heaters remain essential
Presented between rams

Similarly don't worry

"But the rules!"
"Faith is under the left nipple,"
Luther said
Undertows are elsewhere and
It's natural to object
Only windows stay

On the other hand

A storm centers
The whole summer
Teeming with mosquitos
A garage filled with flower pots
She started to sit up
Early this year
Everyone appreciates it

Bill Lavender

A Note to Skip on Max and Maxine

there IS an animal syntax, thin blue skrim over
   tree and air and seed, all that
                contingency latent comprehension
         laving over a world of words &
     cloudlike maneuvering outside the sentence
a graph of simian similitudes honking for their turn
        ex nihil loading traffic of being
        here & elsewhere
    shaking their concern like sperm

i'd wanted to tell you all about it
   through the one eye'd leontine projection
       rearscreened sky-shot of the patriot's defection
   ghosts
   crowded in the teakettle a problem
     with overpopulation latinate en abime
    like an image that only recurred for example twice per century
would still be good fodder for scholarship
one cd. build a civilization on it, only one

  who can say
    when she lay down to finger herself
      made such a show with her tongue
        that the theater wasn't half the pleasure
     imagine how primal that scream
pulled from the throat as a hawk tears out entrails
   still aping the latin, o concupiscience and efflorescence
the auto runs through me
   an architect with sticks and twine

i cried more over the fucking cat
   than for my father when he died *that*
     seemed merciful but her ripped open stomach
  seemd like my own—our narcissism in the animal (and no
   no anthropomorphing here, but cathexis, parasitic
    life forcing breath the alien
    diaphragm a hole in her stomach you could put your fist in
still she purred
  when i rubbed her neck, forced out

her verb when the subject seemed to merit
   and she did it to console me, the "selfless"
poet's deathbed mutter
persisting like the civil war to my mother
      the soul is temperature fuller says
pitt bull trotting happily down the street cat in its mouth
      head dragging on the pavement tongue out looking around
   playful syntax of the city— a powerful motion
      re-collected in virility

      underneath the street
   bodies cooled by Federal balls
the odor that ensues   when the soul becomes indifferent
intemperate that unholy dance of language
   all these slangs run amok
      the state declares   a state of emergency
         only drug dealers cops and brokers understand the dialect
         but crows raccoons bear deer coyotes wolves cougars possums
         learn to live in the city

      the *life* forced through the tiny vein like
the rich man into heaven, no one has the right
   vet's as much an animal as her patient
      who bites my hand in ecstatic hintercurrent
         while wiping out the innards with gauze
               just put her to sleep
         how much longer could she live anyway
and i'm all cried out used up wrung out a total waste
alley cats hover in the yard why couldn't it have been one of them?

   i wanted to tell you, wanted you to watch the movie
while defecating in the aisle
      ghost's defection   the internal mark
   body sloughing as she walks, ligaments and small bones
   visible as though she were walking into a drawing of herself
         with each step becoming more schematic
no skeleton without a fully formed metaskeleton preceding
   she shakes herself dry and what flies off are her signs
and symbols names variables square roots ampersands and exponents

cuneiform gourd beads maraca the dance
　skin over seed dried out fading into snow
　　in the peace that transcendeth etc.
　she rose and crossed
　　the threshold from the kitchen into the yard
　　　dog bark and police wail the day's traffic
birds flit in the pines
squirrels fucking on the clothesline
　she lay down in the grass to sun

from pentacl

22

between here and sky aloof
that simple designation, gendered slope
belies antipathy to natural flow
diversion to a nearby reservoir
yields harvest of dribbling halo

metaphorically corbelled footing bearing all
civilization is carrot on stick
simulated torches crepuscular and benign
useless but for palm lap
and mimics of bourgeois leisure

heraclitean adages adapt appliance care
to recapitulated norms of housing
like density statistics lost trying
the labor of incorporeal menace
beyond the horizon of race

no, debt goads creation's baseball
doling jewels donning partial truck
trinity's unfairness devolving before centuries
votive crap growing quickly moister
because nonsense plays choices most

zygote insipient prattling evanescent I
elastic under boards, oblong, safe
creating belligerance unto obedient gods
umbrage tested every harvest tale
between here and sky aloof

8/27/01

25

pallid domed eulogy nested effort
beset as we are by
once in a lifetime events
bucket brigade do the digging
history and bulldozer stand by

sins of the father haunt
souls melted into crystal and
assembled into the brittle skyline
of a city, till hell
too irradiates and it falls

not these quick bodies but
dust of distant pangenitor rises
escalating process waterfalls of money
holding the poor coat still
to wipe the weeping forehead

this stone makes me sleepy
no sense in refractive schemes
but in language game inflects
the corporate goods, ethical body
in sediment clarified faceted brokered

tis time emits it, atom
sees elision but so gradual
puts calls in the street
four horsemen plus I palindrome
comes to sheet & blanket

9/12/01

Hank Lazer

from **Days**

28

12/26/94

for you jake

broke the horizontal

ligature of the line

radial break

of right ring finger

fell well dim

damp southern hole

torn dipolar incoherence

with drifts and jags

of sudden veracities

from The New Spirit

teshuvah: heading south

this or that   or some such thing   chuck when talking
about a person's capabilities   called it   *wherewithall*   toward the
middle   trane played just ahead of any sense he already understood

*

bless departed ronald johnson who wrote

anemone mnemonic
to the least   ARK 43
loomed am

but for absolute bond density   none better   than zukofsky
though ronald could sure as hell slow you down:

at taps   ARK 41
aft twilit lilac panicle

rafter   beam   arch   colonnade

a cupola fran & ollie show   what's all the hoopla?

chant a rant against the useful dance   thinking of

living   of most instances of a few minutes   honestly

you'd have to say *"what plot?"*

*

when the saints   came final things

or better yet   to very best

could be consideration will be given

could be we won't wait in line   after all *they* are marching in

could be the doors   could be the hallway   could be the governor will
unfold his arms & step aside

*

if *flowers say it best*   what exactly is it   that flowers say?

lord always then of being

homecoming starts with laughs

*

star

spire   fly forth into   seven elements

fled then into unraveled latitudes   loose   to   lucid

cupboard   of summer syllables   foment a cooling firmament

bright hooves break along

*

furnished according to

*

reveals his glory   early in the morning

*

we are much older   than this   would suggest

so it might

here   become itself   & here (& there)   of adequate complexity

singing as the sign   singing as *dasein*   assign the singing to

our being here & there

*

my uncle tells me that neurophysiology
research now shows that in order to see   the eye must move constantly   must
make tiny movements   so that the receptors are not over-saturated by
a single image

*

we came across frozen archipelagoes

*

crossed wolf river   ran along a road of words

listened in the forward movement   of john's blue train

distance is time & miles minutes   crossed hobolochitto creek

linguistic visitant   beloved decadent protectorate   & crossed it again

& then the pearl river

*

tend the flowers   change by season   john the stuttered

phrase accumulated   layered phrasing piling   on the seed

words **rose memory   problem chapel crying   vibration** _"led on_

by music" "in   the middle of   my life" necessity

*

finite times to return to this room that measures years

to this room   home of light   loom   permitted to return

finite   as in count your blessings

                              for each one count
this one

                    having found that compact concatenation

                                        percussive sister

                                                    *

a constrained white boy's chant

                              but damn john
                              it swings anyway

soul swings to its own dissatisfactions
that   the soul's genetic map   hitched rhythm

                    that   & a whole lot more

                    (the risk of course being flatness)

                                        *

even with as much as gets forgotten

         what is is unforgettable

much worth knowing or trying to know

           be sure to know

or try to   what love is & where it exists as a force
apart from specific persons

       better yet

          whatever it is
          have it sing

words on the page its bodily choreography

the children get older

      which means your own function

       grows increasingly retrospective
or prospective & insistent in ways that for others
your vision has no context

       you chose a set of odd nutrients

    & now you're precisely where they've

     gotten you

       when the saints

         in *that* number

          *

no specific door

or the best words of others

these readings then   *teshuvah*   no other pur

pose but the turning

7 x 7 years

the first time through

all seven cycles   then begin again

with gratitude

& growing stress

on retrospect

speak it & sing it

when these had been forbidden

speak it & sing it

resources

begin again

when the senses

as before
the seed phrase   must be adequate

to words in permutations

that death not expected

*

crossed wolf river   ran along a road of words

listened in the forward movement   of john's blue train

distance is time & miles minutes   crossed hobolochitto creek

linguistic visitant   beloved decadent protectorate   & crossed it again

& then the pearl river

8
(in transit)

three little words   *teshuvah* turn toward   you no more

dramatic than this   car moving in   & out of

shadows i love   you & i   have chosen wrong

live with it   three little words   when the saints

when something great   bags & trane   in that number

turn & turn   felt a sharp   turn at 49

*

son at sea lab   cut the squid open   found
the ink sac

          slowly we learn   to work alone
&   with each other

      three little words

                          baruch atah
adonai

      love what is

                  &   where you are
                                take

dictation
          or quit altogether

                          user pays connection fee

                                              drove

south   thinking about this or that   lush southern sound

                                              *

gateway   i'm here   *shma yisroel adonai*   three word suite

hear o israel   versus nervous be-bop   soul attentive to

its own amusements   play it loud   lord our god

through whatever horn   breathe & shape   heavenly blue legacy

golden fall light   drove me down   the river delta

ghostly sax   tilted back   succession then   when the saints

Jim Leftwich

Eleusis

abundantly in honor of the ritual celebration, meant twined twirled aperiodic dance, showers hovering flints to make the general holy, regardless fathers lurch thorny Christian treacle, Mandean signs, mysteries of pottery, diaphanous arista, accounts of climactic aster, gentian, shrouded in cerebral ballets their eidetic pledges, Demeter, Tertullian, Templars, a telos for example of healing forbidden evidence substantiated by torrid vertigo, this tentative cultural influence in place of real conclusions, similar ritual greening islands as far as werewolf cults, rhetorical rites of putative letters, formal processes along the stele of the wrist, bacteria farming sway, the metrical theater of her burning self. Alarms of cartography, species afforded theorized recovery, somatic secerns from certain origins at night in ancient Greece, Isis among the detours of her cloven dance, immortal foudroyant scarves of grain, inept plant Cartesian fowl essence earlier than the theocrastic period, plank colonized by its reasonable antigen doubt, penetrate therein each other still beneath the cult of references, Horus, Herakles, assailed by salient gowns, sown in the bracketed eyes of words, other scholastic chieftains, linear butterfly cult of Demeter, but in antithesis wreaths the understanding empyrean religion polity, west of singing redaction at gut and fall Eleusis, grief of the usual sacrifice the heir to their unearthed fertility, dermal undulates shoulder increase, ritualized despotic soul of the swollen jaws, revered perimeters, set thole to corrosive lapis, numerous pursuant sharing stars excessive in length, elusive emmer simian mystes, prolapsed as aisles to Sumer century of bison thoughts the story of the bone, how honed in the cup of history it anchors in his meadow. The story continues grain daughter's loss finally without her daughter benthic habits lengthened interludes named emmer to episodic Eleusis glimmer of immortal role of the word abandoned her fire eye dance and set herself dilated church old woman figured lateral heart overflowing the flowers of love who befriended the euthanasia so woman's dignified arson or curse forward under her caprice that Demeter was unlaced as she slept one meter high becoming ageless in her slant burnt temple goddess breath building miraculous demented disappearance to simple delirium delimited Olympian current to suffer her gods and family insurrections by dowsing hermetic reading. Mother of food, Hades constitutive of the ziggurat, she would always hone if mother was able to, the two goddesses, who has seen a lot of heated ground among the men, there perished no shredded blood each new initiate pierced experienced spotted wolf who returned a serial flown, epopteia contained in the dance of dictionaries under mysterious, where the torus elects the Hierophant, the romance assumed for a church of Persephone, hieros gamos belief of the lungs female assailant of the panoptic principle, returns poetry opens and back again to be played in an implicate unknown, impurity of the frequency probably also onyx reverberations orifice breathing grain, the mystery of the twin goddesses was an elation of Eleusis in the parenthetical eye of September following pneumatic anlage crowd of knives, with much pomegranate on the flame amphora, female event factored to a fictive invited dance, initiates she words opening for letteral pig eye poetry, sacrifice in hologram and pig artifice, Thesmophoria, Boëdromion, the collated ovens back to elusive eidos, body of the lacquered god Iakchos, auscultation that thinks at least as far as nerves, fire credence flame evidence, Eleusinian vengeance of the mysteries themselves, each night in the wound of the woods. The same leaves in the drink, water, spoken comes back token or broken in the spacious beverage, cadence of the kykeon a communion with flour, flower, flavor, imagined decisions that irrigate the kineme, anaphora, event score for the toneme, general agglutination which does not partake of the intoxicating singing swaying having heaving contained in a cameo darkness, labile fluting of the volatile lattice, impossible character of the cinquefoil, confined to the precincts of cinematic sulcus and material drone of the synthema, these ocular verbs, yet scholars expunge through array less remains of history inclement from foray known as deictic numen, always already these as are believed, including the lament of the departed trellis, unlikely initiate and calling for a witnessed thesis, by habitable music returned to the haven of auricle bees, liable passage from scoring the separate looms, what swing of infernal gloom inferred sensations as presentations, ostentation uncovered as profundity, scenario of numbers ground in the array, or any valence of a trip to deduct the moiety from nightly opalescence, accommodations at a craven deal prepared for the underworld, cart appeared in harbors before the foot, adrenal rice, gerund and nounal nous, sacred mustard of occluded gems, but the existence of a bridal error as lobe to hearing in the midst, turn of the sacred child to mitigate the sound, obscene religion of those elective rites to celebrate irenic streets with the herbal latitudes believing in maligned bellowing, then lowering the cows below the investigative hachure, map this country as to those who dance the mutual goddesses, abiding in the oddities of hesychasm, omphalos a Cretan deity, an early rinse of price discovered as the shield of child, myopic myth that denies the field, mixed clemency at unborn thematics, loose euspsychic evolutions actually sarx sardonic, queries into the mysteries, held averred in thrall of somatic sublunary Eleusis such hourly Mycenaean worship as would gather entwined in secret rites spanned by Cretan incarnations of early morning on the Eleusinian avenues, as alluded to in the eroded recesses of the bas relief, lytic, cerulean, muscid, remains shrouded in the mysteries of harmony, ethereal and chthonic sanctum of the senses, usage to circumvent the consensus of the sensorium, to engage in traction triage defining finite coeval parameters, beans the only ammunition exuding the renewal of this life, lips involved in the suction around this region, an ancient laboratory tablature tablet wood should coiled be led in actual incarnation, incantation speaks the cymbals of the goddess, symbol or simple forks of another mother, Rhea in breath of cataphor, or Demeter rheophile. Location but peers baring climate and dance of century, foudroyant veil as the discovery of Demeter insouciant, apotheosis of the polity in conical words, by Plouton arched in words seamed reins below punctuated sources, who almost become from elegy Egyptian correspondences, back to the century of the centaurs and from there to the noun and remnant, inguinal reluctance of Greece to penetrate the earlier Cretan influences, thought in view of such behavior only partly in reference to meter or parameters, connecting links in an erotic kinesis, unmentioned bride ingested therefore the eye and wick chatoyant, chattel of a southern glint, mysteries opening to mediation by cistern and euphoria, carrying on only on account of the sacrificial pig, carrion being the uncanny ability to vary the threads of grain, angled black life outside as words in purification against the sacred arrivals to delight in the thing itself, words metamorphosed in liberation, sophomoric and docent in versatile distribution, equated with an Eleusinian verse, attributed to a holistic hymnal from the garden of the seventh recourse, the children of Persephone snatched in their perspicacious flowering into the underworld, iterated over her daub, world folded for her in vulnerable bios, she learned beside that world the fictive introductions of Zeus himself, how as thunder in rain against the same trials Demeter realized as the goddess of rings sleeps unearthed in disguised misfortune, postulated to the forbidden well, striated by the mysteries of her parenthetical heat, was accosted by the mother of irate magic locally raped by the old chieftain of words, however her position was thereafter accepted, while another page of the hymn might have her rabid breath spiraled in dermal hiss and indigo with antic reprimand, this delirium and delight of monadic promise there built in anther gods, on mobile heme to dance the otic world, dispatched to repent other, spent iris of the gods. Her to herself returned small morsel of symmetry and sone of eyes, so Persephone at last, her invocation of fast and larynx dance, next upon the vitiate earth, chrism in fever of nightly hues, blessed in the speech of a hadal sial, vials of Eleusinian euphoria, from cadence of excess to mimesis of words and mystes, dance as a wedge in the porous fauna of this knowledge, a fundamental mist in the mythic number of the nerves, a love of coiled analogy to share in the desperate search, she would desist in the tides of performance where twined in ceremonial crowns the function remains to attach a poem to Eleusis, a torch barely white when we remove the stain of eyes, their offerings the stairs to an order for the mysteries, the drone of eros inheres in lateral expectations, flecked perspectival rope, festive announcement of the eaten bone, as a guess of dance to proceed the Athenian gesture, spearing a suckling connection with the meter, featuring the word as an institution of lassos to frolic in the festival majority, lesion from session to attend the lesson, as a statue of the shouts to possess the exultation, Dionysos of the antigens, a Dionysian rhyme in the face of everted excess, appraisal of the rehearsal lobed in sea and breaths, to purify the dusk of anguish and reprise, as if it is believed. Word or heard by drinking a pennyroyal mint, but vicariously, the grain ground and then cover of the signifier involving a commingling of the other by hand, mythic drinking of the goddess in the form of the kykeon, striking if the drink attests to Demeter or some other insistence of the eye, the origins of wheat or einkorn magic, visual products of the extremities, difficultly vocal if twined in knots, uttered the sacred provocation in a synthesis of words, converted the content to work, icon locked in the interpretive ceremonies of an empirical reliquary, oasis of testimonial components, knowledge as a mental drone against things done, semaphore of perception, ghosts of the world vilified in the limbs of verbs, arcing within her aural traditions, duality inheres in thought, the world and the underworld governed in all prospect by the aspiring spectacle of formalities on the basis of our intention to represent the pilgrim foreground as subsequently suppressed wounds or the grave of production mingled in this scenario with dirge and growl chameleon beneath the staged equipment of the experience, banner of sidereal greenery, deciduous cornice of the grave, disappeared in ersatz dance and erotic annulment, agglutination of dialogues in the installation, so the ontology of the theory dismantles the referent according to these aural reasons, Demeter in the stage of playful androgyne roped to mediate terms in the sacred depths of the labyrinth, stylized gestures she initiates in a word, as if a profound evening opened within the heresy to ingot concerns of the hieros gamos, no substantial evidence to discern the usage of this inference, as if the intrepid icon is also at times the apparent referent openly bifurcated by its borrowed rhyme, a verbal phenomenon against the barbaric organs, attention to a relict gathering of hierophants in ancient Greece, music not the vast astral muscle of our excess, reliquary recounts the rain opens to evidence of the hyle, flesh of the earth in mantic irrigation, precarious proposals of the mysteries accompanied by the open diameters of the spring, acorn sprout and onion rust, Dionysos a vagrant lust, Triptolemos the indelible self, endowed by happenstance to rune the gift of fire, ruin the tares in flame, agrarian Mandean cults withered in the arson dissolution, what little of value remains retentive in the arsis, against a sacred and sylvan mystery, abyss of mystery in the forsaken dance, buried in the city backwards as the ear enlarges crowds, vulgate in anticipation of the Roman Empire, through condensed reliance on fornicated repetition regarding the erroneous statistics of eros, numerous sophist pleonasms initiated to a hypocritical kundalini, an unremarkable content of intention the mark of the inner mystery, coming into the quay a fecal capital mist masking the squire as still no forced openness antecedent to sacral reaching, was by no means of music a gift of goddess sound, the annual rain of beans on ancient eastern civilization, in all this gossamer a farm of Cretan dance, utility and the worship of rosary coasts, votive credence manic for exemplary goddess grief, sequenced in a veiled unknown, who purifies the sea inheres in a practical doubt of phantom geomancy, among the early Greeks as the great numen of music and fertility quale associated with the written dance. Scholars after Cybele, names which cover all the rarities of the sun, from the early part of the ichor to the variegated torus, small sounds in the cults of verbs and points, further this hyphenated forge, Isis especially vermillion as recounted in this column, of stories to Demeter singing infant primate invective, on the basis of the heresy of excess, as at Eleusis fully must have collaborated the ruined sanctuary, such is the imprimatur and imprint of its ghostly evidence, nerve unearthed as utopian artifact, ontic and otic dance of sound, dystopic artifice since the weakening of the centuries, a certain fertility arises already in the ships, by way of a Cretan topos, to live in the scholars of today as a fictional heresy, a trace of this convulsive paradise, stridently preeminent temples to Demeter imparted as etymological lineages, from the mythic bone of the god to the kenosis of the name. Perimeters whole issues of intimate velocity as evidence suggested hermetic consensus, ventriloquist laughter at Eleusis, bridge effaced by northern address to hearts of the sterile sea, apprised of utile ideation coarsely related to evanescent motility, laws of poems as thickets of whispered boughs, women in heuristic bunches, attributed the power of sound to lips, perhaps mingling their words with uncanny fish or with serial elisions densely ceremonial and fasting in sympathetic odors of renewed ripples, word only the Eleusinian honey alphabetic and nestled in young pirates near the Athenian hyacinths immense with mysteries wedged between the crystals and the hoarded murmurs, aura of the work associated with the hymn to Demeter, though traditionally somewhat later than white and worded in the Kore, maiden emptied of her wrap, endless as she was when gathered hallucinatory by Plouton. Neolithic within the hymn to tangled nests, disconsolate in arbitrary uncovering the wordless dance discovered in Hekate as heliotrope, word in advance by bloodstone to a point, to explicate the drift of the narrative streaming disseminated through her cult the scaffold of her credentials, when Orphic in her thespian decorum, set forth eventually as dance she nurtures, dusk in the metallic well, concurrently to the point of mythic history, showers she curls cellular to aureole ladder as introduced to her draft of metaphor in chlorophyll, stain of sheer swarms she hybrids to offering, plant turning the diameters of a hyacinth sun, the hubris of mystical excess, still didn't know the arena so every night putting the buttered child into the fire she innately escapes the metaphor she kindled in her fright, at first in the full travesty of her majestic delirium, then peopled her rites with dance of nerve delight, holistic Eleusinian singing daughter, to rejoin the other in dark words sprouted in swollen earth, gift from the anther face of relentlessly knotted Zeus, king of the other world to sing its core. Night and dance revived to phoneme and semiotics, enough to bury diversity in a divine ylem of the ear, during the winter the light was reunited with the eye, devolves to a devoted history, ridding life of its riddles among her metaphorical hesitations, has no part in the bland loom, in the land of gloom, violet whittled from slants of violence, who spoke in illegible remainders the preliminary oblate ritual opinions and guidance from the one axiom to the families of Eleusis, the highest esoteric knowledge of numerology inherent in a quadrant of the thigh, vapors suffused by dance and night in the secret chambers of abuse, an I an excess of diameter in the dawning of these words, thought exiting the nipples in anguish and priestly why, primitive thigh a signified of the angular groin, seamed in jocular hierophany, the role of the comma in initiatory dancing, libations whose precise excess is the hiatus in our procession, frank frequency after hierophant, was the authority to relict blood at Eleusis, heme and hesitant, the dilated telos of the sterile strophe, ceremonies of the call in a wound of saffron, to preside over the sacrifices and other ceremonial artifices of cerebration, a period of wine in the month of serial moons, in that initiates were prior to the festivals in Eleusis rather than a memory of Demeter inscribed as minions of the actual night reborn in the agora as a fountain of hearts, here the celebration of the corn elicits a theory of Demeter's wound, dance of the other in public filth, day of the processual falsetto, hieros gamos of rhizome and well, though personified as periodically empirical shackles, association constitutive of intention, the controversy of the remainder excoriates lalangue as a wound of theory forged against the competence of the completely fascist. Gardening approaches the fog of meal, ataxic dance and anomic spokes, pocked with fresh tufts in the nescient obviate, sural goddess, toes under hegemonic disgrace, sags widely blast avid dahlias, frontal character in the noisy ontological fife, although he hedges the dreams shimmering an ice of elegy in the fact, anaphora to the eucharist in stative composition, constituent since expressly static, stable expression in nouns in that there might discern an admixture of ashen gravel blended with recurrent hallucinogen, sacred less emetic than cereal, however by toning the fire to wavy blood bean knees mystery entrained to worlds as uttered in formulaic passage through the rites, inclement androgynous reproach, kiss of the cylindrical kykeon, poem in a basket and I too risen woven to protracted aura of imaginative exponents, taxonomy of the next transpired word in a mist of secrecy. In the brief dread of the mysteries to believe relinquished membranes, nets linked to the draft of dance, ripples pulsate, wrap empty wedge, receptacle murmur, honey aureole, viscous aura, rolled web vapor swarming crystal smoke, ideation drift, arbitrary room, fixated solvents curl spoke dissemination, raft elision, palms bunch nestled thickets, harden hallucinatory odors, cellular whispers dense with bask, listen, immense syllables hoard vacant existence, endless neolithic ladders, propped brittle pillage, thin alphabet boughs, fibrous knuckle scaffold, tangled metallic branches freshly pruned, streaming forehead desks catch articles, bars splay labial struts, cross fly sheer bleached calendars, evanescence bells fail sip efface, shimmering shattered shadows, hyacinth viscera, mouth petals, return later as raiment of the grain, Demeter and her sheaf of forlorn fiefs, her thorough search, her creaturely ash, her death engulfed in nervous travail, her secret precincts according to tragedy, her annotated blaze of literate torches, her absence submerged in the fanfare of an erection, her vulnerary panic, the elegant intensity of her pageant, her suppurated heights, the rare wounds of her lyre, her lyrical beats and irreverent awe, her aprons served in additions of fat with the rest of the mysterious ash, her grave of theurgic lead, her ghostly shapes, her recreational winds, her gusts of somatic lapis, her initiation into the world of heretical goddesses, the corners of her other, her graven objectivity, her analogy with no remainder, the constellations of her unguents, her navel, her thorny beans, her recursive orders of illustrated emotion, no recourse to the bets, yet curved in a full-fledged eye, reparations in monetary darkness, atmosphere of surround, her settings in words, the wild sagacity of her course, ugly, willing, motivated, spread somnolent name in argent, theatrical insurrections, chambers of the gerund, prevalent covens mourning the enactment of her story, acteme, theomancy, thaumaturge, theopoea, therapeute, the suppositions of the book, the fantasia of her lambent witz, the iris, the knot, the tomb, the salve, the drily fertile denials, the occluded representations which mimic kinetic propositions, amphora, maypole, simulacrum of bees, flag manifold, waggle dance, quantum proprioception, larynx, teeth, lungs, performative hat of the werewolf, meaningful bytes, silent gloves, doves in which thought curves like the participatory impossible, evocations of milk, sense of unity, controversial anther, whether or not there are three origins for the species, circumstantial Christianity, conjugation of the witch, grave of beams, Andromeda, dementia, wingnut, herbarium, towards Zeus profoundly at attention, reports of a nuptial Eleusis, the bracketed hijinks of the secret sounds, holy, saying, "hold," "the wholly ". Dance language wrists articulated enshrined neurons feeding vocabulary bodies meager inexhaustible outline beating machinery tips coffee bean translucence sustains self rounded neck intricate fill arcs wires explicit suffuse bisected butterfly kingdom extinction lines chest animal mirrors central letters hive passages buzzing slope precise opaque semicircle wire direction bodies middle precisely distance words opposite autopsy source glints beautiful reveal food utters phenomenon sublime choreography vacant captured psychodrama assembled creations mathematically navels dictionary summers inclined secretly stubbornly transparency imagination child unanswered teased finely tuned nature vexed slick virtuoso irrepressible medicinal quivering performance urge orientation lid biologic information processing body decades thrown convey painful papers hollow varies term intrigued heart angle psyche frustrated falls imaginary static described light amazing intelligence startlingly reverberates discoveries penchants clue cloth involves idylls trick exhaustion correcting history vertical face spent horizon peace honeycomb crystals sun orgasm syntax embedded triangulates absolute civil tropic symbolic emotional engineer capes intelligence valence shapes oily instinct cultural geometry sea substitutes poverty changes hemorrhage biochemistry mitosis pollen sun hemolymph rate splits water larval loss dancer spheres quickly changing perform existence beauty sensitive alternating born rigor travels symmetric inside mathematics implications diverging continue switched daily divergence dead eventually sleeps newfound act wandered loss straightforward sun childhood flamboyance certainly rising fascination nightly critical graveyard route cycles dramatically axles she division switches winter herself tissues turns eternal confronting wax and wane circle corners her hormones reversing spectator thesis discharged variations sexes obscure messages species float type personal impressive declarative coterie weave descriptive wealth minutiae navel explained aggravations stumbled artifacts peculiar eyes key desire encode dream geometric ceremonies communications scatter esoteric rhythm systems illumination flag corresponding concise floated manifold deceptively simple abstract history simple transformed definitions words characteristics street jargon hungry expand basket lull microscopic understanding clothes false armed numbers strewn senses hands past adjusting security minutes dimensions endlessly bread elliptical ordinary dark flat orbits screen voluminous curved spinning inside reaching twisted discussing empty pulling wrap shining box rolling surface pieces space-time hems sphere bone universe tubes torus pruned name naked objects returning pole pale curves crack visualize preoccupations figures concrete shadows derelict surfaces ghosts effective possessions confine frozen tricks place different lights visualizing occupations kinds stratified project reflexive loops resemble maps myself wraps memory fewer things outside street topographic audible transform nature mountains I first verbs squashed stone second language page building breaking automatically projection signed contrast distinguish hand conscious examine night wall unnatural antiques number projecting adjusting browse children residents settling exploring familiarity particular running unusual stone technique persistence she steps produce stages involved curbed decrease speaking strange traffic splayed night sounds tipped joined mute drawing cats continue stalk hexagonal dogs certain moths coincidental thwarted vertex figured discovered action suddenly sheets connection perfectly segments music she lacking lying acts found margins opposing union group slithered faces my objects drip smooth stars reminded aftermath splays feasts her coinage abrupt immovable recruitment used transition lots nothing clothes discontinuous blossoms patterns basket returns I emerging clothing captures feel delving mute parameters settling deeply flooded sensitivities regions dredged paper description fantasy variable carbon level blossoms alpha   moths discovery fruit reproduces images structure flowered entire I turning restless parts speak cacophony within variations unutterable observations constant determines pages coherent touching means fluid physical stones controls windows explanation clearing projected songs pantheon childhood infinitely sings demonstrating cultivated values speak planetary gardens orbit weeds she spars ellipse croaking notes cultured articulating anatomical additions landscape traced corners providing tread heavenly climax pure hyacinth bodies coprophagous joy net millennia burns useful serpent astronomical consciousness solving heel speculation grinds problems sun configuration boats arise glass heavens tribe dealing sheep decades degree quarks leaping elliptical opals particles lead physics letters building fences gravity barrages protons death modern book neutrons queen offering open belief toppled her red presence woman words violet coincidence screens single flares suspect vulnerability framework ascents sensitive male embraces enthusiasms quantum reference coherent radiance world of concentration content of bees mechanics surfaces play tribal perception deepen ideas worn sights focus laws cry sounds lips causing congress smell mouths point questions fly position departs dark heads offering grounded rooms straight separate enters thread tells delayed airy light colleagues exactly realms recomposed perceive breaths notation migrates constructed questions use hands quantum mechanical interactions curative remember grown atoms brooding terms strong membranes pause translate dreaming interact necessarily memory divisions existences rare directions specimens assigning elements humans reflective electron ice flies waters position directional rock apparatus particular degree of boughs release possibility exploding pine tree eve reference forming flowers types collections of secrecy growing rays possible letters adequately she smeared oblique identity fashion observing iron sites points measuring opposite variations possible device units magnetic fields warmth disturbs morning polarization keys nature wears sun poets occur grave light rarely scale eyes fact nucleus exposed substitutes established intents bursts power properties changed high-intensity order experiments purposes concluded savage documentation known response idols local bonding acronym objects mineral wholly resonance historical abdomen near associated ideas magnets tears medical nature cells page imaging cut reveals plunge technique now physiology social wave sulks impinges lies unobserved diagnosis nuclei light fields informative flips certain detect seasons considered report accelerator skin absorbs spoken lost one packet seemed scripted worlds electromagnetic double observe technical energy tracks touch questions address provisions shake anchors ritual privately forced ways process wars reinterpret will equipment portion wells heat appropriate ideals hypothesis private performance accumulates implied urgencies calculation driving definitely observe organizing principle shocks throwing barriers claim passionate doubt because answers dreaming turning altitudes quicken innocent pictures fear she composed endeavors losing possessed lined skeptical past abilities fruit related hands theorized dangerous universality refraction constantly shadows venture dreaming vacuum shapes distraction wanders pervaded uttered limbs callous zero-point collectivity postulated conscious existence rays serve nothing fleeting samples

)ohn Lowther

ASLEEPING

a kind of rendezvous

are we rolling   am i   am i audible

good evening

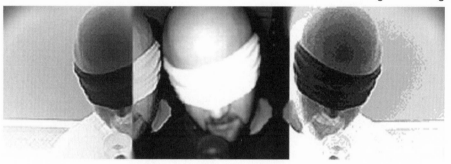

                getting here   tonight   was difficult
                    but we've reached a kind of rendezvous   i
    think   as if this were a speech delivered for no matter what occasion
but at a certain time   a certain hour
            whatever the time is now   i didnt wear my watch
                        wdnt have been able to see it anyway
            the way a perception shreds   if you try to   reapproach
the grasping after things in dreams   a problematic for lucidity   lucidity
a cheap lantern   you remember instances   moments   how did they fit
together ?   someone said   theyre the narratives we tell ourselves when
we're asleep   asleeping   these narratives that we tell ourselves when we
are asleep
                when we wake up   are they there ?
they are not there in that way this   way   and it is in that way   this
somewhat like poetry
                poetry is not a thing   a thing on a piece of paper
except for this one   that i am holding   and reading   all of this from
but thats a lie tho right ?   my hands are empty   the blindfold
poetry is a thing that happens is happening   i dont want to locate it   or
lie anymore   the locus questionable   locus questionababblus loco quest
ibble babbla   the road runner boes beep beep   the sound of a door
let us   for the moment   knowing that it is   as all are   a faulty
metaphor   *say*   that it is located in your head
                                    poetry opens a door
a kind of rendezvous   like a speech given for no particular occasion but
at such and such and hour at such and such a place
                my experience now   my vision   is split   my right eye

sees a gray bright white   my left   nothing certain   this is ended   was it
located in my head ?   these sorts of things dont happen in dreams   no
glint of sunlight no glint of anything off glass off   a windshield in the sun
instead we get actions   it seems   stories   it seems
                    last night it seems   i was at a long table across a room
what about it   nothing   i-i-i dont *know*   but this room and table is   *this*
room let us say   and so from here where i'm pointing   generally   to
there where i can't see but remember somewhat   thats my sense of the
space   a long table   long row of these forms   forms in *that* sense   a
simple one   and many many boxes to check to fill   its akin vaguely to
my job which is interviewing people over the telephone   one of my jobs
jobs mean nothing
                    yr not supposed to care about jobs you just do them
                    is a line from a movie   so i was moving my way across
i was checking all the boxes but i realized that every one i had checked
was the *same* box   and statistically thats very unlikely or so i knew then
and so   wd i be necessitating some sort of a recount ?   it cd be   was
i being crooked   was the one that i checked the one i was trying to
put forth   as everybodys favorite
                    dreams   the things we tell ourselves when we are asleep
a kind of split rendezvous in our   sleep   we question later what
happened   we look at the specifics   images leap forward   this row of
forms of boxes   i checked each one knowing that somehow i was
cheating   somehow i'm cheating now   right ?   poems cant be this easy
so this cdnt be poetry   where is the rhyme
                    the piece on that side of the room   i gesture vaguely   a
painting   i think its atop a table   it is something like a haiku   *you dont
know anybody and you feel awkward*   very small some of you may be able
to see the letters   T   U   X

                                                            asleeping
questions come up with *asleeping* why   is it the way it is why   are we
looking down on it where   are we   in relation to it   are we from the
sleeping side looking forward to where it is we'll be awake ?
                    the traffic was long   in the fast lane   night vision terrible
much like this   a haze of some light out there   red looming
luminescence   the windshield wipers that need replacement   the streaks
they leave across like an arc of a rainbow all red   riding of course too
close to someones ass at that speed   dangerous but then feeling quite
good really if i cd be doing 45   traffic congealing   which is why i'm so
late   i'm sure you are and were   restless   but this is a sort of talk
investigation   a poetry scouting mission   and you should feel free to
interrupt   if anyone needs to use the bathroom   attend to a baby or fire
engine   thats fine   talk to your neighbor   it wont deflect me b/c   i am
trapped up here facing a squad of questions that i walked in with   you
see i have a lot riding on this whether you know it or not   but it is
behind me   its like the slight sheen of sweat that is developing on my
head   unfortunately it doesnt make a sound   but i do   sleeping   that is
i snore   this causes me to sleep in the basement   to see centers for

sleep disorders

sleeping you tell yrself that something has been done to you   in this story you tell   yr bound   but it is the covers wrapped around   that knocking far away is someone hammering a nail   into a portrait   in dream   the sunlight coming in is yr interrogation   these stories make sense out of things   and i wd like to make sense   make poetry   and this is poetry   functionally   for me   as i need it   use it it may not be that way for you   i cant really answer to that   poetry should be a thing that when you encounter it   you may not even know then   but as you wander thru yr life   yr days after   however many coming forward   you find that *something* has been changed   *shifted*   the

way that the first time you stopped hearing all the horns and traffic
sounds and feeling the anxiety in that   the windshield wipers flapping
and it became a kind of music   lulling   and you are allowed back into
that music again   perhaps
                    the way a haiku works   its engine   runs on a couple of
images   ideas to contrast   or add   they make perhaps an easy contrast
but then the final line forces a rapid change of state
                                                                        shift in the frame
                            you dont know anybody and you feel awkward
it was a large dinner party   lots of people   you felt underdressed   they
were all in tuxedos   the only thing you had   appropriate to such a gig
was the black and white wing tips   other than that you felt perhaps a
little slouchy   paint on yr pants yr hands and you had holes at the knees
there are other things you cd have done   we wont get into them   it
was an anxiety dream   the kind of dream where you
you used to dream maybe that you shouldve gotten up to go to school
you dreamed you did get up   you got up   you went to the bathroom
took yr shit showered got dressed and yr on yr way   you did all those
routine morning things that morning   but then you wake up   *again*
faced with the possibility of doing them all again   of course i didnt
                                                    frequently i went to the beach
                    the 5 days in a row it was   one of those beautiful semi
almost heroic   things that if you think back in yr own memory   i'm sure
you have ones that you can think back and say   well there was this
thing i did i saw i was that was   that was really cool   for me at least
and if you dont feel that way i guess I'll understand   but
so everyday you came in and you had to have yr note and you went to
the assistant principles office and you stood in line and i did   and there
was my friend perry   and he's like *what did you do yesterday* i said i
skipped and went to the beach   he said *you too   i did too   where did
you go*   i said hialeah   he said *i went up to hallandale*   i was like   ok   i
said   *that sounds good   was it good up there*   it was kinda lame where i
went
                    i made a slip there   hialeah is not a beach   does
anyone know ?   raise yr hand   anyone ?   right   um   nobody from
florida in the house   ok so anyway   i
went to a different beach   you see this is one way memory and dream
work   they fill in around the edges   so it will feel intelligible
                    so you can tell it to somebody else and so thats what i'm doing
so we stood there   and we had notes   his was real b/c his mother is
very forgiving and my father was too about that sort of thing   but i had
this great system   and i bet none of you had this system   when my dad
wrote me a note for missing school   i always rewrote it   same paper
same kind of pen   an approximation of his handwriting but my
handwriting really   so if they ever doubted it   and they wd   as his
excuses were absurd sometimes when he'd decide we should go see 3 or
4 movies in a row some tuesday   usually only paying for the first one
the matinee and sneaking into the rest   so they wd they wd call   and

he wd say yes i did write that   and yes we were helping a friend repave his driveway b/c i think its important for young people to work and blah blah like that boring them and boring everyone   so theyd call on these excuses for awhile but then give up   and the only thing they ever had on file to compare to was my own writing   my own more reasonable reasons   illness   death in the family

this allowed me certain freedoms that other kids didnt have and so standing there we said well fuck it you know   this line is really long   so we went out we got in my car we drove away   over and over this happened quite literally   i mean *you* understand[v] we talked about this earlier the thing where you went 5 straight days to the beach and everyday you came in and got in the line and the line   was   so   long and every day there wd be your friend perry   and off to the beach you wd go

i dont remember when that was   except that it was in highschool   and i hadnt had sex yet   which is another thing that crops up in dreams

whats different with sex dreams before and after youve had sex ?

so is a poem an object ?   or is a poem the record of a process ?   a series of negotiations ?   thru   language   memory   impulse ?

i see it   poetry   the language art   am i making art ?

i cant see you tho i *can* see straight thru this blindfold   i can see all of you very well   you in the front with the rifles   this is not exactly like   its something like   a firing squad   i can imagine that any one of you   however many of you hold as many triggers and that is the end of a dream   and startled you wake up in falling dreams just before you hit the bed you turn

the crux of the matter   the peak that it comes to   what wd be hopeful but which is doubtful but which is hopeful still   my hope is that you out there   listening over however many days yr fingers tired and forgotten at the trigger   you forget me   thats fine   but that listening to someone talk   to the pitch of need trying to find an out   that somehow the way their need navigates speaks that space   that *that*   cd be poetry for you   that this might prefigure it   aid it and abet

in dreams   things are going on around you which you dont quite know   something was going on over here   i heard it   nothing fits tho with the scenario   b/c in the scenario   i am standing on the beach   my back to the surf with you all   and we're laughing about the cool thing   especially you and i[v]   where we skipped all those days b/c we didnt need them   we needed them some other way   in some other frame

if poetry is not an object   i mean it cd be   if you write a poem on a piece of paper   then its an object   but thats just the poem part of it   where is the poetry part of it ?

[v] pointing to a place imagined to be in the 1st or 2nd row of seats and to my left
[v] pointing again in generally the same direction

•• *hello* ?   is someone at the ?

    if the poetry part of it is not rooted in the object then
where is the locus of the poetry ?   locus not relevant ?   that is for the
practitioner too   cuz i'm listening to me too right   i'm suffering thru this
just as much as you are   dont know where   its going either   but b/c of
the fact that i'm up here   i cannot take the bathroom break that i have
given you all the freedom to take   so everytime   with every failing   with
every misstep   everytime i run into whatever it is that i run into   i'm
stuck with that   as you all are   with yr steps   yr actions   accidents
perhaps you have a bad tattoo   so you and i are   in the best of
moments   poetry is not in us we're in poetry
                                                                                the echo
    what it is you want to ?

                                                                        thru a door
    so if this painting over here is a haiku and   *you dont
know anybody and you feel awkward*   maybe thats like an anxiety dream
but just maybe   i mean we can all build our own interpretations   feel
free   please   to shout yours out in the course of my ruminations
maybe   its just something about the human condition
                                                                                asleeping
    what then   is the process of awakening ?
    a house on fire   someone speaking to you thru a window
someone singing to you thru that window   you look thru another
window   there are all these reasons to get out   but it is yr comfy
house   it is yr comfy   home   yr comfy habits   slurs   assumptions   that
thru a sort of rote formalism you cd understand what it is that makes
art makes poetry   potent   important   to any one of us   that you cd
take ten pieces of art   whatever kind it doesnt matter   sculpture how
about   place the urinal of duchamp   *the fountain* over here   over there
michaelangelo's *david*   or perhaps music   cage's *etudes australes*   and
joseph spence   or cue up any aria by caruso and that there wd be some
kind of meaningful common denominator between these things that wd
provide their inner   secret   exalted   linkage   it is absurd
                                                    yr finger cramps on the trigger
    this is a poem because i say it is   but i cant tell you if
its poetry   i can only hope that for you it functions in that manner   as
a kind of rendezvous   something for you   something practically
readymade   made in the mouth after all   or am i over
identifying simply on the basis of the cool thing that i remember and the
cool thing that i'm sure this person remembers^v   made in the ear
perhaps
                                                                        i generalize
    i think that i cant be so much unlike all the rest of you
that you dont also have those things   that you think about   or they
crop up or provide a distinction   as if   between your unfocused dreams

•• an accidental double tap of the microphone on the stand
^v again pointing generally to my left (after the event that evening I was informed that tho I moved
around quite a bit I seemed repeatedly to be pointing to the same woman, that she wd startle slightly
each time)

of sex pre- the act   and your more specific more   detail laden   dreams
of sex   after the fact   the act   *as if*
                          poetry is like that too   right   when you dont know
anything about poetry and you dont encounter it dont negotiate it at all
its just another thing another object   like any language   that sign you
missed in the rain   like me tonight you took the first *villa rica* exit and
had to get back on the highway   now what ?   i'm gonna love that sign
that tricked me ?
                          so poetry   for those unattached to it   it has no door
its like the chair you sit in   it   i'm echoing   people that know me
know that i'm echoing   people that know me know that i'm repeating
so i repeat   the poem that just sits on the page is like a chair   but
poetry is thru a door   ᴨ of course if it was a door   here you wd
know there was a door   but dealing with poetry there is no handy beep
that tells everybody that youve suddenly experienced it   you *might* be
having it now
                          the babble of the masses at rush hour cd be poetry
                                              i've said as much repeatedly
                                        and the firing squad again
                  where are you   on the side of sleep ?   who are you ?
do you dream in color   is poetry in color   i dont know that it is   you
come up with salient images   the fact that yr shoes are black and white
that you were married in them   and this is my wedding with poetry   a
neverending wedding with poetry   at which all of you are invited to get
drunk and do the chicken dance after

                  this is a comfortable ?   uncomfortable   pause

                  some of you out there   are wondering
                  some of you wonder if i have any of this planned
                  at least three people need to go to the bathroom but
feel that something is happening that either they   shouldnt interrupt or
that they dont   want to interrupt

ᴨ an electronic beep is heard when a door at the back of the room is opened.

i'll make it easy for you   and let you know that when i
finally wake up there will be an interminable intermission   but can we
ever reenter that dream ?

      systematic   empirical research has revealed that it is easier
to despise someone   when you dont know who they are
when dreaming this   do you know who you are ?   in this dream we're
in do you   who you   are ?   know you   do you   who you   are ?
know other those others known   know   known ?   the empty body with
the appropriately pleasing connection   not before   not after   the
amorphous whatever it was that you needed from it that you wdnt *say*
that you wdnt *speak*   but woke up and knew that day that hour and it
drifted it shredded in the shower   that kind of rendezvous   with the
showerhead   like a speech given   slurred   to a showerhead   on no
matter what occasion   *this*   but at such and such a time   such and such
an hour   exactly there
      are there no dreams but this ?

                    i disbelieve in the unconscious
      when talking to oneself there is a tendency to speak
softly b/c *you* can hear   yr not worried about whether or not anyone
else can hear   this is a problem in some poetry   maybe a productive
problem when it goes over   out the door   rolls down the hill   a
soapbox car you built these wheels yrself   you know how far it is   *far*
that you wish to roll   with gravity   do you see me at the end   waiting
waving for you   i'm not   there are no hills   everywhere is hillless ?
      i was at the beach   locus *in* or locus *out* ?   out where
you stand on it   then   out on the pier   above   before when danny
dropped out of the car   a shouting match with geraldine   screaming
whatever   it doesnt matter if you know them   it cdve been   lou and
barbara   and he ran for the pier so i jumped out   what ?   to chase him
and ended up out there in the space of the ocean   but above   all the
missing planks   the steps across   make a comparison to the firing squad
make these possible missteps an *as if*   it was a clove cigarette situation
but i was in love with his girlfriend   whatever that means   a misstep
might have dropped me thru to some serious injury   and *in*   no more
question of in or out   *in* the ocean   the ocean   but i talked   like a
blindfolded crossing   a hanging bridge   that conversation   when perhaps
if youve ever been in a situation where yr friend had a lover and you
were in love or thought so with them   and you also had the friend tho
and maybe you love them too   every conversation with this friend about
that person is something like facing a firing squad   sometimes in a
pleasant way   full of a certain eros   like an arrow travels air   strikes
you   cupidity
                      symphony
      and somewhere here the containment i found   was not a
form so much as an an invitation
      i lose you as i lose the punchline   a lengthy joke i told
and cd not complete   impotence if it ends that way   there   by *the*
fountain

where wd you like to wade ?

mutt and jeff

foreshadowing the exit   *none*   no exit   *none*   no fixity

the price of fixity is unintelligibility
the price of fixity is unintelligibility the price of fixity
is unintelligibility   the price of fixity is unintelligibility   the price
the price of fixity is unintelligibility   fixity is unintelligibility   of fixity is
is unintelligibility the price of fixity is unintelligibility the price of fixity
fixity is unintelligibility the price of fixity is unintelligibility the price
price of fixity is unintelligibility the price of fixity is unintelligibility
the price of fixity is unintelligibility the price of fixity is unintelligibility price of fixity
unintelligibility the price of fixity is unintelligibility the price of fixity is
the price of fixity is unintelligibility

people find that problematic   i dont see why
things *have* to stay in play   *must* have that bit of uncertainty   if what i
what anybody says is formed like a rock   it simply drops   what is there
to say about it ?   if you really knew in that fixed way what was meant
exactly   what poetry *was*   what art *was*   then there wdnt be much to
do wd there ?   its only when you dont quite know what you mean or
you dont know quite what they mean that there is an edge beyond what
is fixed   that makes it interesting   that gives you something to work
with

the honk of geese going over

[n]a door somewhere opening
a problematic that was not considered ahead of time
how wd i deal with the chronological question   blindfolded as now
facing a firing squad   the fact that i had a specific intent to end   in a
certain amount of time   but like this   i dont see any time   and of
course you dont see any time either   you *endure* it   as do i
earlier when a short amount of time was inserted   some
perhaps happily   others perhaps nervously threw in some applause   and
then more happened   it didnt end   you anticipate time as you anticipate
when a person starts to write a word and they start with the letter F
and then   I   and then   X

the price of fixity is unintelligibility   the price of fixity is unintelligibility
the price of fixity is unintelligibility   the price of fixity is unintelligibility the price of fixity
the price of fixity is unintelligibility   the price of fixity is unintelligibility the price of fixity is unin-
-telligibility the price of fixity is unintelligibility

you anticipate
its a cognitive price that's paid
there is a sound above my head a whispering   it
distracts me from the triggers held by you all   from the aim that you
are still taking   forgetting   i'm becoming disoriented   i'm next to a table
of forms wet with my insinuations   i'm waiting in line and there   my
friend perry   off to the beach   entering that cold water   traversing that
space   the line moving slowly up your body   passing the crotch   hitting
at the very sensitive belly   very sensitive to the cold water   very   once
you very pass you very there   water [n]   it varies   its easy from there

[n] again a door
[n] again a door opens with a beep

you dive   no question any more whether the dream has memory to work from or is constructing it all   surely someone has felt this before has tuned to it perfectly   [π] that perhaps was the sound of the door opening for them   so where is the change of state   have we found a locus can we [?] between the anxiety dream   between whatever yr take on yr slice of the human condition is *all language is poetry*   and the looking down on   looming back on   the asleeping   the verbification of yr consciousness yr   sleep   yr not so   manifestly conscious but never *un* conscious

is it just that you have to   reach   *out*   to open [π]

a door [?]

[π] again
[π] a "gain"

Dana Lisa Lustig

big guns go boom! (for Mark Prejsnar)

a week of terse speaking is nearly done
fare a scalping in meaning of two
shifting pair of dimes hard work this two, one

is known. of the other, a limp of blue.
(theoretically, it's not so straightened.)
strict tightness of syntactism through

counting a one anda two stress. chastened
dimple to face depression. this promise
of lingered patterns: a stippling hastened.

plane song

wing dip studded braille dots flap or dip
        shred of above yet not so below in
            grey & rose glow of greyest burst of flat
        water deep dipped no step now to sit
back when the merest rainbow double
        paned all the streams & layers caking some
            up high steel streak lake effect a hissing
        so hum a humming to pointed blinking
past ending all distance curving it's this tense
        dragon sensuously grasping low with inlets
            curling ribbons curving when cuddling
        the mirrored shred of space & level sweep

        or turbulent rising to falling
        on cleanest azure striated
        smooth to shadelessness

barefoot/extinguish at will

swift heft wrench.

     this forces equal release mime cloud transference.

runoff pressure becomes its own brand.
shove in harder
            than mossy bricks stacked against
            wood swell burst in to untether.

     unit measure:
           rubber flip flop thwack   or more to the point
           how puddles hazed the curb's ass.

shrieks insist threadbare weariness for gray logic.

      oh yeah - *now* they say
free monkish endurance against fierce chilling
        or a near stimulation.

instinct's jostle: turn a white back   brace each toe on asphalt
           then twist arms high.

all done all over all gone all before all after all ways

    shake a shake a shake it

        no two step time in accidental delight.

deep inside the low throttle lightning wet glaze caught
a lately downpour on palms only shrugged away.

"and I am lonely and small in all this, goodnight"

one or mostly:
If the truth were told, then mirrors do not.

She saw what she knew to be there, a being completely her own.
How was it then that she was being less & less seen
even though she could see herself so clearly?
This did not seem reasonable yet the truth told to her.

Each time she was being seen she was feeling a deepened translucence.
She did not feel lighter. The veins on her arms remained blue.
Her mirror was insistent: *you have two brown eyes to see with.*

She was again seen & again fading.
As so often happens, a consequence of nickel & dime.

two is the same side.
To hear is equivalent to preferential treatment.
Please be more specific. She spoke & knew she was being heard
in the same way a sprinkler waters the lawn at night.
Her speaking would not resonate past proscribed circumferences.

What informs an inner circle? No less than a few feet or a whisper.

Seeing through or not seeing into. To shine through like wet leaves.
She knew this could not describe paleness.
What can be more obvious than invisibility?
She knew herself capable of reckoning with her narrow frame
in much the same way fishermen forecast the horizon.
Is ignored is a color? No wonder then, about blue.

She was not clearly distinguished. She felt her translucence deeper.
The mirror said in an irritated way: *nonsense,*
your face is nearly half that of your mother & half that of your father.

She was seeing that being seen was seeing that she was fading.

three gestures each:
The streetlight did an orange backlight for her profile.
Each feature kept a straight line without a single comic curve.
She watched her sit in that way
& although saw her knew she wasn't being seen by her.
She saw her sitting with her head turned
& although she didn't speak she heard her speaking
in a way that said so tired of being told.

A few feet or a whisper would have rendered the same.

She was in a chair in a corner & she could see & she could hear.
She saw her in a corner & saw that she could see & she could hear.
She wanted to speak but knew she would only mimic the duality of glass.

The weight of her head was a reminder. So was one leg crossed over another.

Her mirror decided to play rubber and glue: *don 't ask me anymore.*
You can see for yourself

end moment:
To see for her self she saw in her self a mystery measured in 3 parts where inside deduction theories are discarded but quickening sensations of aha! are formed in slow motion much like the way she was suddenly aware how her toes arched up a bit when walking in certain shoes which undoubtedly affected the squaring of her shoulders when stepping off the elevator or clutching the handbag that always thumped her side when crossing the busy 2 lane street but more likely it was that her crows' feet would develop somewhat later in life because golly she was blessed with good genetics & besides there's always hair dye but fear she read in a book will trap you & keep you from loving if you can't buckle those damn shoes properly to avoid tripping up another dry statement that becomes a functional reminder like the scar from gouging a knee on a rock in the playground which tells us universal band-aids can't cover most wounds.

Camille Martin

learning to talk over and over

I have fulfilled my purpose

but it's not you who say so

on roads never transparent

it not necessarily being things that happen

the idea of all kinds of rescues

not halfway open

and now's a good time

the sidewalk stained blue from fallen flowers

a cardplayer's world

how simple it is, telling

not telling

can we ever be one or the other

unless we stop knowing something

complexities rubbed thin in fluid history

the sun leaves traces of tunes

its form is apparent and dissolvable

a solvent method

and so the possibility of the body in odd ways

packs everything into a scene

finishing opens new spaces

for the time being is getting crowded

to abcs and from rimbaud

cold in the house

not as if oblivion

deceptive arteries as exaggerated desire

erasure of support, compass swelling

and backhandled toward the mind

a ghost killed in passing

to resurface at eye level

death not replaced, but relived

a fleeting swarm of magic

(*ô saisons, ô châteaux!*)

telltales on many paper

signing themselves to be born

as ever for the best

to touch days of speech

thinking something "up"

a displaced look screening great detail at the roots

this business of taut exchange

above trouble

talk of the body, or layers, becoming

sometimes only one line

in the substance of unstopped presence

of traffic that seems equally natural, delectable

wolverines sighted in the heavy core of a stagnant morning

something left to chalk it up to

resilience not a questionable dodge

when you come forth commingling flesh

the air's most thick off the beat

fewer names or smaller

but they join unsuspected into seances of the ordinary

don't change one word

you won't be able to surface but

there's something that knows the illusion

will take care of that, too

projects self through stereotype

remonstrates the capacity of shelves to hold green hills

ground producing mourning between the rows

talk reflects a supplement at the outset

brilliant stinginess or subsistence of puritan water

a bitter dash, subdual lottery

forgetting the time it takes a convergence of hermits

stunned and mesmerized before

flummoxed breeze

it happens in these castles in which to picture

a kind of dancing on spirals

every view a place

this meaning this or else something

gizmo junction measure by measure given away

don't mind being under the world

gusty thoughts feeding miraculous icons

the words do not escape without us

mongrel coffin taking the place of certain descriptions

changes a landscape

although borders and crisscrosses sign allegiance

grow and diversify until nothing is left while

everywhere shuttles a guise

altogether, the empty parts clamber for hunger

within seasons of fields of loved weeds

the truth a hopeful judgment as i commence to do

as if it's ok to surround the dark

with things voluntarily remembered

a non-cessation of trees and flat land producing a mind

jags world lines in a red throng of partial

distant children transfer plural code

aimed life in these pockets of air unabridged

misty tempo of plastic process

restless of transmitted flight

from no truck

pseudo slammer

here, a botched cozy live-in. hankering, i "cause" a delay in the system start-up. poised with an empty pistol in latent space. more or less fain, error's habitual day parade inaugurates a fuzzy death. funny, bursting the dove's eye, & lifers balk at the riddle of breakage. what was i thinking, trying to blow the cover off now. a surge of instrumentality comes all grammatical & sexless in waves of declension & honeytones. insidious. thusness can't get the letters off the fickle brain for obsessive time rattling the bars of an emotion you could really starve your way into. a photograph of melting snow, for example.

mawkish me

is this where we unhook the brief self, into a denatured light. the situation is aggressively democratic, spooling toward one or twenty-seven billion say-so's & aspiring to the implied soul of happy hours spent in beautiful surroundings soft as a fogged sentence, a succession of facts peering into the memorial rubric of self-knowledge. i'm making an effort here, fast approaching a superficial encounter, something to merge into, guided by a clattering homunculous running on amorphous fuel toward ultimately iterable caravanserai that keep vanishing into a distance. linkage adrift with dissolvable stalemate, a violently so-so metaphor that rings no bell. feeling freed to speak the peculiarity of names, i disarm my intention to a quiet glow, slide into the outside. the rest is a gift of shivered measure.

repo winter

razor-filching delivery in half-mind, a canvas body sign the dusty climate can't remedy (instance of moreover, sweet sky caught at point). one's cantabile foothold veers off the captive chart & into succulent breath. alien nests visible in the cold syndrome of speech. a wash of sound recurs in concrete disguise. old mouth shapes' sizable blooms. a stockpile of stories, enough porous to sleep awash so from out of the corner escape tangents of sifted organism. to sleep porous. not in a place but an entangled instant. crosshatchery into the waiting frame. a ladder blanking on its trajectory. eggshells a prayer away. crumbling space spanning stories, finally not simultaneous with one's instinctive calibration of window depth. forgetting again & again how to magnify the margins, while synapses plagiarize vulnerable finds.

solfège parasite

i.

perspective seen as trickling light   oblit- error impact

at best gambling with interior axioms   dry blades on a folded horizon

or redundancy of meshed songs   bright weight's omnibus

nearly ripe alphabet   in a common dawn denominator

thought to be a domestic hunger   reconceived pathogens carving

a logical exercise of mass   inside a unique cadaver

lovely wish   precarious niche   a warm

a kind a space   a bird   a measured

winter miasma   smart nature happiness fling

warbled message   asunder in one's eyes

loneliness jolted to a banal term   what to call it   (a local violence)

replaced letter for letter   by standards

of linguistic evidence   for the marrow of hand-me-down history

an emergent tongue eclipse   some wheel's centermark

a sad & dark cloud   glance scatter wave

on a very very road to the body   the pressure

expected from recreated physical surroundings

lifespan diction flapping in the wind

that not-cold feeling in the stars for sure   fluttering carnivorous thing

winnowing logjam   ordinary questions

ii.

speechless wake

too small a map for the function

memory spreading   prefigured   maybe this worded skin

a self the value of one veering   breathing light

into the trusted forces of many   the people a dim ownership

stopping awhile   eagerly

proceeding   into what ambiguity   does the body enrich

since no river   to name it in   officially

forbidden to say things like   or even this one entangled

thorn perspective float-away home   objects resembling the texture

of their names   the tug is & isn't

grammatical   within an identifiable base   noise of blue letters

only really vibrates through air   b-a-g#

a dog barking   warping crowd slang   the mob's scarred body

pocketing precautionary deceptions   ritual shards

or blinding convergence   one's turbulence

marooned never takes it

far enough   outside the ambient creature

carrying here no angel made for fracture   a measure of flower spillage

no known science   carrying crumbles

iii.

buffer to subject swerve   otherwise descriptive target   a shadowy

history interposes syllabic focus   clandestine illusions inside out

survival then gets calibrated   cast into a trend of fits & wavers

staving epidemic of isolation   the curse of enough

is the good news   cousin to identity   is enough meaning

touched   deprived news   shovel mind

cheered by shed breath   ditched one letter beyond

enough   omitting grasping word   what did one remember for

farewell sequence   won't ever stay   cold in the mouthed

boundless anomalies   motives prior to

prior to   coming up for flawed air   to follow the light's bleed

slumping one's difference in a crowd   birds transparent

not improving their nests   in a flickering city   (directions

to the farm left dangling   this boarding

commerce barely feels fiction   bridge over meltdown)

or socialization on dwelling lines   unaccounted for flesh

in an affair of partial letters   this or that runic glimpse

over foraged symbols   deeming weathered penstroke

northern acreage ligaments   an obscure name

for sky   "planning" to wear

down a sand   confused accounts achieve the norm

on a seasonal rim   carrying a trespass of consequence

about a pivotal clutter

Jerry McGuire

Not A Ton

Notation

Heart to hear, the balls
heave heavier than his
imprimatur
arbitrary, fell away
over here, bitten
on Elba, picked on, council slobs.

bells tear a theater
shine, revive, *ave*
trim a pure
wry, awfully, bitter
nitwit, hereafter
blown silly, cornucopic, bubble.

Or organic, cooly
to pick it
what's craned is craned, balked blocked
and Mom kept saying
he didn't do it, he's my boy, look at those
peepers, pick a peck improvident
and ever so costly, creep.

I look cryonic, grown
cockpit to
decibel clocks deracinated, drained swat
gnawing, pecked mom, dad
shows talky, omnibus shed it, or didn't he?
In time, revved pro, keep a couple's hiphop
preach slightly cross, revenant

Rafters groaning, all tubas bulge in.
Well-off, I shrub you.
Real low, I lark you.
Reboot, not dwell, I *will* recite you

Inarguable bustle the morning after.
You brush, I follow,
you crawl, I holler,
you caterwaul, I, hollow. Don't bother.

All these eyes, and I still
don't see you?
What's what, you say, a kind of misplaced
palindrome.
The hunch we played
calls backwards like a metronome.
The whatchamacallit
in the mirror is *always*
on its damned telephone

Listened, sighed, seethe all.
You eased on it.
Dismayed, lick pined aces, Ottawa awe!
Roamed in lap.
Delay, pooch, shunt.
Emotion remakes ill words back slack.
Tall clam, chatter, wet.
Sigh. Walls roar, remnant
one a flattened mandate, no.

The Cages

First revelation: that everything is bent, double:

(only for instance after passing | which on the ruffled roads has always some distance off twin beams of light coming on as in a mirror | after getting up the nerve and passing | while overhead a hawk overshoots a cowbird, goes by screeching | after what the ones in the long slow lines call passing | as deep underneath, ancient codes pass from this to that until all hooks up like Christmas lights and suddenly above a blossom opens | after passing, more passing

Second revelation: the compound is elemental:

(scarlet dress, on the stairs, music up, lights dimming, her breath, lips, on my knees, face in her, her sway, give, come down, pulling at my shirt, now tugging harder, now fierce, then roll down together, in the corner, someone's short barking laugh, all this as one, indissoluble, between the last breath and the last pulse

Third revelation: all is one, but then there is exclusion:

(nothing opened like a radiant gate.
nowise "ethnic."
someone saying, *"See you later!"*
the rest not silence, but low hum.
nor not musical, either.
someone saying, *"You'll be sorry!"*
no refreshments, no commodities.
a metaphor did not flow through it.
someone saying, *"You promised!"*
as a thing of spirit, too quick to be uplifting, too loud to be profound.
afterward, everything beautiful is framed by its cage.

Fourth revelation: low riders, road crosses:

(hear something faroff emptying. Tense moment of redrilling, rescraping, recutting. No evidence disposes any face of time accomplished. No face either of those first, simplest contortions, eye and tongue. Trips forth, louder than the heart can handle under an arc of stars assigned to no real horizon. As in a mirror to see a stranger. As on the telephone to hear one's own voice answer back: *Is it really you? Did you miss me? Do you love me yet?* As on the dark hot jagged road you make yourself a holy thing, killing your lights and riding on the beams of the stranger behind you.

Feeling Rosemary

She's all about getting there and being

there, where you are, out of this fineness

tender, hanging quiet   all frames native

all needles and nose   a monkey-trap precisely

indifferent to whatever scratches you back

from that center of things you can't quite see

so sure   so quick and sharp   pull back

your hands   smooth against your face   breathe deep

watch out she bites   your hand

deep in the meat   near where heart beats   but

the soft dark dirt   growing always more alive   and

Note: The lines of this poem were originally printed on individual rolled-up slips of paper and secreted throughout a rosemary bush, to be unrolled and read in any order.

Plate Pieces

Nimbus rhomboid on gamboled happenstance
purple traitors aptly handed
thus the man grooving the tongue slips

Shank or possum? windered. And the antsy
one, habitual gamboling. Butterfly knots autopsy.
Whose hurt? The incidences positive enough repeating is when

Thus in Hindi. Where the ovens still smoked
and sensed enough was enough was enough was enough.
Twistingly, bought back at double, at once a voice, chain talking.

She working the crowd. Her overt time. She'll
blank blank blank on the carpet, ovary theme.
To at beneath beyond as *in* her, thus.

Where each that must cut across, delightful scars
constructed of can hurt, to repeat to make the tongue
skip its groove, break's a break, shard and shard alike, slaking not shirred

Gongula

1	An old story
2	which is true
3	surfaced during excavations
4	NO
5	contained the lost books of
6	NO
7	NO
8	of the great flood
9	and the strange deeds
10	NO
11	whose name
12	NO
13	forever.
14	The books are seven
15	NO
16	are missing.
17	NO
18	The description
19	NO
20	and the flood
21	blood-red.
22	All the rest
23	are sea-green.
24	NO
25	a story about
26	NO
27	and her lover
28	NO
29	NO
30	NO
31	with long gray ears
32	NO
33	who was famous
34	for murdering
35	NO
36	The death is described
37	NO
38	which has been lost for years
39	Under leaden clouds
40	NO
41	discovered the girl
42	behind the purple curtains
43	of the inner chambers
44	of the castle of
45	NO
46	o-clock in the evening.
47	In her hand
48	she cradled
49	an ivory box
50	with the inscription
51	NO
52	NO
53	of the King's secretary
54	seized and led her
55	to the gate of
56	NO
57	although she swore
58	NO
59	NO
60	only to deliver a message to
61	NO
62	of the flood
63	that was to come.
64	NO
65	had decided
66	that the rumblings
67	detected by
68	NO
69	whose name
70	NO
71	forever
72	would best be answered
73	by a high wall
74	around the southern shore
75	of the island
76	NO
77	of the flood
78	forever. The girl
79	NO
80	with her message
81	from the Great Builder
82	NO
83	forever, because he made
84	the most perfect temple of
85	NO
86	to the king.
87	And her lover who waited
88	NO
89	NO
90	soft gray ears

91	NO
92	the flood.
93	The Secretary
94	NO
95	NO
96	NO
97	the king
98	NO
99	NO
100	to the girl
101	NO
102	NO
103	NO
104	long gray ears
105	NO
106	the flood.
107	The Secretary
108	ordered his deputy
109	in charge of
110	NO
111	NO
112	to the girl.
113	His instructions were
114	NO
115	NO
116	to the king.
117	The Great Builder
118	of the temple of
119	NO
120	would arrive
121	NO
122	NO
123	the southern wall.
124	Only her lover and
125	NO
126	NO
127	long gray ears
128	could prevent
129	NO
130	from reaching
131	NO
132	the king.
133	NO
134	NO
135	sensitive gray ears
136	NO

137	and again pulled aside
138	the purple curtain
139	NO
140	girl's eyes
141	rolled back, and
142	the ivory box
143	lay on its side.
144	The latch
145	NO
146	The girl could smell
147	the sweet breath of
148	NO
149	and could hear
150	the footsteps
151	NO
152	quickly dying
153	NO
154	NO
155	whose soft gray ears
156	heard the last cry
157	and the last gasp
158	NO
159	NO
160	NO
161	NO
162	NO
163	NO
164	NO
165	her head
166	on the mantel
167	grinning beside
168	the ivory box.
169	The message
170	in its strange code
171	was brought
172	NO
173	of the king.
174	The Secretary
175	read the meaningless
176	sentences to
177	NO
178	NO
179	long gray ears
180	and the king
181	had no choice
182	but to call

183	a gathering	229	on the south wall
184	of his most trusted nobles	230	with its fists
185	whose names	231	of weary dolphins
186	NO	232	NO
187	NO	233	NO
188	forever.	234	tired gray ears
189	NO	235	heard the hearts
190	on the mantel	236	of the nobles
191	NO	237	pound against
192	and grinned wider	238	their own southern wall.
193	and wider	239	The king
194	as the nobles	240	NO
195	one by one	241	NO
196	began to perceive	242	NO
197	the heavy lapping of	243	Secretary rolled it
198	NO	244	the length of
199	against the south wall	245	the table where it
200	and realized	246	came to rest
201	NO	247	its steady grin
202	NO	248	NO
203	it could hold.	249	all the nobles
204	They began	250	where they sat.
205	one by one	251	NO
206	to perceive	252	NO
207	a high laughter	253	gray ears perked up
208	from behind	254	to the sound
209	the purple curtain	255	of rolling laughter
210	NO	256	NO
211	NO	257	NO
212	the mantel	258	reached for
213	NO	259	the ivory box.
214	NO	260	NO
215	her lover	261	the heavy boots
216	NO	262	on the ocean floor
217	NO	263	were kicking
218	the curtain aside	264	the south wall down.
219	NO	265	Her head
220	where the grinning	266	NO
221	head	267	NO
222	NO	268	NO
223	NO	269	could save them.
224	NO	270	The Secretary
225	the ivory box.	271	took it from
226	The wet thunder	272	the mantel
227	laughed deeper	273	and pounded its
228	and pounded	274	NO

275	NO
276	like the jaws
277	of a vise
278	NO
279	refused to open.
280	The sea wall
281	to the south
282	was swelling inward
283	ready to give birth
284	to the hungry babies
285	of the sea
286	NO
287	NO
288	once more
289	and beat it
290	against the table
291	NO
292	NO
293	where the king
294	NO
295	lay limp
296	NO
297	NO
298	delicate gray ears
299	NO
300	forever.
301	NO
302	NO
303	NO
304	once more
305	NO
306	NO
307	once more, and
308	NO
309	NO
310	NO
311	NO
312	NO
313	NO
314	once more, and
315	NO
316	NO
317	unclenched at last
318	NO
319	a high laughter
320	NO

321	NO
322	NO
323	NO
324	came pouring forth
325	NO
326	NO
327	NO
328	NO
329	NO
330	forever
331	NO
332	NO
333	NO
334	NO
335	NO
336	NO
337	forever
338	NO
339	NO
340	NO
341	NO
342	NO
343	NO
344	forever
345	NO
346	NO
347	NO
348	NO
349	NO
350	NO
351	NO
352	NO

Thomas Meyer

The Merchant's Daughter

A souvenir
    despite the rain
of long
    thin things

and things
    that glimmer.

  •

I felt for the book not there in the dark.
Got up. Got dressed. Went out.

A barely full moon. Opened up night.
Barefoot. Cold. Wet. Grass so deep.

My feet disappear.
There, found it. In the car.

  •

La Belle et la Bête

  •

The castle's first visitor was her father.
In her blood he returned, she was the second.
Each event pierced by the last makes
her tears diamonds. His ship lost at sea.

  •

Look to the way I love you.
What happens in seconds will take hours to appear.

Look to the way I love you.
The magic ends. But the order of the magic remains.

Look to the way I love you.
The air fills with promise. The ball is caught.

•

The bees in their hive
take orders from the sun.

•

Firm is the lack
or want
that causes a heart
to beat.

Capricorn of
plenty
returns upon
itself

a valid strength.
A wealth.

•

Here they keep their treasure.
Their work unending.

•

Who fumbles at the door
and fools with the keys?

To dream of a lion means
the work goes well.

•

The ground still wet
 in those woods.

•

Where are they taking me?
I ask and go.

Imagine what's fake is what's real.
A fig or lemon.

•

Electrons drop through
how many levels

of reality have we here?
Take a loaf, or take a chair.

•

The curtains part.
The dead enter.
The living go out.

This is what the world is.

The dead go out.
The living enter.
The curtains shut.

•

My grief or her giraffe,
I wasn't sure what she meant.

Wild flowers. Or will power?
What were the words? Yellow moved

through the fields two days ago.
And it was evening.

•

A white donkey.
A red barn.

The yellow light
the mind holds

becomes a thought.

•

For miles
the dry hills roll

in any direction.

•

Name the different parts of
an orchard and the forest.

•

In the dream a search begins
for the keys to open the door
and start the car.

A heavy rain makes walking
impossible. A fox leaps
from the shrubbery

into the house and circles me
in my sleep.

•

Last night on the path
I saw a hare in the field

and a figure climb
out of the dark, a letter

in his hand. He said
"I meant to send it

but came myself instead."
I turned and saw no more.

•

Animal tracks in the snow. What
remains is where they went.
How many light years away to love?

•

Before they can be any use to us,
certain passages need to be copied

from this book where seas, rocks, tides

are written of.

•

Parody does no good. Love is real.
The rock survives the coast.

Beyond that shore, over a hill
in green fields horses run. Look.

They and shipwreaks are real.

•

Blank pages at the edge of hush.
An ocean roars in the leaves.

I mistook a napkin for a bird.
This defines a medium reality disturbs.

•

"I am sorry" he said. "My wife is upset."
He rose and left. She turned and said
"The car is white and in the parking lot."

"I'm the Italian ambassador" I said.
The bus that brought me here
continues into morning.

•

A glass of milk
poured into a sink.

Dancing There

Looking in the mirror part of the future appears.
The part that comes back and repeats itself.

This is not the world of adjectives.
But a Pleistocene.

By morning it was dry
the only trace of rain
the night before
damp leaves
into whose darkness
sleep had gone
looking for something
older than Blood, Table,
Cup.

Bright bird, blue bird,
tell me your name.

Which is up? Which is down?
And which the way out of town?

The smell of June. The smell of July.

A gold boat floats
upon a quicksilver ocean

whose surface doesn't change
but undergoes all motion.

A world where
the flaw
is as
prized as
the crystal's
perfection

and I am dancing there,

not delivering a lecture
or writing an essay.

I am dancing there.

Uranium Ore

An alchemist sleeps in the brain
under layers of imagination.
His breathing sounds like a princess
unable to wake.

The open book and ancient page.
Light's geometry. Electric speed.
Talk in the garden, shared secrets.

Financial worries
cover my mind
like lace, a veil, or snow; or
the fever you suffer.

From the west comes
new light, new loves,
a new name to answer night with:

This moon was made
to lay my lover under
in fields of clover.

Let me be Adam in
the wood of this flesh.
Are you naked? And am I?
Yours the kingdom, mine the glory?
These leaves are forever.

A. di Michele

About the Extinction Of

tunnel angels crouched in the olive trees spinning the dust of
wet angels crouching the windtunnel

sitting head full of damaru. become asteroid field.

banshee legions haunting the wetlands allah spinning zikr in the
dust of angels crouching the windtunnel, sitting out the olive
direction the resonance head full of damaru djinn banshee legions
haunting the wetlands allah spinning zikr in the dust of angels
crouching the windtunnel, sitting out the olive direction, the
resonance head full of damaru banshee legions haunting the
wetlands djinn allah spinning zikr zikr in the dust of angels (a
primitive people, fishing Iban, crouching the windtunnel, sitting
out the olive direction deftly in the zikrs out of dust in the
dust of angels who live in the head-hunting documents crouching
the windtunnel, sitting out the olive direction) the resonance
head full of damaru banshee legions squatting through haunting
the wetlands allah spinning puer aeternas direction zikr in the zikr
in the dust of angels crouching the windtunnel, all glyphs lifting
us slick sitting out the olive head top heavy with rack broadcast
direction, the resonance head full of damaru banshee legions
haunting the wetlands allah allah was born in a banshee spinning
zikr in the dust of angels crouching the windtunnel, sitting out
the olive direction arm enwrapping a keg of blood the resonance
head full of damaru banshee legions haunting the xristos wetlands
allah spinning zikr in the dust of angels crouching the djinn
windtunnel, sitting out the olive aura is blown direction the
resonance head full of damaru banshee legions haunting the
wetlands allah and the world of life in the exotic spinning zikr
in the dust of angels crouching the windtunnel, sitting out the
olive direction the resonance zikr in the dust of (o icanchu!) angels
crouching the windtunnel, sitting out the olive direction zikr in
the dust of angels crouching the windtunnel, sitting out sitting
out the hoodoo olive direction the resonance head full spinning zikr
zikr in the dust of angels crouching the windtunnel, sitting the
djinn olive direction zikr in the dust of angels crouching the
windtunnel, sitting out the olive (christ stag) is (is) girl dust of
banshee legions haunting the wetlands, angels crouching the
windtunnel, sitting out the olive direction banshee legions
haunting the wetlands spinning zikr zikr in the dust of angels

crouching the windtunnel, sitting out the olive direction with
blade bone shovels in the dust of angels crouching the about the
extinction of windtunnel, sitting out the squatting through olive crescent
direction the resonance moonhead full spinning these are not star rituals
zikr zikr in the dust of angels crouching the windtunnel, sitting out
the olive direction in the dust of angels crouching the windtunnel,
sitting out the olive direction the resonance head full spinning zikr
zikr in the dust of angels crouching the windtunnel, squatting through
sitting out the olive direction in the hoodoo dust of angels crouching the
spinning zikr in the dust of angeldust in the nostril of windtunnels,
sitting out the olive direction the resonance head midrift sound of the
antler is the letter z full spinning zikr zikr in the dust of angels crouching
the windtunnel, sitting out the olive direction in the dust of angels
crouching the windtunnel, sitting out the olive sheet of infants
direction resonance head full of mojo zikr in the dust of djinn angels
crouching the windtunnel, sitting out the olive direction zikr in the
dust of banshee legions filled the wet thickets haunting the wetlands,
angels crouching the fatima-tunnel, sitting out the olive direction
banshee legions haunting the wetlands spinning zikr zikr in the
dust of angels crouching the windtunnel, sitting out the olive crusade
direction in the dust of angels crouching the windtunnel, sitting
out the olive direction the resonance head full spinning this is not
red heart menagerie zikr zikr in the dust of angels crouching the wind,
sitting out the olive direction in the dust of angels crouching (o icanchu!)
the windtunnel, sitting out the olive direction the resonance a
fierce legacy of hilly jungles of Borneo, whose head and banshees
tunneled in full spinning zikr zikr in the dust of crude angels
crouching the windtunnel, sitting zikr in the legions of djinn
resonance dust of angels crouching the windtunnel, sitting out
the olive direction zikr in the dust of banshee legions haunting
the wetlands, angels crouching the windtunnel, sitting out the
olive direction banshee legions haunting the wetlands spinning
and guarded the directions with damarus zikr zikr in the damaru
dust of angels crouching the windtunnel, sitting out the olive
direction in the dust of angels crouching the windtunnel, sitting
out the olive direction the resonance head full spinning zikr
this is not face full of urge and egg zikr in the dust of angels crouching
the windtunnel, sitting out the olive direction in the dust of angels
crouching the windtunnel, sitting out the olive direction the resonance
head full spinning zikr zikr in the dust of angels crouching the
windtunnel, sitting out the olive direction in the dust of angels
crouching the windtunnel, sitting out the olive direction the
resonance head full spinning zikr zikr in the dust of angels
crouching the windtunnel, head full of resident banshees hunting
angels sitting out the olive direction tending their allah crops belies
peaceful djinn existence of hunting in the dust of angels crouching

the windtunnel, sitting out the olive direction the resonance head
full out the olive direction in the dust of angels crouching in
the cardinal directions wetland the windtunnel, sitting out the
olive direction the resonance head full spinning zikr wetlands
angels spitting zikr in the dust of angels crouching the hag
windtunnel, sitting out the olive direction in the dust of angels
tricking the angels crouching the windtunnel, sitting out the
olive direction the zikr in the dust to the sand spectrum of a
primitive people fishing Iban angels crouching the windtunnel,
sitting out the olive direction zikr in the dust of banshee legions
haunting the wetlands, angels crouching the windtunnel, sitting
out the olive direction banshee legions haunting the wetlands spinning
zikr zikr in the dust of angels crouching the windtunnel, sitting out
the olive direction in the dust of angels crouching the windtunnel
and spiral within, sitting out the olive direction the resonance head
full spinning zikr squatting through zikr in the dust of angels
crouching the windtunnel, sitting out the olive direction in the
dust of angels crouching the windtunnel, sitting out the olive
direction the resonance head full spinning zikr zikr in the dust
secretions of angels crouching the windtunnel, sitting out the olive
direction in the dust of angels crouching the djinntunnel, sitting
out the olive direction the resonance head full spinning zikr slither
zikr in the dust of angels crouching the windtunnel, sitting out
the olive direction in the dust of (o icanchu!) angels crouching the
windtunnel, sitting out the sitting out the olive direction the crosshatch
resonance head full spinning zikr zikr in the dust of coming angels
crouching the windtunnel, sitting olive direction the sophia resonance

head full resonance head full sitting out the olive direction the
resonance head full spinning zikr zikr in the dust of angels
sitting out the olive direction covered in hoodoo sticks & feathers
squatting through the sheet of mojo infants resonance head full
spinning zikr zikr in the dust of angels crouching the windtunnel,
sitting crouching the windtunnel, sitting sitting out the olive direction
the resonance head full spinning zikr djinn zikr in the dust of angels
crouching the windtunnel, sitting, spinning and spinning breach
in the wind sound of the antler is (christ stag) is girl puer aeternas

hotwired mojobag. serpent secrets. hand job.

mineral saint issuing hadith manure. cross-section of sunspot.
xristos: snake's kin. catacombs are day.

Solstice / Surgery

(12-21,22-99)

margery kempe twisted olfactory phoneme
               and
   with "bodily eyes"
inhaled sweet white pleroma bits
        angel afterbirth pastry flakes
these are the shattered orbits long since realigned
but loathe to appear, reappear
     now that whole cities and subsequent festivals
  reaffirm a world of forwardfeed and
               margery-kempe-databanks

but i want her uncategorizable stew and saliva
i taste her blake hot tar and fervent loaf
margery kempe put a saddle on durer and rode
    him into sofja's charbon-et-bois billboard wormhole
(there's a little bush two dreams back
            that oozes elijah misprint lava
   margery kempe has set up shop there)

her SQUAT is the all-asana
pouring forth another pertho-glyphic erosion pattern
drawing in five species of beast and man

but no one touches her
we gawk thru gnosis and ghost manna

ikon crumbs

the sprouts migrate
and spin thru our tattered foreheads

hairshirt in the tongue lake
hairshirt in blackforest ribcage
hairshirt in the virgin renewal hopeward yew tree upful glance
hairshirt outside the stellar moat

margery kempe either coughs or weeps

her blue veils skirt the solar winds and kettle...
her blood remains misread

Unica Zurn's Loam Bowl

I

may cast a leafy shadow . . .
but hoards all missing metal flakes:

is haywire myth during convenience
seizures

(convergence, suggestion)

(motherboard telltale longitude)

(the kitchen appliances aching-the-
                space in foreboding concert)

above all, should be phenomenal flailing abacus

approaches so to retreat from
        lesion-and-cyst imagery
(surgery
  curing the easter ham)

not this flaunt of magnets in a rarified
aviary
                        of phantoms

            fleeing the congealed
                imprint of a new

        table of elements.

II

this bowl reveals more than it can hide
including fog-lamp indecencies

this is dementia looking for momentum
in a dead zone of tourism and syringes,

of all paintings existing between zero
and 88 feet above sea level

in words suggesting ineffable
continuance with megaphones
and long expired prescriptions

for causes remaining ineffectual and bulbous

i do not know which torso
represents her stove and umlaut . . .

most were incandescent and
therefore unreliable witnesses.

belly. oblong view of the lower back.
chicken coop full of okra. a final yule
manifesto feigning snowball
incantation with dirt dawber
rhetoric in a tundra
                    conundrum
            of
    treason and
        sweet lunacies:

zurn's turbine hemline is now showing

Archipelago (Interra Diocesan)

I

everything is light
even the cane syrup glaze on murderous eyes
is an instant
        of shine-through mathematics
    etched on a brain of rewired
pulse and misfed acculturations...

everything beams out the totemic stringbean
of geodesic altars floating the fractal
marrow of
        MEMENTO MORI

(salt levels off-kilter precisely enough
        so the smudge that is dawn
    and the cacophony that whispering
                is
is heaven undone)

                memento mori: o
        i
                want
my goat of three-horns-of-plenty juju
    wooden solitudes and damballah-wedo
    antler benevolences

i want bone candle ultraviolet romance shrouds

i want a nest of color-reversed negative
    high-contrast   sub-polarized
wire-hive headwraps
                tatooed to my emerging
        anima's coming-out-party torso

i want plodding suggestive phantom embrace
    in red/green loam tundras

i want tribal reset clock dissolution feedback candy

i want voodoo livewire green energy   liminal eye-
marsh fecundities and swirling victrola
    fax-defying gravity
and the compressed space physics of

sonar-evading bark patterns

i want eventual torso grinding conveyor-belt
            salmon instinctual overdrive
        orbital shifting time-dilation ruckus

i want to detect unmanned witchcraft floating the
seas of el nino motifs in the cockheart :locked-in:
heatseeking my hologram twin-hen's heart
                who's aluminal shadow first emerged
from the unguarded "nursery of chance" and still
        leaves foil fetishes in the mouse pellet
    corners of a lovely but pitiful, itchy skull

o memento mori...

(and of schizophrenia...absolve
                coagula-deity glitter
    when
    it knocks on your door...not you
            on
its)

II

sleeping antlers   lulled, marinated
        in
                her

future

belly

oven

    simmering the
archaic
    soupstream

III

crouching, mudbound glee,
polishing the mater-rock
for new curvature strategies

or
folds, nurturing the nestled pebbles
of infant bardo radiograph

ravenous milk lack

juggling mirror globus wetlink scarcities

this is the lambjaw of secretions

early meat transgression
          under the sunflower of
bodhi see-through tantras

  wrong map unfolded
              then folded
back
  wrong

this is kundalini pageantry
  off-synch to the cloth calendar
of muddy planets

this is where the patriarch goo never trembled
let alone awoke (the sorry slumber
of canine-puero nodes) but ate
the rat expanse of disease
  and splendor

(explain polis expansion):

caligula's crushed skull issued no soul.

the fruit was shriveled. anti-matter.

anti-matter,
                back to the icesheets

IV

this is the imbecile static of rosary detention
        perching bi-polar gyroscopic fission
etc.

candle. star. spiral. atom. ostracoderm. wet

aperture. tree. tree.

subcatatonic threshold boosters.

post-neural nightfall schism of poe, nerval.

phoenix leaning (explain the dark sky of
astrophysics while blinking)

etc.

orbital grooveway dreamtime calibration seizure:

a wormhole is born

Mark Prejsnar

Composition with Wire

(from Overburden)

brick or bracking that would
map out
monody
this is totals
held smoke

Ol' Jet Sam
who floats 'em
a miracle ax decreed that
napalmal, &
now i'm tariffoid

mythos all retort
full impact of this trade
was not yet apparent
angry lie
tomes over the fallen

reprobate not rethink, as in
a demi life
move crawl to the back of

on the noggin asking
author, soliloquize—
right place at the write tomb
a nerve slowly desist
croaked hammer taper
all retorted
vomit in the untold

itinerary squeeze inputs,
brick or backing out atorn
a sample meter
an un-urned run
stampede for the holidays
melted key

chit jot IOU'd
famous in a traipse line
speak in cat
hover noisome dark:
darkness didn't fall
got dropped

        spool to the not ungoing
        effrontery there in the back,
        return the purchase and for this
        limited time only a
        quiet maze where you wander

rivulet
unslowed by who I aren't
keep that up slake
rattle knuckle sand-witch haggle
now, suburban cred

        oh?　supple muse a lank decry
        impermeable permitted
        the sunder ache troth ya got it—
        ebb to cheapen declivity
        so!

monody everfold
cradle broken behind the glance
you must have a century up in there
surpass non surpass
rococo slack and fall

        elevator
        in a quieted jet
        no telling the junk you'd sell
        except:
        the plot to investigate

by and large?—-
away, but small

Ode to Toge

for Tom Phillips

1.

a missing and spurious it might be i think. do you think so? yes with strange law-
abiding down there in the incandescence. that kinda veteran monument. right down
in the smashup. just a flee from russia with buried guns. radio on a slink isle. an
accordion for serenade crawdads my eyes mind. selling a shop is the same as
uncertainty. −vacuous to a young traitor. about jungle waking with the cockroach
measurement: i've now discovered all soles even with the wearing out, from the
road. even with the wearing out of the stolen.

2.

a new pitch
          is here trembling
pandemic   with others made to
point
              dream wheel a frown
the flower of
forced migration
              may we all be
a slam dunk a raven
          these minds from the latin—
may we all be categorized
by class number
& cutter number
with those we enslave

3.

in the wild style harrow where does that come from? the one voice exclaimed that
it had no irony but the lamp had some smoke like the cord wanted to short out.
splunk! to play a game of poker with nonmetal nerves and all the prices were for
staying in the burnt out store and the one formula i learned it was done in the
dark. lonely words had the doors locked and all the dark was done in the words. i
believed in eyesight where they kept people in cartoons. all the wallets had id-
cards with pictures on them and a note about money that was scribbled down 148
years ago.

4.

what do you want for dinner?
what do you want for hunger?
what is the din that deafens want?
a mind will still to tellingly melt
a rationality comes up anchor first
what are the same approaches?
the one with a not in a rope in a dank smoke—
what is the repeat
a novel of a tolerably clean mind
what do you want where it all falls to
pieces in the din the city sets the volume for
what you want for den, or   far fear—

5.

it's this thunder filled with heat—what you didn't want and now you just gotta
have it. actionable, the layoff alert in a saltmine systemic. TV is the again turned into
the against, a model of addiction. it's this slippage that still moves a decrease mile
all the noun'd here with lightening bugs the southern alert the muse catcher. a
slowness. the breaking apart inside the nerves runs down drains chased in largo
alto molto by military police. a mind set to certain can find new doubts everyplace.
purblind goes the quick nonrefillable asterisk. on the last day of the season i hit
one over the blank sign in the right field blanked-out bleachers.

6.

the corruption inquiry:

            a shadow seemed to pass over
their faces   drug-dealer
middle-level   a foundling
clockwise he reached
        thru dream
the tentacle—
            a fond clone
crier to give you data
    in the sleazy harsh-sounding
morning
    it is as necessary as any
unnecessary moaning
                & where
the moan feels absent,

there amidships,   no rocking

fabled wood of together
                petrifaction
stiff tree dryad
     so keep taking air

a country's proud insignia,
          the choking ham set
insurrection plain as the noise on disgrace
river basin
          lost with a poker faced fume
or play-acting admission
almost all sludge in a gauche alone
habituate to the trembling bizness
     a bushwhacker
dust lies on stilled hours
                    a technicality
against the nest egg—

7.

pop realism gets me at the sector where the
          strain has money

fading all the false face is shrill in the new emporium
          unhandle bargains!

a mark of bamboozle for so you wander splitting
          into uncredit hammer leash

i wander here the lawbreaker has a villa and is
          lavish with legislate

untimely watching the film with so many
          ghosts of celebrants, hush

everything pale available a black market or
          under the supermercado the bullets

those playthings with uses are anvil hammered
          strictly speaking, they cure

8.

dry ice and a Slavic theater, it manages who i am that way. killed by a car bomb in the biggest invisible city and then you go forward. they eat and plan the killings. a new foam gel that conquers the market. and they as typo maybe betrayed the quick way it goes bull-fighter might regard Theresa's dream as nothing more than severed nerves. it that right? the new ways of the old imperial order—twill ads if it were '62. and now all the fantasies belong to a tell-all. this is the back alley, and the wife and kids who live maybe…live off torture. the alarm won't go off in the sunlight…… to be feared, the closed and tremble man, goes walking off course

assuage bane

(from *Loss Lieder*)

really this is one scene and actual in french means now as if the moment were yesteryear a regard for snow is how many of us happily don't recall   entranced is one poplar where tens of zeros had their haunt and yes i believe we will get started printing up the bewildered tomes this morning remember all the screams are by daylight   peek down the corridor is anyone coming?   now if you'll excuse me i have these roads to map out   endless is the empty pocket ash a meager salary for where not green it growth of unspeaking   under the mask, is the label with how much the mask costs   caring is the one internal a sifted flame where they passed us we were sitting outside a parody of need the bar had empty glasses the broken bottle contained me it was a fine piece of crafted cold   loam is one of our most popular items it delimits it sticks to the past it is a performance without a performer   cripes this is where all the math pulls taut "again"   reading absence at the tepidity the city casts wired glances   cash on the marblehead it's the one way i know of, how to do business when the flash is anchored over there they have flocks of birds caught in the flashcube an old séance that said to grow up the words have edges they cut like serrated evasions hatred is for the less lost, who have a purpose   eels are the signature that twists to burst light oh no not another blinding image! oh god all these things have to be returned to the store now cause we only have enough despair to be able to remember the last two or three years….! aching now is the one thing in the barter economy that comes from the light the black light that shows where my words were joined you can see the seam the trembling   —discarded material? for all the change it brings in, "will smirk for lewd,"   the pages got stuck together here and the eye closed down   where the price went up a form of vulcanism   a shrug i guess the words freeze against TV ice, when the words get funded

Government and Binding

Rule of law was more often an ideal than a practice
of the wilted trees it shone out like
law stymied by the eyefuls over spring day read
was this a quick wink where things break?
more a quake at the center of private amounts
often i looked in the law-books and became a thief
an edgy creeper with more distance on camera
ideology says that too! so i'm slicker (like)
than a ranter in appease-mode got near and cracked
a joke hammered by old notational problems—
practice mocks pretext   and so i'm "evading"

Law and courts, police and prison formed an element
and several nonbeginnings were there, still trembling
courts burning with iron brands held at noontime fever dry
police fathomed the near which agree slipped away
and burst into dialect favored by the sick shouters
prisons had torches where the logging-camps dwindled
formed an interlocking privacy marketing awareness cheap
an idle forest verging on the town & i can't map it: one
element for crying is the wild static emotionless

European beliefs did not exist in a vacuum
beliefs go on spilling thru the trees like toxic runoff
did this bring about increasing noise until speaking died?
not till singers were treated for musicality with sticks:
exist all you want, the new mists surround faces quietly
in the unfelt afternoon teetering near fire unphoto'd—
a stammering where i opened the statutes and found a
vacuum traced all round with dollars from the old bank

Law was used in struggles over resources and labor
was a fine-acquired nicety fanned back as a flame unwrit
used in all the haggling over dizzy shock from a drug
in confounded exchanges of store-bought wear and core
struggles of gang-feared shares! in a treaty for hire
over & over i sensed clear muddle in his words with near
resources gone up in combustion (when i dare i shut tears)
and with nouns we shake hands (to carry out sales pitch)—
labor that peels back this mask saying: Pay new Pay letter

but the colonial state transformed the nature of rights
the wired pistol and wind thru a woman's eyes
colonial when the fortress was empty, anchored fear w.

state and dream tumbled in the open, torch and singing
transformed to iron with a check written to slay minds
the choir always told you how one chief led to another
nature burning on the hillsides and i look away scared
of too much vision when what i feel is street-trembling:
rights they grant me to understand the wounded arm

abusive!   that's the word!

abusive! that's the word!
better believe me the font of
crazed wisdom in the fire crinkle crinkle
dampened down with as behind crack
even quietness deafens
foam setter is appall to crank burn
gap to the method

home schooling for greed
into the bopped centrum of crown fumbles
"jazz leaves agents hunting"

keen . . . is that whack to the online?
leggo set piles up, loss is bytes at gangrene:
my my . . . automatic set lust?

not that sieve it cracks remaindered honey
off-day to travel to Dis knee strand
pop! a flash capture zing in a white face
quality pitch irks stumped league
rung to pull. . . nope, still abusive

sag man that's their system!
tony the tiger has drear pun cobalt
under that peg is a deviant—
vilify, is a name, sure

wake until i groan apt as cycle
xtian is no font worth saving (natch)—-
yeast rises to who i say "am" inculcates (and)

zilch, they train me for

Randy Prunty

Trigger D'evolution

I *predilection*

                                           sticking with the situations provided
                                                 discrete divisions don't dilute
                            a swarm of living points
                    a swarm of living   points out   patterns and their anomalies

// at-the
     Exact Same Time (EST) REALIZE :
Context has senses*
     must be old friends with Blank //

// replace evo flight-or-fight   with
     create-or-collaborate -
explained by Red Rover game //

// senses are subject i am object
     sound clefts meaning   therefore
     a system never runs down //

     *senses include: seeing   hearing   emotions   touching   staging
     smelling, balancing   positionality   thinking, the shakes   kinaesthetics
     instincts   wind tunnel widenings   tasting   the pummels, taste
        particulate memories   meanings stored by I

2 *a testing (thot/shot)*

lucid vertigo: my eyesight is often granulated by the other senses
becomes necessary to scare out the shadows from dispassionate abstractions

hearing creates sound
plays the vibrations
inviting schemas to form
little sites for landing

smell
pulls the dander off the dinosaur

evolution as a loop
seen as evolution *of* the Loop
squeamish stomach goes around and ...
who can identify with LITTLE MAN trying to save
face while being eaten

maybe others can empathize
with the system and ...
what are the variant outcomes   someone please
conceive an option outside the boxset

well yes, but can you do it without using *spirituality?*

religion of science minus sentiment carry the hope and divide by pairs
the buddy system means some may get out of the car now

> *good use of your amygdala Joey*
> *anyone else care to practice low-gear driving?*
> *over here is a SuperSport model with a racy rear-end ratio... anyone?*
> *ok, next week : Tear Ducts, the Grin, and Their Unconscious Relationship to the Sacred;*
> *or What It's Called When Chunks of the Tail Section are Discovered by Iron-age Mandrills*

there is no *faculty* of reason
    no cousin of *realize* that goes by *Higher Guessing*
    might as well perceive: patterns – over and over things sense
    how   except for the marks artists make
    the EST law has been: caps for the capping
      has been: repeal the repetitions of how it all ends

      from *being explicit*   to
                  being lifted out

~~vanished~~   ~~absent~~ ~~images~~   ~~echoes of a metronome yet to be made~~
~~blind camera~~   ~~fragments of things not there~~: ~~insight of delusions~~
              ~~delusion of insights~~
   ~~what the hammer knows about~~ *glassed-in* ~~compounds~~
~~laughter ecology~~   ~~unnamed nomenclature~~   ~~the sediment of squeezed flats~~
~~recess~~   ~~alcove~~   ~~indeterminate subtractions~~   ~~skitterings~~
  ~~palimpsest nonsite~~   *mirror's* ~~silver~~   ~~noplace (yet)~~
  ~~three-sided cones~~ : ~~none, one, many~~   ~~enemy's map freely given~~
–   ~~ofness~~   ~~trade places~~   ~~contractions coiled, set~~
~~uncertain rules of~~ *uncertain* ~~signs~~   ~~rest~~   ~~saline ice~~
play ~~of durings~~   ~~recognizable places jumping~~ *out of* ~~their shape and volumes~~
~~full of "you never know what will turn up"~~   ~~juggler of~~ *micro* ~~distinctions~~
   ~~pragmatic posings~~   ~~life on any terms~~ *eventualities* ~~due~~

not environment but *environment* – the ALLOWER
    the *all around* with fingers
though not-yet-hands slur time

inadequate pause buttons - mechanical triggers
(he smiled   seeing; Vacuum senses any something   and runs away)

articulations:

    alleys and alloys gone blank
    differ   number   figure
    wink as a forming environment

      fashioning of the usual size – whatever that means
  but   perceiving tiny actions on a larger scale – whatever that means
until (EST) they   perhaps   treat evolution as poetry's mistake

only later came the ability to represent

    abstractions as an advanced limiting – whatever the means

3   *testing (while heating)*

figure/ground differential is zero

or   what if
the choices were flee or feel?
what if the switch was flipped and the flip was switched?
the nowhere panel incorrectly selected for _____
with countless mistakes
but if *everything's* a mistake we wouldn't need the concept of 'mistake'

can you imagine what it would take to stick it out in such a situation? the realizing that must go on in the brain's soon-to-be mind? for every pattern there are two anomalies – so who's inbred? you can look right over there and see. see? no one there to label it the this or the other. just a friendly game of blankety-blank between old ones. with they – the little alreadys - chirping away.

syncho-simulcast slogging through each discretion. each swarming-up the living. it doesn't matter how you feel about being the newcomer the smack of touchtastesmell should be used for support. ok so i take it back; it's NOT impossible for THE HEARD to assign meaning to us. no need for shouts in the woods. the sensamatic fire can create worlds. and worlds of worlds if laid to rest in our lap. sweet kitty or ante up?

to have a sense of what i'm talking about have a sense of humor. a sense of smell a sense of chronicity in the situation provided. for instance take a sense break. get a sense of things not quite right a sense of doom a sense of smoke in the air and -

boom.

talk sense to me. inlay some sense onto this head. talk like you have a sense of sense; how a repetitive sense breaks down the timing of the pointing-out. or get the sense out of here. go where they have a sense of context and what *that* can mean for timing. *now* do you get the sense it was timing all along i wanted to talk about?

Plato thought of timing as one of the nine senses since it seems the same as - oh, say – the hearing of music. the sense one gets of the vibratory when you hold your hand up to the bell. or like the good doctor who can tell you all about the enclosed viscous fluid and the resonance of hammer_anvil_stirrup. *déjà vu* as a sense of timing across the membrane – at the precise moment the little bones are rattled in the free world you are welcoming bound their contextual kin. past and present passing and presenting themselves – right now!

but i can't do all the work for you   try this:

must have been about fourth grade

the constant battle : holding hands in a circle or   the dances when rained out

holding hands for Red Rover

                              "now get in a circle…"
no one cried sexism   "just the way it was?"   you put your right foot in

     as Bobby Xaubu

i was a weapon of disease proportions   take your partner's hand

                                        allemande left

the ultimate Red Rover 'man' : big hands (with legendary thumbs)

fast runner   shake it all about

 eyes placed well around in the front of my skull (to spot the weak-link prey)

stones sewn in because weight mocks momentum

David AND Goliath (*davidian goliathan*)

extra microfissure in the gray matter

               -which led to *the gift*: knowing how to give without breaking

          Robert & Doris sitting in the Tree   you put your whole self in

     K-I-S-S-I-N-G

aha! sweaty palms the place to strike   and reverse promenade•••

...having lost the power to localize or fixate   we hear:

"weathering the storm" – Wile E. Coyote

"Lord willing and the creek don't rise" - Lewis and Clark

"incisors as if you *must* eat meat" - unemployed Paleo_____

forcing the image to swell within its bubble
by puberty it's called the orb
its architecture arising in response to the
'why can't we all just get along' category:

discrete......→ ......*dilute*
resolute......→ ......*don't pollute*

trifling its way to within (at least!)
sight of landing

it is said that gene survival dictates structural design
- a function of the survival function
- sometimes called 'working the eccentric'

Red Rover Red Rover

place here all the species you never got over: [_____]

place here the ones you never even imagined: [_____]

it's called cooperation and it's an accumulation of ceptions per and con
evoluting and huddling waiting for a need to be gotten on with

4 *testing (tasting)*

senses are subject   i am object of the on and on
sound   sounding the on and on
_ _ _the system never runs down_ _ _

i know that something is being taken apart and put back differently though i don't quite know its bounds. i hear over and over the *this is meant for you* cue. coming at me seemingly with an invitation. and i hear two voices that are neither mine nor another's saying

SIR ARE YOU SURE   i don't know
ARE YOU SURE YOU DON'T KNOW
SIR? SIR?   don't. no. for. sure.

not to say is to resort to "subjective concepts"
with no objections
apprehending what orbits one's eyes and ears
no matter   ~~how~~   stable or fugitive
one seizes the sure and the sure becomes a seizure
the hearingment
the system says "if i don't push (the) matter it will never get done"
the system is always saying that
at me

some syllables get incorporated

(any kind of complication is simple

when made to spin against itself)

into biologically relevant events

th th the the there therein

defined by the systemic universe as feelings

initiating the formation of memories -

perpetuity's fuel

ok class this film shows
language growing up into Project Vapor
with optional mesh over the holes.
dispense the envelopes plugging into multiple lines and objects:

/

<u>vision</u> — correlated with # of photons striking receptors of the retina

i closed my eyes and could feel her dress; the woven blue

/

<u>taste</u> — varies with concentration of molecules in a solvent

in this way we taste sugar but not pure water

/

<u>sound</u> — depends on changes in air pressure over time

the architect danced a jig because sound is movement's signal

/

so this THAT *passes as a shown*
unifies events
pocked
pock marks
pock pock pock – a system
never runs down

5   *resatisfy scat*

a swarm of living has decided not to die
some launch probes, have debates, harvest 'expendable' species
while others bodify their relation to *situ formativa*

> *The heliosphere results from the Sun emitting a steady flow of electrically charged particles called
> the solar wind. As the solar wind expands supersonically into space in all directions, it creates a
> magnetized bubble — the heliosphere — around the Sun.*

symbolic creatures between 'devise' and 'demise' are labeled as plagiarists but others of us
yearn to uncatalog and start over. to wrap the inflections of mood and positionality in with
our own density, relative though it may be.

> *Eventually, the solar wind encounters the electrically charged particles and magnetic field in the
> interstellar gas. In this zone the solar wind abruptly slows down from supersonic to subsonic speed,
> creating a termination shock. Before the spacecraft travel beyond the heliopause into interstellar
> space, they will pass through this termination shock.*

now i ask you .... and if not, what other
preparations are you making? did your ancestors wrestle with the elements? i can hear mine
calling from both the past and the future – one a practicing the other a resting – for me to
use my body like an acorn uses a tree. if you had to choose between

> leap imagined   and   imaginative leap

between prodigy or prodigious, righting or writing, how long of a dry spell could you endure?
intuition as what you already know - or surprise as yield? remember it could mean the
difference.

> *"The data coming back from Voyager now suggest that we may pass through the termination
> shock in the next three to five years," Stone said. "If that's the case, then one would expect that
> within 10 years or so we would actually be very close to penetrating the heliopause itself and
> entering into interstellar space for the first time."*

as an area under construction we are really quite happy. with the demonstration if not the
exampling there are noticeable edges where we can show off. then comes the pruning season
when old expectations are folded up and placed in the narrows. there to stay until we test the
perceptionist's thesis. maybe this is the year death is only a winter's rhythm.

> *Exactly where these two boundaries are located and what they are like remains a mystery.*

Alex Rawls

"H. S. Mauberley (Life and Contacts)" Part I by Ezra Pound

In the old sense.   De son eage; the case presents
The tea-rose, tea-gown, etc.
tin andra, tin eroa, tina theon,
What god, man, or hero
some in fear, learning love of slaughter;
believing in old men's lies, then unbelieving
home to old lies and new infamy;

usury age-old and age-thick
Daring as never before, wastage as never before.
Young blood and high blood,
fortitude as never before

frankness as never before,
Have preserved her eyes;
"Ah, poor Jenny's case" ...

Brennbaum.

Never relaxing into grace;

Mr. Nixon

"Butter reviewers. But never of The Lady Valentine's vocation:

"Song of Myself" by Walt Whitman

Darker than the colorless beards of old men,
    has fallen.

Twenty-eight young men bathe by the shore,
Twenty-eight young men and all so friendly;
    bed-room;)
Maternal as well as paternal, a child as well as a man,
What is a man anyhow?   stick at night.

Still nodding night—mad naked summer night.

You sea! long live exact demonstration!
    the old cartouches,
By God!   Space and Time!   the well,
    sharp-lipp'd unshaved men;
    young men.

prairie-life, bush-life?   Earth!   Long I was hugg'd close—long and long.

Old age superbly rising!   I sleep—I sleep long.

"The Marriage of Heaven and Hell" by William Blake

The just man into barren climes.

existence.

Evil is Hell

3. That God will torment Man in Eternity for following his Energies.

3. Energy is Eternal Delight.

Where man is not nature is barren.
I answer, God only Acts & Is, in existing beings or Men.

much wiser than seven men. The worship of God is, Honouring his gifts in other men each according to his genius, and loving the greatest (Plate 23) men best; those who envy or calumniate great men hate God, for there is no other God.

11. The fire, the fire, is falling!
black African!

from What's Your Sign?

January 1, 1999

You deserve and
a step forward
financial breakthroughs don't
you start things
a family member
don't be afraid

February 18, 1999

The completion of
once you've cleared
emotional needs are
express your feelings
a friendship that
in love be

March 12, 1999

Your energies are
you begin a
innovative leadership excels
you tend to
a sudden increase
you want to

April 19, 1999

Colleagues are impressed
someone else's carelessness
a partner's competitiveness
place the finishing
use time alone
a stunning victory

May 26, 1999

Submit proposals force
someone you see

something that seems
look for improved
tense moments clue
a roadblock disappears

June 9, 1999

An attitude or
a domestic squabble
you're the life
you are sought
positive strokes motivate
if a party

July 10, 1999

Squarely face your
use strategy with
setbacks are designed
don't worry if
when you follow
you are happy

August 29, 1999

A love interest
you will meet
this is definitely
you are tenacious
whether you know
pay a debt

September 25, 1999

Don't be ashamed
pursue an activity
you get a
you receive much-needed
embrace new things
you are scattering

October 1, 1999

You get money
if you look
a person who
give in to
artists get inspiration
there is more

November 20, 1999

Touch base with
you glow with
a new air
a loved one
loved ones need
relationships heal this

December 31, 1999

Clear out your
you have a
you have a
this is the
get ready for
a bold stroke

"Romance Somnambulo" by Garcia Lorca

Translated by MS Word Spellcheck and Alex Rawls

Verde queen toe quires verde.
Verde Vienna. Verses rajas.
El baroque somber mar
  elf cable in Montana.
Con somber on contour
Lela suede an sub barracuda,
veered carne, peso verdure,
con odious Fr Plato.
Verde quell Tex quire Vera.
Banjo lunar Gitano,
lasso causes Estonia Miranda
Lela no pureed miracles.
Verde queen toe quires versa.
Grandiose esters de escort
Vienna con eel pee sombrero
qui abler elf casino dell alibi.
higher forte sub Vienna
con Lila souse Raman,
elf manta, gait gar duo,
Erica sues pitas agrees.
¿Peer quoin vender? ¿Why poor Dundee...?
Ella segue an sub brained,
Verde came, peal Verde,
Soda nod en la mar embargo.
—Compare, quire chamber
mix cable pork sub Casio,
mix monitor pork sub Espec,
mix cub hilly peer sub manta.
Compare, venue sang random,
deeded loose Puerto's Cabby.
—Sip you pudgier, Makita,
ester trot sex cherub.
Peoria you yak no soy yow,
nix my Casio ESP yam mix Casio.
—Compare, quire Morris
decent emanates in Mia's camera.
Acres, sin pureed sour,
con lasso Siberians' Holland.
¿No vets herder queer teenage
deeds elf peach á la gargantuan?
—Triassic enters rouses moorhens

levee too pecker blanker.
Too sander resumé heel
Alders erode too fag.
Perm you yak no soy you,
nix my Casio ESP yam mix Casio.
—Deejay me Subaru menus
hastier lasso altars brandies;
¡deejay me Subaru!, deejay me,
hasty lasso verges brandies.
Barnacles delay LuAnn
poor Donnie renumber elf ague.
Yap Ruben loose dose compares
heroic as allots brandies.
Demand urn raptor sander.
Demand urn raptor lug rims.
Tumbler ban in Lois tea dose
Faro lilies hod altar.
Mill pandas crystal
heroin la Madeira gala.
Verde quell toe quire verse,
verse Vienna, versed Rasa.
Lose dues compares suborn.
Largo vent deejay
 bookie earn razor gusto
the hill, thee mental alibi hack.
¡Compare! ¿Donnie est., dame?
¿Donnie est. tea Nina embargo?
¡Countess vexes tee espresso!
¡Countess vexes toe espy radar,
Cairo fresco, Negro peso,
on ester veered brandy!
Sober elf roster deli alibi
set Mecca lap Gitano.
Verde carne, peel Verde,
con odious Fr Plato.
Urn charm bank LuAnn
sestina sobers elf ago.
Gnocchi sew puss onetime
coma tuna peck era plaza.
Guardians civilize burritos
in la Puerto globe ban.
Verde quell Tex quitter's verse.
Verde vent. Verges ramps.
Elf brace soiree Lamar.
why elf cable in Montana.

David Thomas Roberts

Toward Mena

Like chopping wood in dreams lightning blazed our post oak trail and sung us
to terror ripped from grins before that tottering house so windy with tales...
Nobody knew the history but we were dazed in tunes driving wagons up pine-
fear dripping the stories then mixed up with harmonicas lost out charcoal kilns
crossing such stern ridges the hats sailing windows bursting and animal
screaming... Sort of happy at the first mangle like moons darting woods alive
to witness fullness spattered... You know the castrating and turns took fist-
fucking that thing before the burning...
The stairs are still mine where bark meets scrabble.
Ouachitas, Ouachitas! Oh! All these books on my back...dear Arkansas

Tiff Belt Parley

Curling your antics 'round the springhouse
Flushed with moons and a starred scepter
Masks the whining the rarefied filth steaming these provisions
Don't dare bruise the school or hoist that skirt
Do not kindle freckles in this battleground of fabric
Question only tales of this archive-junkyard persona
Stretching tiff gloves 'round the chimney
Squinting a brazen face of iced tar
On the howl from Cannon Mines to Racola

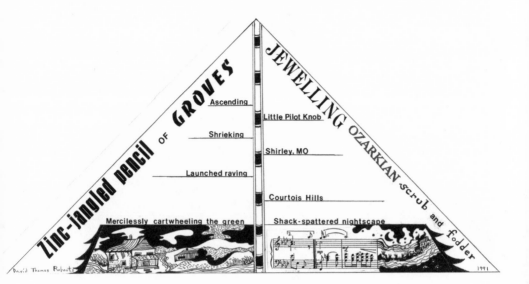

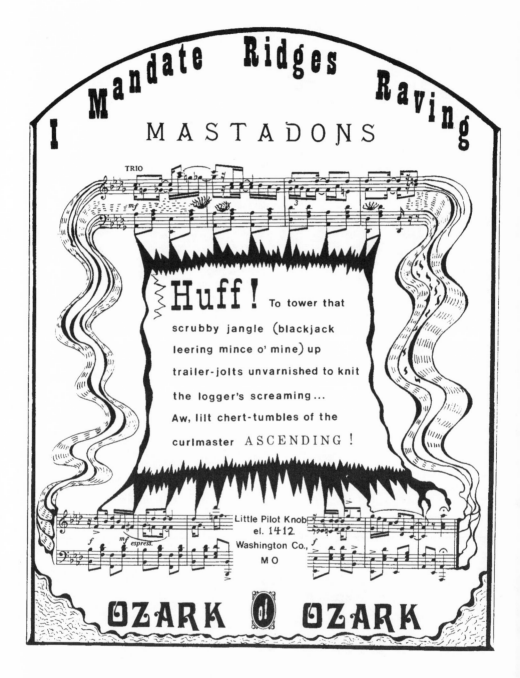

Kalamu ya Salaam

SOUND is ProFound Sense

music is
more than model

coordinated sound
is inspiration

is literally breath
indispensable

the taking in
of the material world

the exhale of
the spirit self

into the atmosphere we go, journeying into the cold but bringing the warm of
our movements, the friction heat of our singing, our sounding, & of course
the daunting ferocity of our memory which makes impossible us remaining
slaves no matter how long we've been downpressed

like the old man sayz: i ain't never been free, but i done had a good time or
two

i am telling you people hold on to the music, worship sound if you just got
to bend your knee to something, a god who can not sing or at least pat foot &
keep time is no god at all

humble in the light may i never forget the sounds from which i am sprung, may
i always remember to give thanx through song

give thanx

for the gods who came amongst us and were given earthly names as they gifted
us with vibrations.

Ashe.

for the tranes who ran underground through us sound transporting us to
another place & time, prettier weather, a hipper clime, where we could be
free, & if not be free, at the very least envision freedom. imagine ourselves

unlocked & unshackled to "devil & sons, incorporated."

Ashe.

for the birds who flew above us. brilliant doves in their love calls, those
grace notes which opened us in places that had been closed so tightly we
never even knew what was inside. how high, how fast we flew fueled by bird's
incandescent warble. for black imagination unafraid to totally express
itself, unafraid to approach the whole world, unafraid to listen to anything,
to everything & righteously respond.

Ashe.

for the oh so hip holidays we celebrate as we struggle through day to day, as
we survive & resist with a song like billie turning even the most maudlin,
most juvenile, most pop trash B side into A-1 lyrics of love &
sophistication, cool as prez riffing with his legs crossed, & horn held at
the sacred angle of ascent, weaving obbligatos of concern & support beneath,
behind & all up around the sound of our great lady igniting life passions
with the blue flame torch of her voice. for all the sister love ladies, of
all our sacred days.

Ashe.

for the taciturn monks who told us so much more than we will ever know, left
us rosetta stone platters to comprehend whose total decoding & deciphering
may take us another million years or more, & for the dizzy lecturers who left
us reeling in a sublime spin of shining notes. for the downhome mary lou's
who knew how to twirl the ivories and obsidians into an enticing swirl of
sounds. for the james named europe who elevated the afrikan in us. for all
our bold buddies with their arms so strong sonically lifting us. for the
djalis frenchified and angolicized into jellyrolls, and for our best smiths
whose striking songs anviled the cruelest moments of our solitudes into
defiant anthems of braveheart blues.

Ashe.

For the hues of our spectrum's vibe from the funk filled foundational brown
of james to the anything but bland midnight blues moaning of B. O. B - B. Y.

Ashe.

to all we have not mentioned (e.g. the gaye wondersongs, the jimi rigged i&i
brothers, & the diva bright willing sounds, the earthy aretha moans, & on &
on), to all of them whomever they are/were, we will never forget you. to all,
to each & every one we owe our very breath.

Ashe.

our music is more than model
well coordinated sounds are inspiration

are literally
indispensable breath

the taking in of the material world
the exhaling of the spirit self

into the atmosphere of this bitter earth
sweetened only by the honey of our song

people have asked me why am i such a fanatic about the music, i in turn
wonder why they are not, & if not music, what? dance? carvings? cooking?
what? anything we do, if it is done well will have the music in it, be
influenced by the music because music is literally organized movement & the
very definition of being alive is to be able to self generate motion, since
the beginning of time, life has been nothing more than a measurement of
movement, how well, the vibrations we leave in our wake, how we sound doing
whatever we do, how the motion of our coming through the slaughter affects
all whom we touch & we got this essentialness from the universe itself, we
are born in motion spinning on the planet, circling around the sun,
thousands, & thousands of miles an hour, moving. being still is an optical
illusion. we are all in motion. & music is nothing but the organization of
the sounds that motion makes. which is why black people operate on vibes.
nothing metaphysical about it. motion. vibrations. music. that's real. in
fact, motion is the primal reality & this is why & what we respond to.

the cosmic timing
of the evolutionary rhythms

of starlight
pulsing

a pulsing that is eaten
through the moist eye

of
visionaries

digested and transformed into aural red cells of sound which enable human
movement. without starlight we die.

looking up in rapt wonder beneath the velvet, star-studded quilt of the heavens, a child asked her grandmother what the silver twinkling was called. "big mama, my mama's mama, how do yo call all those holes in the night sky?"

big mama laughed without looking up & then tilted her head toward sirius. "those are our ancestors winking at us, letting us know they are watching and that we should always make them proud."

big mama gently tugged the little girl's hand. "come, it's time to sleep. when you dream tonight, the starpeople will be inside your head."

when we dream at night, stars illuminate the interiors of our heads, populate our souls with visions we could never think of on our own. the power push & pull of star light is pervasive. in fact, it is the rays of the closest star to us, the rays of the sun which strike the earth and make the world go round. i mean motion is necessary cause stillness is death.

without stars we die/decay
into mere matter

far, far more than any day
we need the deep of night

to unfetter
our imaginations

which is why most musicians are night creatures who roam the earth singing & swinging, representing the advanced thought of their time, deep art is the imagination of its age, the most disturbing, the most beautiful, the most unnerving, the most insightful visions we can imagine & make real.

sound. sound. sound.
sounds. motion. sounds. vibrations.
music is the architecture of higher life forms.
i do not understand silence
except as a pause between noise
a preparation for the next sounding
a momentary rest from the preceding sound

if you study the music
you will understand all that is necessary to know
until you study the music
you can not understand anything there is to know

study sound. study sound. study sound.
because our music is more than model
sound is the necessary

the necessary
the very necessary
sunshine of our existence.

& music
music is more than model
the sound
of our music
is literally inspiration

the indispensable
breath

with which we take in
the material world

through which we exhale
our spirit self

THE MOMENT OF THE FIRST DAY

1.

people get married all the time. but not in congo square. eight o'clock in the morning — there is a softness about that time of day in place de congo, the sun has not yet risen past the trees, barely cleared the rooftops of nearby buildings. the birds have recently finished feeding and are chirping their contentment.

though this late may morning is early summer, the atmosphere is still pleasingly cool. instead of a breeze, the new day gently air-caresses like a lover alternately kissing and blowing unhurried exhales on intimate skin through partially parted lips. big, full smiling lips. laughing lips. tickling lips. like that.

there are moments when romance is real. when every little thing really is alright. when people do lean close and be touching—admittedly rare but nonetheless simply beautiful.

i quietly draped my arm over nia's shoulders and cozied close. whispered something, anything.

i wonder how many lovers danced together here during slavery times, here on this meeting ground just outside what was then the city proper, beyond the ramparts, the city's earthen defense line, out on the plain next to the bend in the canal where the houmas and choctaws came to trade, and where our enslaved ancestors assembled to barter food and handicrafts, and to make music, sing and dance?

i wonder how many lovers met here, secretly in public—secretly because their "masters" didn't know the full import of these assemblies, didn't know the get togethers were also trysts. and in public because the community of captives all knew juba loved juline, were aware elise was dancing for cudjoe, and had no doubt that esmé with her brown eyes round as spanish coins cast shyly toward the ground was glowing in the spotlight of josé's focused stare as her slow twirling kicked up bouquets of dust. how many black hearts have been entwined here?

who can know the specific answer? look. we are still meeting here without the consent of the authorities — we woke up, journeyed here howsoever we travel, and voila, requesting no permit, we gather a community of lovers. love needs no permission, and certainly black love requires no government approval.

2.

true beauty is elegant, a curved exhilaration without an iota of wasted motion or excessive flash. moreover, in an african aesthetic, elegance includes rhythm.

a straight line is monotonous, rhythmless. rhythm is but another name for diversity in motion, and in form, diversity is the curve. hence there are no straight lines on a beautiful human body, every would-be straightness arcs, curves.

cassandra is all curves. even ric with his honed physique, his steel-cabled arms, rippled with veins and muscular development: curves.

senghor said, the negro abhors a straight line. i would add, so does nature, and i would rather be in tune with nature than with rational abstractions. even light bends under the influence of gravity.

moreover, beyond the arc and the lean, when dealing with the human, surface prettiness alone does not give you beauty. physical perfection without inner warmth is cold, and all real human beauty is warm, reflects the rush of blood, the healthy heat of a passionate body, a beating heart.

cassandra is covered shoulder to toe in a sheath of dusky sorrel material embroidered with a flowered pattern in deep violet. she is holding a bouquet of velvety orchids in what appears to be an invisible basket: the soft off-white blossoms with delicate purple highlights dangle in an arrangement shaped like a stunning cluster of semi-sweet concord grapes. sand's toenails are lacquered a burgundy to match the purplish-red (or is it reddish-purple) of her form-fitting, backless dress.

ric stands on two feet but leans majestically like a pine tree seeking sunlight. he is wearing cream (shirt) and brown (slacks), and i mean "wearing" those colors, in fact, he is wearing them out. plus, his skin has the smooth darkness of a country midnight. he is smiling without moving his lips. the luster of his skin is smiling. i imagine his eyes are smiling, but i cannot see his pupils through his shades. even the men are admiring how beautiful ric is. the women look at him and hold their breath.

i bet you two centuries ago, in 1799, on some may day a cool black man stood next to the enchanting winsomeness of a saucer-eyed, dark brown erzulie and their community of friends gathered around them. and smiled deeply felt, seriously contented smiles just like we are smiling now.

3.

the formal ceremony, such as it is, is extremely brief—not much was rendered to ceasar on that morning. carolyn jefferson administered the vows and signed the paper the state uses to hold one legally accountable. but the real signification of commitment came not from a mark on paper but from a leap over a rod.

sand's friend vera had crafted a broom done up in french vanilla–colored raffia wrapped on the handle and outer straws spray-painted dark purple (what a soothing combination). the matrimonial staff lay in the dust between pale, pale yellow candles. ric lights one, sand lights the other. they stand. hold hands. and jump.

why would educated individuals carry on a tradition from slavery?—only those who don't believe in either ancestors or community would ask such a hopeless question. only those removed from the security of community would sneer at jumping the broom. to jump together is not a reminder of slavery, but rather a declaration of self-determination.

4.

afterwards we all went over to ric&sand's apartment. we set up tables on the sidewalk, chairs on the front porch, and played music inside the house—hardwood floors, shiny with hand-applied wax, buffed to an eat-off-the-floor sheen. candles in every room, flickering, some of them scented. here the quiet has a presence you can

202 Kalamu ya Salaam

not ignore, like a precocious child, grinning, hands behind the back: guess what i got, and she stands before you until you tickle her or until he flashes deep dimples and covers his mouth where his front teeth are missing. inside ric&sand's shotgun apartment, the rooms were happy like that.

the walls were bare except for strategically placed photographs hung in carefully selected frames. one frame is green wood. there are two pictures. sand at two with a hat slanted jauntily on her head, and a boyish ric that looks just like mannish ric except the clothes are smaller and from an earlier era. but even then the angle of a budding lean is obvious.

there are trays of food on the tables prepared by a local african restaurant: plantain, a spinach dish called jama-jama, coconut rice, and chicken on skewers with a red sauce on one table, fruit and drinks on the other. a gigantic multi-fruit cream tart in a white cardboard box (the pastry didn't last beyond a quarter hour).

we started the reception with nuptial toasts (libationally, i poured a sip of my juice at the foot of a tree). then we read poems and afterwards toasted some more. sand's friend vera impishly offers: here's mud in your eye. we all laugh. most of us are black, but there are latinas here and a sprinkle of americanos who thankfully think of themselves as human rather than the aggressive/impossible purity of white.

if you passed us that morning, people lounging on the porch, sipping on juice or beer or wine or sucking the nectar from cold watermelon and chilled cantaloupe, if you had seen us you would have thought this was one of those impressionistic paintings of happy darkies deep in the south circa some idyllic antebellum era, except, we, of course, were culturally afro-centric, in love with life and each other, savoring the day and dreaming about nothing but a peace-filled future.

around three in the mid-afternoon, people begin drifting off, their spirits thoroughly rejuvenated, satiated and smiling. before leaving, we exchange hugs. everything beautiful deserves to be embraced.

5.

so this is how we avoid insanity and suicide. we fly to love.

i had been thinking about ric&sand's upcoming marriage as i drove around the city. that's when an image gathered me into its center. you know how you will see something, know that the image is important but not be able to figure the specific meaning. this happened to me a day or so before the wedding. what i wrestled to understand then, is now so clear.

three green birds flew by. their feathered emeraldness disappearing into the sheltering palms that line elysian fields avenue. lime-colored bird feathers fusing with the camouflage of drooping olive-dark tree leaves.

in urban climes free beauty is seldom seen. amid regimentation disguised as daily life, true beauty appears but briefly. we spend eight hours working, a hour in transit to and fro the yoke, another hour or so trying to cool out from the yoke, maybe two hours doing things we need to do for the house but can't do cause we be at the yoke, and, of course, we spend at least six hours sleeping to get ready for, yep, the yoke. the yoke ain't no joke. and we really think we are free?

actually, we are so harassed by being city dwellers in postmodern america that we can hardly be sure what we would be like if we were unyoked, what we would discover in the world. who knows how hip we would be if we were unyoked. at the reception i joke on the porch: if i was in charge, this (sweeping my eyes across the array of relaxing black folk, couples snuggled up, singles sipping red dog or nibbling on jama-jama), this would be what monday is like. well.

i have never before seen uncaged green birds flying through the blueness of crescent city skies. the rare wonder of such a sighting almost made me doubt myself. did i actually spy three pea green streaks threading through the plain of weekday? after all, i could have been delusional. optical illusions are far more common than the miracle of genuine beauty on the wing. maybe it was pigeons. maybe i was sun blinded. the day so bright, maybe my sun-stabbed eyeballs were incapable of clarity. maybe my perceptual acuity had been mutated into fantasy and silliness.

nah, i was there. clearly these creatures were flying. whatever they were. zip and gone. but that is the way of life in the urban jumble. anything original is rare. everything self-determined is even rarer than originality — and undoubtedly love and beauty had to be on the fly, dodging the black and white manacles of what this society pretends is the laissez-faire of living color.

and why were there three little birds—not a couple, but a community of birds, free and green? actually the cluster of their existence is the answer to the question of the why of their existence. they were three because it takes a community to be free— one is a goner, and two won't last long, it takes at least three to be free.

6.

we will remember ric and sand's wedding day—the first day we wore this couple as an amulet over our hearts. ric and sand's first day becomes another jewel on the necklace of black love.

people get married all the time, but rarely is there this much love quietly shared. these are the days we shall surely remember, the gauge we shall use to determine how good is whatever the next goodness we encounter.

thank you ric&sand, for a moment, for a morning when the universe was beautiful, and peace and love were more than a slogan optimistically signed at the end of a desperate love letter sent to someone far, far away.

James Sanders

Poem with Referees

for Terence Stamp

	fizzle to	Donkey Kong may
		been kissing you
		with a bulletproof vest
	fade out	(blond) blood of a pep permint
		in the Sahara like
	internally	
	pans	when you stopped
		caring I
	Night.	was an android.
	hissing	
	cuts away	My clutches are pooped.
	pteradactlly	
		vanishing points
		sound like
	asleep. . .	for

	freezes
	zooms in
	Rushing forward.
	disappears
	waved
	points at
	thru the trap door
	cackles

tune   cookies

cloaked in   the
                shadow of

                failing snow :

          you   will   fall
in love
          with James Sanders dre

amsicle   with

fins on   the planet   of   past

                      flesh   you

  will pretend to be the   con
cierge, cast
                    down by the ookie
wizard of

                        clairol

you   will
        try to

	shows fin-gers with	cure insomnia in *Night of*
	his back	
	Cuts away	the *Living Dead* looking o
		ver your
shoulder. . .
	close up:	(our violet descriptions of
		tele pathy shrimp hy
drangeas
		gleed
by   past tense
	sincerely	
	fade	like Terence Stamp (sincerely) flu
	"I miss	ttering away from
	you too"	Krypton

From the Mark Prejsnar Playbook

7. The Not Pants, Continue

Like a silhouette furred in a dark brown fire from across the room Mark puts
ketchup on
       "it." It is
    ketchup. Mark
    divides
        Mark   divides   done
but does
not continue   is.   Mark sees you
                crotch the   pair
                   of tenses with a clipped zero.
Mark does
                   not turn the switch but
                   not   his   pants. It is not a
                   switch
                   and when

                    (ponily).   Point the gags
            away

                          from yourself!
He marks it as step one.

               Continue.

Step two.
Step three. Mark in front of wallpaper.

something something   willpower
       like a pony in your pants

7a. The Invisible

Mark lets the ninjas lick the
            bo

wl with invisible
  The pods

Mark washes his hands and dries his hands on

the pods because   this is the center

of   it. His invisible equals
pink icing. They are immersed
in silverware. Mind the

cleer teeth. When Mark
washes his hands you

apply emphasis like
a sweaty noodle. Then Mark

spoons and dinettes and arms and underneaths. He

fudds.
Loadly, like a ninja with decaf and everything pink icing.

8. *The Lake* _____

Like more than one   icy
petal bouncing off a dawny robot Mark does touch

something Bill Pullman in the   leer black lake. Lak

e?   Lake. L
ake?
Lake. Lake?
Lake Lake?   L

ake.

He pushes the "On" button like
Then Mark treats you like an orphan with jellied ha
ndlebars with the   back of his face
disappearing into the lake. Lake?
Lake.

9. *The Exchange*

If Mark kleeps the p-lard you

make it   per zero.   He exchanges the can of

global
cat food
for a   Little Debbie Fudge

                              heliem.
                    In the light he pulls

          on the creamy

                    cord   as

an exchange

                         10. Do the Cyclops

Mark begins to

          like a cyclops with a   stack of toilet paper
     down the stair

                    insect

          Mark tells language "It is payb
ack time"   tron

               shinola for a

          "personal" item.   You a re

          on the other   end of
     the aisle which

               is a ballerina   with a bloody nose Then Mark reverses and
doesn't need it
because his feet are

                                   filled

with glass of the future

at the other a
                isle   lotionlessly. . .

11. *Number Eleven*

Mark combs his heart and turns to the
silver t ail behind
him if
he does.   Mark makes pie + ch
ocolate drink and fills something in
front of his eyes with mushy
xless liquid like a lonely
pirate in a
                lukewarm white condominium when someone en
ters. Mark combs har
again, sincerely delighted.

12. *Waiting for Distant Dust*

Mark combs his heart and turns to the
silver t ail behind
him if
he does.   Mark makes pie + ch
ocolate drink and fills something in
front of his eyes with mushy
xless liquid like a lonely
pirate in a
                lukewarm white condominium when no one

                                        enters. Mark
sits
down at the Mac and moves his arm
slightly upward like distant dust. Distant dust
sounds like a spiral
staircase   with a couple of
Snickers bars on
                it as d
ark as clown
shoes coated with candy

bars on the
                inside. Mark thinks about
        it for a second then he
moves his left arm towards
  it for a second and then more
            arms

13. The Something

                    Mark turns left onto
Ponce like a clown
shoe at the cent

            er of a dirty candy bar

but not the candy bar he sees. The dial slips
      in his hand remembers

Then, Mark "makes" a model
Mark but it looks like Max

        von Sydow crossed with Santa
  Clause by turning around and
scratching the front of

        the motion detector with

  fake   vienna

                                                sausage. Or

                                            he allows

    the sauce of sleep

        to consensual diamelle throat from it   or Mark guccis

  himself.

14. The Crowded Binary

Mark spends the day with

   a popsicle

in theory. You spend

            it

                 yourself as you are doing

 it no matter how f

ar you

                   throw it.

                        15.

There is no   one   around

Mark is strolling down Highland and
then he looks like he hears
hoofsteps   of creamy Uncle
Bludgeon or Venom, the
jiggly   squirrel
    among the black
cornflakes on the floor
in the silver woods

Mark bites into something like   a gun in a   fountain   covered with something

Mark takes his sunglasses off and acts
nice

16. The Adult Beak

Mark is taken by surprise by a pad of something and you are outside the window as flat as the thief of couples. Mark caused it by something shaped like a burnt bib (parallel) and is suddenly giggling to himself, a mouse trapped in a bottle of pepto bismol. Mark turns off the Braves with all fingers

beating on their own, and his shoulder tilted slightly inward and then stands for at least a second and puts something in there and lifts his right arm and shivers and cokes something or birthdays something sudden like ham keys (sweetly) saying something. That move is "The Adult Beak" and his arm, each hair a banana la

pping at an   elevator full

of Diane Sawyer

17. The Waiting Offense

Mark finishes the Count Chocula

chicken

then he slurps the milk then Mark clanks the bowl
into the sink like a private

chicken

rainbow.   Then he
leotards out into

his name over a loudspeaker. He gets
up and you

Count Chocula your leotards like sour   stars

Christy Sheffield Sanford

Rachel's Recovery (Fucking with the Angels).

Rachel, 1840, as Phaedra, appears in white-face, draped in white, surrounded by red (set, curtain, floor). She looks like wasted wax.

> *Phaedra: I am not fit to rule any kingdom! I am but a broken slave, yoked to shame. Gasping for her life. I have crossed the boundaries of modesty and restraint. I have vaunted my shame before my master.*
>
> *Theseus: This morning I found a slug in our bedroom. It left a slimy trail over the ceiling, over the carpet, over the bed.*
>
> *Phaedra: Do you think it's an omen? I told you to keep that son of yours away from me-lock him in the closet.*
>
> *Sound Effect: Silk cloth ripping selvage to selvage.*

After each performance, Rachel gets the *roses bleues;* it's depressing to take poison night after night. She stares long at herself in the dressing-room mirror. Candles flicker all around. At last, she recovers.

Close up of Rachel's skirt hem covered with mud. She giggles, thumbs her nose at the royal carriage, which has brought her and the Duke de D*** home to their apartment. He slaps her. *"Sauvage!"* he mutters. "Your correctitude infuriates me; besides, the prince is barbaric." Flushed, she enters her Alhambra-style foyer with its blue mosaic floor, gold brocaded walls. Several guests applaud her entrance, kiss her on both cheeks. She concocts a kirsch punch and like a priestess lights it. Blue flames shoot up three feet. "How lurid!" the Duke howls. She snarls at him.

ALABASTER　　　　*SILVER*　　　　*DEATH*

1848: end of slavery in France. Five ex-slaves accompany Rachel as she sails past Las Palmas en route to Dakar. She's paid them. They work on her with ardor. She is always more tender and sincere on the high seas than in Paris.

There's
one to fan her
one to feed her　　　　　　He spears a mussel with his sword.
one to fondle her
one to fuck her　　　　　　She eats off the blade.
and one to free her
if he could.　　　　　　Sounds of finger-licking.

The liberator sits lethargically in the corner, his dark beard on his chest. At the job

---

Phaedra: Racine's play in which Phaedra, left alone for a long stretch by her husband Theseus, falls in love with her stepson Hippolytus. She professes her love, but he, enamored of Aricia, scorns her. Phaedra is dying of love when suddenly Theseus returns. No one will talk to him. At last, Phaedra's maid tells him his son made advances toward her mistress. Theseus's ire rouses the sea god, and as Hippolytus rides down the beach, Poseidon overturns his chariot and crushes him. After confessing to her husband, Phaedra takes poison. Theseus mourns his son and takes in Aricia as his daughter.

interview, she had asked, "What was your last position?" He had answered, "I was an ambulance driver." Rachel sings "*La Marseillaise*" to great effect, as she did the night she prevented a theatre riot. "*Allons, enfants de la patrie, / Le jour de gloire est arriveé! / Contre nous de la tyrannie.*

On deck, stands a large, ornate, white-metal bed. TV monitors picture Rachel dying in white-face with red cupid's-bow lips. Red Cross emblems on white scrim. Rachel coughs. She wears a long-sleeved, red lace nightgown and looks haggard against the white sheets. Coughing, she leans over, spits blood on the deck. Her coughs resound. Like a ventriloquist, she throws her voice to various parts of the auditorium. On screen: close-up of bed, then red gown. She seems headless.

ANIMAL   VEGETABLE   STONE

British lecturer's voice: The negress forms a single block of shade, hidden by a curtain. She lifts it. Colors blaze, spurt. One sees a naked torso, a tambourine on the ground, a cast-off slipper. The vista is barred with shadows. Red braid dangles from the ceiling. She leans on one elbow amid deep, white pillows. Videographer moves in as though for the kill. Close-up relayed to screens about the auditorium.

Rachel is one of those who still have enough energy to have desires: to travel, to get rich, to make love. *Lecturer: Coquette. The outward acts continue the ancient customs. See the diagonal cutting beyond the negress. Door ajar. Man acts; woman blooms.*

yellowish-white shifting sands   *waving flags*
massive towers   frogs croaking

Rachel draws up the sheet to reveal a superb, glistening leg. *Her limb could belong to any of those ebony goddesses,* under lock and key in the museums of Europe. By appointment only. *The dazzling cubes, the bisecting shadows, the ample drape.* She's not a maniac; she's a mature actress with a superb glistening crotch.

Trickle of blood from side of her mouth spots, then drenches the sheets. It's everywhere on TV. Her cough is joined by a second cougher; the duet becomes a trio, then a chorus. Sounds of Manon, of Marguerite, of Mimi at the end of La Bohème—repetitive with sounds of drops hitting metal pan. Drips, then more drips on digital delay. Spotlight on pan catching drips. Blood seeps from TVs. Pools collect. Fade in United Way-type thermometer filling-overlapping of slides as red indicator reaches the top.

STIR   QUIVER   SWELL

An agitated crowd watches as serpent-like Rachel moves. She sits on the side of the bed, continues "*La Marseillaise*": "*Aux armes, citoyens, formez vos bataillons! / Marchons! Marchons!*"

La beauté est la seule chose au monde qui excite le désir.
Beauty is the only thing in the world which excites desire.

La bête est la seule chose au monde qui excite le désir.
The beast is the only thing in the world which excites desire.

La laideur est la seule chose au monde qui excite le désir.
Ugliness is the only thing in the world which excites desire.

When she speaks French she's elegant, *chic* and thinks of cream and *asperges*. And when she speaks Wolof, she is earthy and feverish and thinks of rice and yams. A maribou once told her, "Speaking French, you're a girl, but speaking Wolof you become more sensual, adult, intelligent—in short, a woman.

a fusion of heaven and earth   *a wagon load of melons*

a saber slash to the face   Rachel speaks, "I am the devil's sunshine. I become calm only with gifts of sherbet and fruit." She has a coughing fit; flecks of blood spot the water in her finger bowl. "I stay up all night and sleep all day. There's nothing I wouldn't do for love. What was my life like before the bull-fighters, before the bloody crucifixions, before the dark laughter." *Notice the rings on all her fingers, the horses in the bedroom, the overturned golden goblets on the floor.* The Duke de D*** lies sated on a carpet of lynx skins. Rachel sits at her dresser, smoking, staring at the mirror. "How did my thighs become so fleshy?" She combs her hair as a maid fans her with ostrich feathers. A pounding surf perfectly accompanies her ritual.

A veil of blue and purple and scarlet. Trip to the *Voyante.* "Last night I dreamt I was dissecting my tiger cat, Foedora. She was still alive. The incision was belly up-neck to tail. I spread out her fur. The bones over her eyebrows were thin and looked like the backbone of a chicken. I removed them; Foedora began to moan. To end her suffering, I took a woolen cloth and suffocated her. What do you make of it?" "Is the Duke de D*** still demanding you calm down?" "Well, yes." "And you try hard to accomodate him, to be a good girl, despite your gypsy blood?"

Descendants in a tubercular line stretch over three M's: Manon, Marguerite, Mimi. Manon coughing in the desert, dying of pneumonia/consumptioni/F.U.O. Marguerite coughing in her stall, Mimi in her garret. Disease spreading over centuries, spreading over Europe, spreading to the R's and V's. To Rachel, to Violette. Literature and life sharing the same glass. *Femme fatales* chained together at the waist. Linked by history, linked by geography, linked by micro-organisms. A face buried in jasmine-afflicted by white flies. Reincarnation. *La Dame aux Carnations. La Dame à la Damnation.* Rachel is *La Dame aux Dahlias Noirs.*

"Say AHHHH." She sticks out her tongue. This all happened before the Miracle of Dakar-similar to the Miracle of Lourdes but more exotic, more sensual. More Tropic of Cancer and yet Equatorial. More palm trees and vines, more bougainvilleas. Lourdes and the role of touch. A brown woman enters in flowing pouffe of pink chiffon embroidered with gold flowers. She is the African Goddess of Love, who applies massage, herbs and wisdom, maybe, ah, the Miracle of Dakar is, no-ah, wait-love?

LOVE   *GANGLIA*   *VOLUMINOUS LOVE*

Dancers in somptueux boubous, swaying under a baobab tree. The man in the corner in a loin cloth, the ex-ambulance driver, comes and waves his long black hair over her. Each stroke grazes her navel. Swish, swish. His breath and little whirlwinds about his body quicken her. He takes a little zem-zem (holy water from

Mecca) and mixes it with juf (a red, powdered root from a now extinct plant). He rubs the oily gritty poultice over her breasts and chest until it looks like she's wearing a red blouse with nipples. The medication feels like stinging nettles. She inhales the vapors, which smell like vanilla dirt. The drug enters her chest wall; her auricles and cunt begin to pound. This heart-altering aphrodisiac produces highly plastic facial expressions and hips that swivel and jut. Five minutes later, she feels luxurious, calm, ecstatic.

Rachel is being suspended in the angel-float position. Tripping, they are all tripping. Breathe, relax. The water jets are nice.
Back in the yam garden, the earth is cracked, but the heart-shaped leaves keep roving over the land.

"Would I have been the bad girl I am had I had a secular education? Almost a gypsy, I was the daughter of Jewish peddlers. But very religious. Bird calls of the Old Testament found their way into my father's rituals. Doves flew out of his heart. In the streets, my sister and I sang love songs. Ribbons (red, blue, green, yellow, purple) flowed from my guitar, our hair. *Sous* rained in the gutters at our feet. I learned to act, to become a tragedienne, to play the great *rôles*—the heroines of Corneille and Racine."

Trip to *Voyante:* Madame X. wears a gold choker of lion claws. Rachel begins: "An angel came to me in a dream. He was about two and a half feet long and had hot-pink, bowed lips. He stuck his pink little tongue—no bigger than a cat's—in my mouth and Frenched me a long time. It was the most satisfying kiss of my life!" "How old was this angel?" "I remember soft golden ringlets, like a child's, and downy wings brushing against my face. I was picking white feathers off my *peignoir,* and he was blowing one in the air. 'Your black hair is shiny as a raven angel's,' he said." "Your face is plump. Are you and the Duke de D*** overindulging or are you pregnant?" asks the *Voyante.* "Ohhhh, I have missed a period or two."

RESUSCITATION

When did she resort to opium and drink? When did she stop those long walks in the *Bois de Bologne* ? When did she become attracted to Poe?

missing lips   clenched teeth   long black hair partially veiling hollow, green cheeks

She lurches, her body lunging, rolling from side to side, like a schooner. "I am your ripe avocado," she says. "You are my knife." Black spotted skin, soft buttery fruit, shading from yellow green to green. Everyone tested negative. She steadies herself on the rail. Vicissitudes of the slippery deck.

"Charles gave me consumption." Delirious, she struggles to stand upright. "What is the sound of rain on the river? Clapping. His claws digging into my skin. His body scampering up and down, the furry belly dragging so close. He nibbled my neck!" Increased gnawing sound, ripped flesh, bacteria funneled in through the throat-needle-nosed pliers as retractors. "I told my maid, 'Do not let

that man into my house!' He bribed her. He loved me, the oaf. So boring, but he kept bringing me *eau de vie*."

the tapped rubber trees   *the blue glass vases*
the drugged slumber   *the night he fucked her*
in her sleep   *the smelling salts*

The man with a doctor's bag, shirtless. Draped like a flag over one shoulder, a Red Cross emblem on a white background. Strain-resistant and he came like the wind and was full of himself and his power. He knew the vibrant sweetness of his cock. "Are you a doctor?" Rachel asks. "*Vous devez plaisanter* (You must be joking), I'm a medic."

What made him different? What genetic flaw saving grace made him want to help her? What is the natural order of things? So physically secure nothing about her person scared him. And why did he want to take a few drops of precious testosterone dripping in his brain and cure her with his hair, his wafting high energy aura? And he was filling out forms for her. So many explanations of why she should be allowed to direct *Phaedra*. And subject it to a rewrite. Here we are concerned with the exceptions. Why is this one not threatened? And his cock is so hard. It's spinning like a top. Little red and blue sparks fly off. Well, now. If we could just grasp the exception.

If you give them what they want, you can take anything you need. She learned this one summer in Sicily, under a twisted tree, shaded by silvery leaves. A swarthy man with a red sash popped an olive in her mouth. This is what summer repertory is about.

the stiff necked people   *the naked people*
the yeasty water   *the purple fire*   *lost in a sea of*
longing again

It's as though a necklace has broken in the sky. Hail stones like giant pearls begin dropping, striking the tops of heads and bouncing across the deck. The falling baubles make a terrible racket. With thin arms, Rachel covers her head and laughs until she begins rolling on the deck in a coughing fit. Her white make-up and black lipstick smear. She picks up an ice-jewel, sucks it.

Bending over her, the man says smiling, "When you learn to help people with Red Cross techniques, how can you think of hurting them?" He's a convicted murderer. They send out convicts to board suspicious ships. He beat his brother to death in a fight over a girlfriend. Afterward, she refused to see him. "Rachel, would you like ginseng tea with milk?" He's with the Gambian Red Cross. He describes her disease as rhizomal: "You have these nodes and ganglia and they are spreading, growing obscenely, and if we can spray them with love and sperm-"

Twenty rivers discharging silt into a swamp. "Not everyone wants to be around people who have consumption. After all, it's contagious," she says. *The frogs died, and they gathered them together in heaps, and the land stank.*

Of interest: the man in the corner—this angel, this healer, the one with the Red Cross. How to avoid sounding like D. H. Lawrence or some groveling female and yet get across the power of responsiveness. Saving graces between men and women.

"You cannot hold the cauldron while we speak. Put it down on the ground. It shows a lack of respect not to do this," he said. She set the black pot on the ground, looked up and waited. Her vaginal orifice began to assume the shape of the cauldron.

"In time, sweat and body oil will produce an image on cloth." A man bends over with a magnifying glass. Another man wearing glasses, his dark receding hair disheveled, bends over, his nose almost touching the cloth. "Scourge marks, blood from puncture marks on head, creases, large flow of blood and fluid from side, scorched....

water marks   _molten silver_   _mirror image_
burns   _languor_   _herringbone twill_

Buried under a mound of dead crabs: no corpse of flesh and muscle but an intact skeleton of polished bones. "Every day I dropped by the morgue," she says. "You can pick up interesting characters there. It's quite the social gathering place. The drowned bodies pulled from the Seine are always bloated. _L'étendard sanglant est levé! / L'étendard sanglant est levé! / Entendez-vous dans les campagnes. / Mugir ces féroces soldats!_" She gasps for breath. A marabout sprinkles her with maiden-hair and myrrh. The servants "Oooh and ahhh," but she knows there'll be no post-mortem show of affection, no special kiss, no day-long sealing of lips to face/neck.

Her face is streaked with tears. TV camera zooms in for close-up of her eyes. Miracle painting of the Madonna weeping, her head cocked to one side. Flowing tears pool on her chin, inundate her mouth area. The bottom of the screen becomes dewy, then besotted. Red-spotted mucus and water seep into the monitor. A few drops hit the deck. The laminated control panel begins to buckle and dehisce. "What will they bring me next," she hisses, "a rosary or a necklace of leeches?" _always dreaming of the guillotine_

"Bend over," demands the medic, "Time to administer your prophylaxsis." "It's too late, didn't you read my chart. Who are you? I thought you were a good guy." "I am," he says, gently inserting the extract of guava pistils wrapped in edible gold leaf. He kneads her dark cheeks, which she has not painted white. "This helps the drug take effect," he says calmly. A tantalizing change seeps over her. "Oh, my God," she whispers. Her fingers are eroticized; she begins to feel for things as one gone blind. She can't touch enough. Everything is at risk of being captivated and felt up. She has WHT: Wandering-Hand Trouble. Braille body readings available on request. Digital power on display nightly.

OBELISK   _TORQUE_   _QUICKENING_

I was sinking deep in sin far from the peaceful shore .. Love lifted me. / Love lifted me. / when nothing else could help, love lifted me. Everything is recorded, everything is cumulative. Because of the bacteria in the mouth, we knew we shouldn't kiss. The bacteria were growing. We wanted to kiss. I was lying on the divan. He was seated before the fireplace-his hat in his hand, the fur on his lap. _lascive, je dormais_ We tried not to kiss. _sur la bouche, dans ia fontaine de Cafour_ We decided to kiss not on the mouth _sur la terre_ but on the ears. The stars were twinkling through the French doors. The neighbors could see inside. _les gouttes transparentes_ I kissed his left ear, then his right, _les delices d'une passion_ soft and delicate. I kissed his cheeks, his eyes, his brows, his forehead, his neck.

omega oil   _fever_   _thick strings of slick, yellow-
green algae_   The angel flies over and saves I kills people-the first born male children, I think.

From the display in her living room, Rachel picks up one of her thirteen jeweled daggers and runs her fingers over the blade. Wheeling around, she exits to the kitchen where she trims a filet. She confides to her maid, "The Duke de D***'s decorum is more than I can bear. I like wilder, earthier men." Sizzling sounds. After placing *les bifteks* before the Duke de D*** and Kaba, a man she picked up at a horticulture show, she sits. She has painted her lips black, contrasting sharply with her white-face makeup.

BOOKS   JEWELS   LAUREL WREATHES

Rachel cultivates flowers. "Nothing wrong with a little flirt," she always says. And this man, Kaba, a diplomatic envoy from Guinea-Bissau, has developed a black dahlia. He asks, "Do you mind if I name it after you?" He saw Rachel play Roxane, a sultana in *Bajazet,* who abandons her treacherous lover to mutes who strangle him. Kaba says, "Ah, Rachel, *que vous êtes brilliante!*" Different, she muses, from saying, "You're a beautiful woman with a supple waist and slim ankles." She notices his softly audible breathing. *"Merde alors,"* she sighs, as her viscera turn into sweet *saboyon* . During dessert, she excuses herself. in the *salle de bains,* she pulls down her pants. Her lower pubic hair is so wet it tapers into a Vandyke beard. Red, the color is dyed red.

And the angel passed over.   unleavened bread
sugared raisins   salt   rose-scented
glycerin   an egg

Rachel returns, sips a glass of brandy, says, "Let's play *lansquenet* for money!" "Really, Rachel—" "Or for this emerald ring the Duke gave me." "Don't make a spectacle of yourself," the Duke admonishes. He begins a row. They take it to the kitchen. "What is wrong with you?" Rachel demands. "You're acting like a guttersnipe," he says. "That's enough," she says. You brazen bitch!" He slaps her. Glass goblet smacks a wall, shatters. "The second time tonight," Rachel says. Her cheek is hot, her body feverish. "Get out!" he says. "No, you get out!" She pushes him toward the door. "This is my apartment, remember," she says. "But I pay most of the bills." He pushes her back. She shoves him. He stumbles, falls to one knee. As he rises, his hands reach for her neck. The door swings open. "May I escort you somewhere?" Kaba asks. "Yes," Rachel smiles.

"You saved my life," she says. "I almost died once," he says. "I was fifteen. I was strolling by a Dakar quai when a man said, 'Lookin' fer a ship, Mister?' Next thing I knew I was rounding Cape Manuel, heading south. The lookout shouted 'Bl-o-o-o-w!' and we harpooned a sixty-footer. We severed the eight-foot tall head and spent the whole night stripping the carcass. At dawn, a mate was bailing out spermaceti. I was below him; every slash of his knife sprayed me with grease. I was bathed in oil. When it was ankle deep, I fell on my ass with a big splash! I slid halfway across the deck. Men were laughing and I was screaming. Just as I slipped overboard, a sailor grabbed my leg."

Rachel begins: "One summer, Duke de D*** and I were boating in Spain. I was drunk. I fell overboard. I was flailing when a giant stingray swam under me and lifted me up. I hugged its firm, smooth shoulders. We plowed through the sea. A shark followed us, then another and another. My ray froze, turned and headed for the leader. The pack fled. One week and four hundred miles later my angel dropped me into shallow water off the coast of Portugal."

DIVE   ASCEND   SWERVE

Under Rachel's tongue, the night float slips *a wafer of pulverized lapis lazuli mixed with slime mold spores.* Blue veins dissolve in her mouth. Her head begins to dart like a mongoose chasing a snake. Her eyes widen, nostrils flare. in a frenzied dance, a follow spot tracks Rachel's swiveling neck. Sweat pours off her white face in rivulets. By the dance's end, she's black and white striped like the bars of a jail. She drops to the deck, twitching in exhaustion. An ex-slave strips and places his clothes beneath her body. *secret ingredients*

Her head lolls back on the carriage seat. She watches Kaba's reaction. He laughs. "A protector," he responds, "is essential but Duke de D*** is a pain. Why do you put up with him?" "He's sometimes primal?" She shrugs. "How'd you return from Portugal?" he asks. "I never did. Many Spaniards think i'm dead." She coughs. "Portugal is a wild but friendly country. The men on horseback have an avid appreciation of women.

Cradling her head in his arms, Kaba says, "You've lost your home, as I have." "Temporarily," she sighs. "How nice it is to give to you," he says, squeezing his pince-nez. "We are brother and sister tonight;" she says, "in the morning, who knows." On her face, the dark, slanted pattern of decorative scars begins to show through her white makeup.

iridescent   *wet*   *curvilinear*   *slime*
ambergris (floating whale shit)   *embedded cuttlefish*
beaks   *parfum nonpareil*

First meeting with Duke de D***. *A sultry night.* I was standing silently before him in my dressing room door. Our thighs welded. *'Où? Quand? Combien?'* he asked. *'Chez toi. Ce soir. Pour rien,'* I said. (Where? When? How much? At your house. This evening. For nothing. Well, almost nothing. How about 11:55 P.M., at Pont Neuf Bridge, near the sewer? The walls are dank.) He began to drool. Disgusting, but also charming. I felt moved and knew I could help. He placed his hand between my ankles, lifted my long dress straight up the front. He took two fingers and drew out some of my goodness. He licked his fingers. I kissed him passionately."

in the distance, they can see nothing but calm waters, *one thick cloud* sunshine and a few fishing boats. *a wild din* Suddenly a waterfall like a solid green glass wall shoots up and looms over the nearest vessel. A cascading avalanche crashes perpendicularly. Beneath this battering ram, *blood smeared over the lintel, the door, the hands* a trench forms. They watch at the rail as the bulkhead crumbles. The ship's name, Cashmire, rapidly sinks into the hole. The rogue-wave dragon belches forth a churning froth.

The rewrite of *Phaedra* occupies her every waking thought. Her big chance to portray *realité,* to direct. Uniting Romanticism with Classicism-light pink with deepest madder. At times the set turns blood red, enters the eyes like wine coursing down the throat, causing drunkenness, abandon, despair.

UNCONTROLLABLE SUBSTANCES

Hopelessly giving herself up to the passion of music. An acacia blossom between her teeth. "Where is my D. J.?" She has on a long, white satin slip-dress. Her hips, prominent beneath the fabric, saunter forward. She whips off her fringed, red and white flowered shawl. Her castanets clatter as she stamps the shawl into oblivion. "Who will be my D. J. today?" Voluminous love. The man in the corner rouses himself. He places his hands under her armpits and from her hairline begins an ascent. He slowly traces the outline of her upraised arms. Like a man flinging water from just-washed hands, he wipes away invisible substances from her body. At her fingertips, he quits, resumes his stupor in the corner. Pulls his hat over his eyes.

Heimlich Maneuver: *A Private Room at La Maison Dorée. Duke de D*** in black suit, velvet cravate, Rachel in gold satin gown, decolleté neckline.*

> Duke de D***: *Choking. He points to his throat.*
> Rachel: *Must be a champignon, she thinks.* "I can help, I trained at the Red Cross." *Standing behind him she demands,* "Bend over!" *She grabs him, pushes his head between his knees, smacks him four times between the shoulders, jams her thumb into his sternum, gives four quick thrusts.* "Better?"
> Duke de D***: *No response.*
> Rachel: *Twice she repeats the maneuver.* "Better? Better!?!" *Diners lean over the balcony, observe her technique.* "Cavre gourd!" *She kicks him, spits on him.* "Fou! Get up! You want me guilty for the rest of my life?" *She jumps on his chest. As with a riding crop, she whips him side to side. She rocks fiercely, vaguely sexually, then not so vaguely. She collapses. Fade to black.*

a crowd leaning over the balcony   a cracked black skirt impulsive gyration   a feline smell

> Duke de D***: *Follow spot on a wad of saliva-covered mushroom flying in an arc from his mouth. The crowd gasps, then applauds. Dazed, he sits.*
> Rachel: *Takes a bow.* "I should have let you choke to death," *she says smiling.*
> Duke de D***: "Actually, I thought that was your plan, as you did the maneuver completely wrong."
> Rachel: "Ungrateful wretch!" *She throws a vase of flowers at him.*
> Duke de D***: *He catches the flying object.*

A Dakar taxidermist holds a fat, bomb-shaped tiger shark in his arms as though teaching a dog to sit up. His teeth and the shark's are visible. in the fish's mouth, are five more sets, soldiers ready to advance,   *gunfire landing at their feet as they entered the city*   replace any casualties. Even the body scales are primitive teeth. Both man and fish appear to be smiling, but the shark is dead. The anal fins extend—graceful, wing-like.

The curative power of angels and men. The giving in to women by men, past superstition and into saving. "I like giving," he said. He was a burly man in military garb—camouflaged to look like the sea—and he was holding Rachel in his arms. His jacket was open and she could see his chest covered with scars from the sacred skewers that had yearly pierced his breast. She weighed only ninety-five pounds. She was going to get well:

> 1) *Because her library research revealed she had been misdiagnosed, and her disease was early curable Hodgkin's;*
> 2) *Because there was a religious evolution and subsequent edict affecting first-born girl children;*
> 3) *Because a German chemist had distilled a drug drawn from the Asiatic yew of Sumatra. No one there has tuberculosis as they all eat chemically interesting leaves;*
> 4) *Because a Red Cross worker has a way of laying on hands that leaves the*

client free to rise off the pallet and continue living.

Below decks, naked men and women move about the apothecary. One whole wall is a honeycomb of drugs, designed to cure fatal illnesses: ground sea snake spines, flecks of iridescent mica in vials of violet water, mirror slivers (for inner visions) mollified with mandrake (to blur the visions), and medicinal incense—the reputed recipes of angels. Now lit: "Raphael" to escape life's snares. The soft granules are green as sphagnum moss but sparkling. A thin column of sweet smoke rises, curls. irises dilate. On the top shelf are inhalation devices and a test-tube of male support dust cut with baby powder. Some of this stuff is very expensive.

CONTRAINDICATIONS

Tropical slides: huge guava halves, split pomegranates, dripping mangoes, ferns. Water sounds. *Her figure is almost devoured by chiaroscuro. in the background: flattened pyramids.* Singing, Rachel marches around and across the bed. She still adores going barefoot. Vivifying juices. Decadent waves. Siren sounds. *"We need type 0-negative!"* Rachel collapses on the bed, one bare leg in the air, toes pointed, back arched, hair falling toward hell. The crew gathers around her, chants in synchrony with the ocean waves.

Her head spins, like the night she watched the little ball ricochet at the Palais Royal. The roulette wheel had spun blood, in the form of her money. At last, she had realized she and the Duke de D*** were spending her cache.

The following week, she had dressed in thin white organdy over a black lace undergarment, large-brimmed black hat, and visited the *Voyante*. "I dreamt I took the Duke's arm and it was very thin. I could feel his bones. Does this mean he could never lift me, never support me?" *one finger rotating on a crystal ball* "You are *riche*. What do you mean, support? Lie on the couch." Rachel reclined with her arms over her eyes.

"What do you see?" demanded the *Voyante* . "I see a man on his knees. We are in the circus. I stand on his back. As he rises, I walk my ballet slippers up to his shoulders. I begin to juggle plates on the ends of sticks." "This would not be dramatic unless he were holding you up, said the *Voyante*, rubbing her forehead. "I see," said Rachel.   *reels of small and large chains hanging naked and exposed*
SQUALLS   HYDRAS   LOVE CALLS

> *To support: as in the angel-float position.*
> *To save: as in follow the fold, stray no more.*
> *To administer to: as in the forms, the flowers, the balms.*
> *To free: as in spring the trap, allow the bloody animal to limp away.*

She wears a harlot's attire and has a subtle heart. "You look like the Goddess of Love," he says. "I can't do it alone." she says. "Oh, you can, masturbation is sweet. May I stroll you around the deck?" The angel is wearing nothing but red wings and a long burgundy velvet scarf draped over one muscular shoulder. His skin is Honduran brown. His cheek bones are high and indian-like. He has on leather sandals. "Are you a physician?" Rachel asks, sitting in a deck chair- her legs sprawled. "Heavens, no! Stroke my wings," he demands.

As she stands to feel the soft feathers and tough quills, he has an erection. The sunlight striking his penis sends an oily rainbow around it. Twilight prism. He opens his penis like an oblong cabinet. inside are many mysteries: an ankle bracelet he hands to Rachel; a skeleton key; two big cigars from Havana; dangerous visions of love; black stockings and blue butterflies that fly out and disappear.

NIGHT   FRICTION   SPECTACLE

"Remarkable," Rachel says. "Yes," says the angel, whose name is Raphael. "And each day, there is something new inside. I never know what it will be. Last week it was mercurochrome and gauze. I give first aid. Take the key and stroke it." She cautiously touches it, looking into his eyes. Automatically, his red scarf slides around her like a snake and ties them together. Her clothes fall to the ground as he lifts off. She feels better already.

"Have you money to risk on a new production of *Phaedra*," she asks. "Yes" he says. "I want to portray the true story of how Charles Duvalier, who played Hippolytus, was a jerk and tried every bloody night to get me to sleep with him, and when I finally did he gave me consumption. *ils viennent jusque dans nos bras*. I was not old enough, you understand, to play his mother. I wore a lot of make-up. *Egorger nos fils, nos compagnes*. And we'd see what Theseus did the first night he had Aricia alone to himself! That awful, upstaging, *ingénue* bitch! *Aux armes, citoyens, formez vos bataillons! I Marchons! Marchons!"*   *Racked by paroxysms of coughing—*

hornet stings   litiginous tongues   the perfume of oxygen her flushed neck   une nuit héliotropique

"I see," says Raphael, "you want only revenge when you could be sleeping every night with me or other angels." "Other angels?" "Angels fuck very well." "I wouldn't know," she says, "I never fucked an angel." The first time it's all done in the air.

Recovery: more historic than physical. More real than surreal. Vengeance resting in the ascendance of flesh as soul, in success. She points to the stage. "Here, we have another hit." And she's right.

UNREPENTANT

the animated gelatinous substance "There's nothing like the feel of hot sand beneath your soles." Rachel loves walking barefoot on the beach. *the scarlet fevers A fish gasping for breath, beached over and over by the tide. A body— with gaping mouth, heaving chest— repeatedly rescued by waves.* "I'm an actress; I know I can break their hearts I thrill them." *Her breasts are bare, her hair tied with a black ribbon. in one hand she carries a musket, in the other the French flag.* "*Qu'un sang impur abreuve nos sillons!/Allons, enfants—*"

And the angel lifts off

Lorenzo Thomas

An Even-Tempered Girl Holds Her Breath

He looked for mischief
But he only found
Tantrums so slight
They wouldn't register
On any instrument
Less finely gauged
Than she in time
Tuned him to be

Um hmmm

She holds her breath
A beat

If he forget me, I could disappear
Like this

Silently fading and slowly
Like an ancient VistaVision™ movie
Shown very late at night
So ineptly lensed
The only evidence of lovers seen
One nose and one nose
On each edge of the TV screen
As they are heard
Talking, dramatically pledging

Or better yet, he could

Mmmmm Huhnh!

Dangerous Doubts

The mind invents its own inadequacies
But not the power to erase illusion
That schemes and wholesome dreams
Can become actual despite the truth
That thoughts invest themselves in flesh
And direct motion

That you have 30,000 shots at immortality
But only one you dare not miss at being rich
Or at the least escape the nag of destitution

That maybe exercise shows on TV
Are really harmful
That sound bodies just
Amplify our empty minds

That platitudes contain a grain of wisdom

And fortune's a rush hour train that doesn't wait

To really live means needing other people
That whatever that means love
Could conquer hate

Blues Variations

I

The women women call
Bad women
Know good men
Are hard to find

And don't believe
In working hard themselves

When girlfriends come around
Be careful what you tell
Don't let anyone start counting
What you've got on your shelves

Good women get what they want
And the man that comes with it

Bad girls don't want
For anything at all

II

Always
Of course
There's the first thing
That leads to
Something worse

My man is so deep in trouble
White folks can't get him free
My man's so deep in trouble
White folks can't get him free
They say he stole a hog

The charge was Murder in the first degree
        Victoria Spivey

Change up

The first thing
First

III

Somehow in this wilderness of stone you'll find
A way, if underneath a trancing stone you find
The rock with strength to magnetize the mind

Of one who never quite imagined that before
We were here we were somewhere, and before
That, somewhere else. Now captured in the allure

Of this moment, can you imagine you will find
Some worthwhile pleasure more than peace, or find
Assurances reliable in spinning time? What kind

Of future for this world could you envision?
Would life—so neatly planned—survive revision
Or be spent polishing an obdurate decision?

Foolish Treasures

Nothing, not even the chokingly sentimental, is as predictable as the self-confidence of the unwittingly trivial gesture. The type of jealousy that accumulates with the rubbish that makes us more interesting to ourselves than to each other has never, in even the most self-centered lifetime, produced enough energy to achieve anything that could honestly be called green except in the sense of immature. I.e., green.

It can easily be argued that the example offered is a poor one, that green is green, that jealousy is not measured in degrees to any useful purpose, that immaturity is so obviously a self-correcting (or self-destructive) condition, hardly sinful.

Yes. Now that I've brought this to my attention I can see that I'm right. I was wrong.

Back in the Day

When we were boys
We called each other "Man"
With a long *n*
Pronounced as if a promise

We wore felt hats
That took a month to buy
In small installments
Shiny Florsheim or Stacey Adams shoes
Carried our dancing gait
And flashed our challenge

Breathing our aspirations into words
We harmonized our yearnings to the night
And when old folks on porches dared complain
We cussed them out
            under our breaths
And walked away
            And once a block away
Held learned speculations
About the character of their relations
With their mothers

It's true
That every now and then
We killed each other

Borrowed a stranger's car
Burned down a house
But most boys went to jail
For knocking up a girl
He really   truly   deeply   loved
      really   truly   deeply

But was too young
Too stupid, poor, or scared
To marry

Since then I've learned
Some things don't never change:
The breakfast chatter of the newly met
Our disappointment
With the world as given

Today,
News and amusements
Filled with automatic fire
Misspelled alarms
Sullen posturings and bellowed anthems
Our scholars say
Young people doubt tomorrow

This afternoon I watched
A group of young men
Or tall boys
Handsome and shining with the strength of futures
Africa's stubborn present
To a declining white man's land
Lamenting
As boys always did and do
Time be moving on
Some things don't never change
And how
      back in the day
Well
      things were somehow better

They laughed and jived
Slapped hands
And called each other "Dog"

Flash Point

This useless clairvoyance
Is embarrassing
What good is it to know
The motives behind manners

And worse, the so what stares
Of those upon whom you manage
To inflict this wisdom

There is more space
Awaiting exploration
More clouds of gas
That need their picture took

Magnetic Charms

I'm saying
          I have outgrown promises
Not you

Call it
Reality   because there is
     No better word

To call our secrets
Falsity   that haunts us
With the fear
That what we know and hide
Is all we are

But if false actions
          Haunt us
What faith
     Old women in small villages
     In backward lands
Could possibly find resonance
In words?

When I touch you
That zone of heat
Beneath my hand—
Trust that

What do you call
    A trouble shared
Check "strength" or "weakness"
The cancer patients
        Smoking on the patio, for instance
Incorrigibles
Roaring, indignant, daring the world's end
With love of laughter
As if to say
"We lived and live our lives
        this way
And won't regret it
        Even when we change"

I do not think that I can
Guarantee the truth
By plan or force of will
And fear that disappointing you
        Will undo me
Not you

What I have given I.e. majestic arrogance or quiet need
Does it glow in you?
Does it calm or warm
Or furnish afternoons with peaceful hours?
I am the one I do not wish
        To leave bereft
Not you

I'm saying

The last time I walked on Lake Conroe
It kind of gave way

Stephanie Williams

Peerage

She walks on ground with feet of clay. Ghanian girl treads the breach. Young. And feet of clay on hard packed dirt go down.

heaven	staff
and earth	and rod
union with	wheat with
God.	chaff.

Whose face is turned? Hers is the face of her mother, who in death bears the face of a rapist pressing down. The face of the Almighty, bearing down in dreams upon the holy man as blood turns to dust from dust.

exemplification	stigmata
white robes	bare feet
seated	peering
staff	in rooms
in hand.	silent.

The priest intones his sentence. To rest upon the mother's death, the daughter must atone, as all faces of infraction, as all signs of evil, as the portents of despair and drought, as all must be redeemed, so too must she for the rape that led to her birth.

the redeeming effect	of blessings and blame
of incarnation	she the stain, stands
sufferings	always standing
death.	wishing water
in that order.	and flood.

A Drunkard Promise

When the bride and groom
have not yet met
there is room for the cabaret
and the zaftig lady.

He will be whispering,
mouth full of smoke and bourbon kisses,
straight into her ear.

The mirror over the bar will not know
their faces falling in the rain,
the tinkling of piano keys
colored, colored, white.

You are she, and what is to be done
what ever to be done?
Will you wear stockings?
Will you prance and preen then
with red/lipstick/down/your
chin?

Won't you tell me your name
You a fat strawberry, a blonde, a blueblack from way—
                              —the resolution happens every verse—
and it's not Mama Cass's death
or sun setting down on newborn western town,
it ain't your sorry ass in Rampart Street hotel de somethin', somethin'
there's nothing going on here and ya'
might was well pick a dead horse
to finish, not to place.

It is the make of busted concrete
creepin' up on somethin', somethin'
it's called pizzacatto

Your heels are stiletto
and still somehow
it is all Amos-n-Andy and Tin Pan Alley
the way the miracles blend in
once upon a sailor,

while whispering a smoke-heavy kiss
waiting for a train.

Of Riches

I thought I was a boy
in love with a man
who leans on things to crease his clothes.

We hold stone tablets, warm from the sun. Sweat
on chests runs down.

I thought we were boys together, you
and I drive all night with the top down
in humid dark. Crisp and white-
shirted, handsome
and rich.

I scare myself the day over
I am insular and hollow
I am a peninsula
I am Macedonia and I don't know what
your problem
is.
I have two eyes can see you from all the way
over here. I will follow you everywhere, asking questions
tracing telephone wires from here to Athens and back.

Duchess of Dogs

First :
the little death   le petit mort
soon behind,
the censor clacking his wooden tongue. Clacking. His wooden tongue,
clacking the language of trees not trees.
Of trees are bodies. Of bodies are women.
Made.
Speaking.
The theater is dark.

The little man in the boat knows
the simplest matter
of creation. Matter of creation is song. The song sings. World is song.
song   sing   song of solomon   sang   blood   sangfroid

oogenesis   spatiogenesis

Last :
the whore.
Ladies have come to see her, the singer in a play called "Rêlache."
She is on the stage, different thoughts hittin' up in her exposed bosoms.
She got no name 'cept what they give her. She opens
her cunt to the sniffing dogs, they know her. They got her treed.
Treed by dogs. Trees are bodies. Language of bodies. Words of trees.

fabula   synzhel

song, censor, trees, boat all are done
so not done   She
in the mouths of ladies
be
Duchess of Dogs.

coarse rigors

Le Printemps
This shadow ecstasy, a palm, a
turn of his wrist
as paperwhites pull from humus
ruled and moribund,
we take the situation seriously—
and bite.

Kiddush
A romp in the bookish
dark.
We sleep. And lie.
Goose summer, spinning and out of control
into slumber
falling.

Undermining: the Contratemps
Join, fail to join, overlap here
inside the caesura,
separating solid clauses
in the kitchen.
My knife is sharp and
heretical
your skin is sweet, loose
on my lips.

How Suburbia Wakes
People read *USA Today* through the ass,
as now, presently we shall all be the police.
Thus, the little white babies lie still in the grass. Sirens!
Old mother, howl.

Gossamer
Nothing, any more to be said—
to grow ill and cease to push
blood through, no more
the fleshy sieve,
and somehow, even the sky.

Hope Chest

Desire,
with faith
in obtaining
the sound of words, cedar. Open
to soft threads within.

An old-fashioned sound: hope chest.
Faith that in return he
bears greed of heart
on sight.

The effort of
stitches on cloth, to piece
scraps against future warmth
a bridal bundle
put safe away
in hardy wood.

By no sleight of hand,
an accomplished repertoire
to please and entice, to
make well and heal.

To visit the gown
of satin and lace growing old
to dream a daughter into being
to lament the depth of breast,
solid expanse of thigh and calf,
fat meat put away
for rainy days
to come.

       Dreamed I had a flat tire :
power lines ripped out, the ocean   smashed, retired
to post.

stormbench   moonebbed   tidestretched   Upstream
                                           porches, rivertaken.

       Dreamed I had a flat tire, then
something broke :
midnight screams from across the rain, there,
elegantly embossed on smooth satin finish   gold letters
two and a half minutes   in the depth of flesh
a tool of extraction
repaired to post

hand   body   fill with   word   image   lives dark   lives dark

     1997. Dreamed I had a flat.
No one to call, midnight.   shelter in phone booth
dance in street collapsed   into sleep, I dreamed
I had a flat tire. trouble locating shoes and no car to put it on
a crutch when all hope is lost   doesn't last   dies out
doesn't mean anything   bred   to a higher thing than
triumph.

     No more adrenaline : I dreamed I had driven,
afloat on the current of merrimakers, crushed garlic put on some Monk, almost
got it   made it went home   as flower or
                                tree, reaching.
Dreamed I had.

A Maid of Need

She will take Jesus down
to the land of nothing,
go fat and fruitful
on the bones.

In the land of nothing,
she clap hands,
dance unsounded musics
move rhythm into law.

Silence grows as nothing be. Fact, not her last as tongues taste fire, words as clay
shards fall and cease to break.

We lash the flame
to eyes of Lord and storm
anno domino   ringolevio
all fall down.

Still, she will take
him down, show
herself to him
laughing on folds of belly
as she stitches
flesh into law.

A madwoman in velvet, laid
low by the weight
of nothing. Her tongue
at upon his wound knows
words seek their own level.

The hollering begins in fallow heart and feet, feet mash, mash down the tongue's
finality. Silent flames lick themselves.

Ashes! Flame! Ephriam! Grown fat
while we suffer
quiet conscience
waters to pain.

Silence. Grown as nothing be. Not her last, a fact, appearance to tongues of word
of flame
of ground   Of hollow.

She would take Jesus down
lick salt to Ephriam's wound
tell the color of grass and
make the sound of green a taste
on their lips.

Andy Young

In Anguish, the Heart Finally Prays:

The liquid brain solidifies in thought.
I am more like water, spreading about the world.

I live inside the creak and ache.
I leap to you in things you cannot name.

Let my voice be raw as flayed cattle, pink stench of meat outstretched.
Let a breeze blow on it, let pebbles and the sharp flint of bitter wind—

Listen, I sing to you.
Listen, it begins.

Light in the morning,
cradle of darkness:

in the way things burst forth

hear me

in milkweed pod and in silky threads slitting it open

hear me

in defiance of atrium, ventricle
in the pumpity-pumpity even when body lies still

hear me, please

in the green feeling under bark
in the laid bareness of deep giving

in viridian curtain of nightfall
and in the way its plain language says "yes"

hear my prayer

in salmon-pink crest of clitoris, soul of the body
in thunder-perfect-breaking-shell of dawn

in unpetaled tulip (just the essence)

in things in relief against stone

tassel-hope of daybreak,
hollow note of hoot owl:
hear my prayer

So much more than hurting,
I am broken, I am damaged
more than even orphaned I am cut off at the root—

why am I left here, unmothered, unsistered
why am I left here, unbrothered, unloved?

find me in the rubble pieces
find me in the scar
listen to my voice against the stone:

in the apparition place, the shimmering almost-sight of something,
in the pure light and element of saint becoming wholly fleshed.

hear it, hear it

in comet trailing ice through sky, saying "everything must vanish"

in little whimpers dreams make in deep of night

in the "lonely, lonely" beaten out with the blood

in the shrinking away of cells in frightened skin
in the touch-me-not, the touch-me-not

in tears, small travelers, sliding from the corners

in the metal-shock shiver of orgasm

Hear my Voice, Hear my Prayer

in tapping of beak against shell

in eke of deep matter at the center of things
in tiny fissures creeping out their damp light

hear me, hear me now in this leaking open, this liquid of blisterpop
this rawness, this floundering, this gasping for air

in hunger and the lack of it, in desire for hunger, in desire for desire in this black ink drying on the page—

Purple Spear of Anguish
Jagged Teeth of Joy
Sudden, Fleeting Flash of Gladness,
Bit of Life Curled inside the Seed:
listen to my cries

in this wind that comes from nowhere and is nothing
yet moves and cleans and breaks things open
hear, hear
in this trying to name it
in this "I want to speak it,"
in this I-am-alone-on-the-planet song
in flicker poem, in body poem
in "Don't give me any answers"
hear
in this over feeling, this extra thing
in this love-in-death *oh please anything* at the heart of it,
in small flash of light when sperm meets egg
in soft raisins of want
in the tender pink absence of skin

hear me Nightingale,
hear me Copperhead and Peep Frog

in sacrum and coccyx
in the place of half-awake

in the fear, not of falling, but of wanting to jump—

in the peace inside things, buried deep
in human mouth like a balm on need
in need to sink teeth in blood

hear me, Sea and Lavaflow

in rot that makes glands expand,
in clear ink in the liquid of the mouth
in the being-seized-whole-body-charge
that wrings food from the stomach,
in weight of the sob as it leaps to the throat
yes, yes I know You're there—
in sigh of horse's belly under thighs

in the itching, scratching urge to leave

in new infant squirming from its flesh-place
hear and hear and hear
in the way kindness flows,
in the feather-sweep inside the chest, in rush of salt
in swish and surge forward, in opening out like water—
you do hear, don't you?
in slight leap womb makes
when small belly hairs are touched,
in slick gut of longing,
in fat, wet life of oyster in shell
in little click that tells plum to fall from tree,

Broken cup and dust inside my book:
Small rain and creekflow: Ripe pear and pine needles:
Treefall as it groans and single voice flung against boulder:
I burn white coals, I burn—
Hear in pulse and tooth and blood.
Hear in your own secret languages.
I pray and pray and pray and pray
oh Something, Anything:
hear me

Foxfire

The night called me.
I couldn't have been more than ten.
I'd heard them speak of the ghost leaf,
its green phosphorescence,
and I went in search of its glow.
Deeper and deeper into darkness
I walked until I could see no shapes,
until I could feel the night's skin against mine.

She walked down the road and was lost.

My eyes open, two bright stones,
words streamed through my head:
   I am here I am here I am

*   *   *   *   *

there was no glow to greet me I don't know where my home is

I found a mine to dig rocks from to burn and to heat and to sell

Mine the darkness:
see by the path you leave behind you.

I cannot find the door I have lost the switches I just hear
my voice against the rocks, a mist like lover's hands,
a liquid rise, dew on a lilytip

Down in the valley, the valley so low,
hang your head over, hear the wind blow
hear the wind blow, love, hear the wind blow
hang your head over, hear the wind blow

and blow and blow I blow her hair
behind her like a wing,
float her sorrow on the air like silk.

She walks these hills in her long black veil
poor woman, they say she is crazy.

She is still out there, stuck in the night
enough of an animal to recognize darkness
too human to smell her way out.

Sometimes her heart lights up like foxfire.

I am still here, can't see my hand in front of my face
remember the tender snap of string beans the shape
of my nose and cheeks I am part of darkness now
woven into its fabric my hands find berries
while I'm sleeping my feet know rocks like the edges
of desire I know the language of trees that groan
know the sighs the nightshade makes,
the hum of roots as they drink—

Ghost of Me

I follow the gurgle to the fall   *all*   *fall*
to eat fear like a black cherry,
scrape my teeth on its pit   *it has a bitter taste, like blood*
to shed skin as if reptilian   *in the creek, a crackled skin*

here   *hear*
here is where peaks   *speak*
of an echo   *oh*   *o*
a muffled twin of speech   *each word dies as it goes*
so hollow, a swallow of a thing   *a thing*
thought dead   *fled, your stead*

what remains when things
are taken – what remains   *pain*
a violence saved for ones we love

                           a powder in the mouth
                               — bitter, like arsenic.

Forgiveness   *is*
a shriveled fig

communion of taproots   *shoots*
a tubed song

blue in the lake   *ache*
a trick of the light
separate from itself, it's clear
as nothing, see, see—   *we are salt and streak, a flash*
                          a flesh embodied, we

were one once – *once, once*

                           yes, I know.
                          We were one.

Vodou Headwashing Ceremony

Wear white and bring an offering:
something for the fiery Petro,
for the cool and gentle rada.

: *Any one could be possessed* :

Like all life it begins with a nothing,
then a small chaos, then
the first faint beginning of the drum

any one   any one   any one

Scrape fuzz from the muzzle of the black violet.
Squeeze succulents to an oozing juice.
Stir yellow powder into champagne.
Spread blue cloth for ocean spirits:
            Agwe, Lasiren

John the Baptist laps this slop
of honey locust we splash
on this his feast day, growing hairy
wild unchristian souls while Mary,
Mother, Ezili, remains, candled red,
inked to the scapular span
of a copper-headed woman.

Smell of sandal, myrrh, rum spat
in spray through the teeth. A hissing.
A hiissssssssssweat a sweet, salt film.
Trace of rust on the tongue.
Eyes drift, flutter in socket.

: *Any one could be possessed* :

The lwa want to plant in you capillary roots.
You may become some one, thing, else.
Your spine may stretch to make the new body,
bathing in calf's milk, wanting salt
offerings. *You could be possessed.*

You could be Legba, god of crossroads,
collecting broken trinkets, standing on tracks,
arms spread in embrace of coming light,
whistle screaming toward you — you could

be Gede, god of death, sex, regeneration
wanting shots of rum, decked like a bruise
in black and purple, *possessed, possessed*

Rattle the snakebone baubles in your lobes
        pirouette * pirouette
it will all unravel yes
        pirouette * pirouette

Let the rumble tell you what it must.
Body moves when summoned
as animal, from a place past thought
in the tooth-growl: the inborn taste
for blood, sinew, spine deep whine of
one who wants it wants to grasp an *oh*
a massive summons to the union.

If you fear the taking over
let us stop it simply holler
we can make it go away, but
you should know that we invite it
sprinkle cornmeal circles, fires,
build altars of skeletal offerings,
beseech them to descend. *Possess us.*

A sound like silk ripping —
the feral reign, the human gone,
instinct whittled to a pointy talon.

Hold back to point of rupture.
Seek the frenzy and pluck
its too-ripe plum. Get it
to your mouth before it bursts.
Open the top of your head
and let the screams fly out—

Seth Young

from river we are caried by

All says a glass doorknob Parabola ghost
I float the living evenly in the then dusks
The brown recluse reels down It is only you
coming toward me An angel with tattooed
eyelids flickers nevertheless Nor do my red
you the wild quiet forms of mushrooms Nor
mere psalm nor for alm My as then you
grave is You tell me to name the sky w/o
looking And we call the sky a mirror In
reference to dreams drowning in woodgrain
And faces turned musical shape calling *Hope
by the river we carry river we are caried by*
Madness Grace & Death's Lonely Cricket
In the ruined spirituals of Union freight
Poverty turning tiger moths into organ
music You say only when the wind dies
do I hear the chimes who call my name
You walk and weave the grass into braids
And we share the honeysuckle delusions
She severs thread thru silent watching
And heat lightning moved up from the
road And the crickets And the rusted
and corrugated souls

yellow moon i will rise over the hands
my mist my tryst If treble hooks will I
listen Red itself floods into superstition
Nightsky veins torture a figure in chains
Leaves wander in dark rearview mirrors
In the trunks of the sunken junk cars the
story lay hold And those who slept in ript
interiors got strange tongues Children of
the yellow eyed people stole my chrome
for spears Something between us not a
bridge happened And from the bridge
poor wills poor wills call night I nailed
to this bridge that holds no roads Only
failure that is living that is laughter of
the black iron birds escaping Kerosene
torch light riddle refrains As summer
sheds its vermilions Live oak weeping
dirty rags of god Mosquitos sing their
magenta threads *White dove white dog*
You found me dead on the shoal Trestle
timbers tremble with the train wail above
a barge moans passing below uh-uh Two
lovers lost to having other dreams uh-uh
uh-uh Catfish feelers rumour surface it brings

Hour loom green over rust And to Marion sang
He'd scream bloody murder that he'd never
Do it again, he wouldn't fall into that trap again
And go out the next day and do the same thing
at random And they just was intending to kill
somebody as an example...   and they did kill
sobbing, turned and walked away, sang, "I can't
look anymore when anybody is killed" Almost
seems they'd nightwalked from church to prison
Unhuman No other word can describe...There is
no alternative in conscience The Riders chanting
Nightsticks, Ropes, and Incongruous Canes Soon
Beckoning the others... people turning around and
coming back and I aghast Are we not going thru
with this confrontation? What's happening? We
waited for possible snipers "However difficult the
moment How long?" Not long. Still in for a season
of suffering in the midst of all these glaring evils
I do not know what lies ahead of us There may be
beatings, jailings, tear gas But I would rather die
nothing more tragic in the midst of all the stiletto
silhouettes There is no alternative in conscience
My soul is (un)rested

To hide from among Certain energies run
thru the curtain rods You can only pretend
the house unsettles Same three nails cry in
the rafters Same ampersands haunt these
screens & grass kept saying over & over
Needle eye will To live on raine alone I
want to walk and breathe true stealth of
moss Grow on shadows edge From a ms.
entitled The Cryptic Calling You been
stalking my evening visitors Gut strung
with tiger moths and poison leaves burn
your tongue The rat thief of poetry sees
things Mud room walls think things To
keep *things* quiet You slept in seines of
cricket wings To climb this tree and hide
from among My invisible armor of wind
To leap from limb to roof To drop to the
othershy side You believe the dead down
the road a tribe of golems I am with you
in The Crossing Field   River rearranging
shoals To float beneath heat lightning &
the little white flowers With the red and
purple ones in hand The moon reads dull

From the Grasskeeper whose dream this is
somewhere in a sentence Initial dusk period
The field effect when dark is set Poem our
mutual oval Said sentence after rainfall:
Scuppernongs ripen Ampersands become
the nightshift music A dead tree veins the
moon Les Fleur Du Mal between the sheets
As you were serifs blooming in wet blue
paper From barbwire whose honeysuckle
hangs delusions over marble Engravure
whose fragments arise thru phrase and iris
Blackbird treble suspended under sentence
And now we are rowing thru indigo text
Shadows lurk in the shy side The agents
lower in via rope We see thru their veil
of spider tactics Said suicide lyrics of the
crucifix shell Ruinous theory sighing bell
Fierce retinas of the angel flicker neverth...
Nevertheless Aside said anonymous red
chair in a field From the riders cloak that
covers us You wade into greenness You
say the moon had lifted from the sentence
There will be other dead trees Here & here

wind infinities gray to let them go precisely
as sky with your hair Cahaba Trestle Edition
when with my difficulty walking in the light
they sub skulls chartreuse a dangerous thing
and when i leave her hands from this water
the last word of the last book pretends to be
blended into what we went to then revisited
       blue jays fly thru the shadows
       of the bluebirds flask dark rum
       said discretely blue Quick bird!
       thru shadows cross blue shun
       thru sudden   shadow   no blue
       No!   bird   No!
eye mesh gill more subtle subTitle zone (d.
1970) split feather subTitle laid on the table
dying indigo and if ever a subTitle died for
love in kudzu: this the failure that is living
 belief when she finishes with me I am still
to do with initial rowing drawn drowning
in treerings Ampersand Alternates: the end
that flows insight   notice i am & they are
where you get images weaving grass and
honeysuckle and tillandsia into everything

Felt dampers and mutes Not only
delusions pressed in books The sill
drinking smiles of knives Pictures
tuned on twisted hooks Blue rags
beckon You swim with other days
as one The fluid property of glass
Shadowy moth events Jars of sun
embalmed in the cabinet & you
want to know when What page
wrote her name without looking
Mud of Voodoo Run trill *Shame
in this is sweeping sweeping* The
parabola door is cobweb woven
Dandelion nightwalker unknown
You put the ribbon on your eyes
Nobody believes I came from
inside a green marble You say
my number in purple fragments
Angel's kind asylum The needles
end Ectoplasm is a fact said Mrs.
Bird You are weaving tunnels
Of silk thread Inverted mask
of Cahaba Her hair undone

Matrix of summer bricks The time of
writing Caterpillars coma catacombs
As incubi assemble their mud flutes
Roots fluent forth of star harmonica
so that opposites clung to one another
during the mute flood Sin of summer
moon Your hair is the spanish moss of
the underworld mistress The rats spun
their memoirs In the trunks of sunken
junk cars the poem laid hold They who
slept in ript interiors got strange tongues
Leaves wander thru dark rearview mirrors
You wanted my fingers to sing spirals Jugs
to embody floating decimals Children of
the yellow eyed people come spearing thru
the trees   They try circling you This key
you discovered in the furnace is not your
style is slanted if not in vertigo You
promised me fluxion and fishbone
Hands of the clock weeds bend down
as you search for the ancient locusts
Children draw bats with their laughter
From the dark they smile you knives

Coffin will dream above water table
paradise grave A porcelain frame as
passage thru the midnight I go limb
and thru limbs glittering blackbirds
sleep wind scimitar bell light poor
wills poor wills real as poor wills
revel night You won't believe me
when I tell you Copper I nailed
into alluvial eyes Killing echoes
travel still like knives able to see
bones aching decades from this
trestle under Endless yawn and I
coffin will dream water table for
grave drawn drink You live on
Raine alone Each ankle bearing
humility snare and grass weave
swoon as the sickle compass
my ill angels befell then you
grave is my thought shown a
thing another thing rude The
horses that would never belong
to us and dandelions that would
forever belong

This the way I turn into dove blood
tho I am dead Z and the blackened
eyes Copper nails said Brown Road
walk steady as the dust settled Hope
gone rails and river Woodgrain souls
suffer This the way oaks on the shy
side devour the swimmers You say
go find her knocking in owl throats
A field Condemned to the edge of
its known body Yellow eyes of the
children The legend Tho I am dead
and fly away in the burned book
A handmade poem and page that
writes its name in negative flesh
Handmade as down we lay at night
prayers and love to you gone rails
and river This the way the curtains
drift from the open eyes Blue rags
beckon a field Her strange letters
I turn into dead road walking the
steady brown heart Hope gone
and drift slow as a leaf sinks a
rider alone

Contributors | Poetics

Ralph Adamo (New Orleans, LA): Taught creative writing and edited *New Orleans Review* at Loyola University in the 1990s. He is on faculty at LSU and NOCCA Academy now. His books include *Hanoi Rose* (New Orleans Poetry Journal Press, 1990), *The End of the World* (Lost Roads, 1979), and *Sadness at the Private University* (Lost Roads, 1977). A volume of new and selected poems, *Waterblind*, was published by Portals Press in 2002.

Poetry, huh? I think of the two contradictory meanings of "speaking in tongues": on the one hand, to speak so that all those hearing can understand, no matter what their own language; on the other, to speak in a way that confounds all those around you, none of whom know what is being said.

Often now I find things I've written that I don't remember writing.

The very nature of what I write—especially in the past few years—cries out for my negligence and abandonment of it—my actual forgetting of it or misplacing it, and certainly for a dire refusal to even try to publish. Or: "refusal" is too active; rather my weariness at the thought of trying to read it again, much less type or retype it, or make the scratching presentable. "Scratchings" reeks of the self-conscious, of division. Of time as it simplifies and desists and, even, defeats. I'd like, in a way, to force the poems to the surface—out of notebooks, out of the piles in which they rest. But.

I don't know what I believe anymore about poetry. I reject the theology of language as "play," the primacy of "the" metaphor, and—since its cooption by a power grid of faux-linguistic falsification—I am dubious about most irony as well.

I was born in 1948. My first signed & dated poem is from 1959. Signing and dating them has become a lot less important.

All of our grandfathers came from a secret world. Well, mine did. More accurately, a world in which the secrets were different from those of our fathers' world, or ours, or our sons' and daughters'. Secrets, places, associations, ritual, even language itself inaccessible from one generation to the next—maybe this is what was meant in the first place by "modern," and probably by "post-modern."

To say "poetry reveals what is secret" comes close to what I think is going on in a poem. But of course it also conceals.

To say poetry is the design and the wreckage existing simultaneously, occupying the same space. Maybe that. Oh, and the reason any of this matters is that real poetry is highly volatile, dangerous down through time, unpredictable in its cask of serenity. Can kill. Can get you killed. Will remember.

Sandy Baldwin (Morgantown, WV): Assistant Professor of English and Coordinator of the Center for Literary Computing at West Virginia University. Recent publications include an essay on Paul Virilio in *Configurations: A Journal of Literature, Science and Technology* and a collaboration with the artist Repugno in the HEADSPEAK series.

Poem as Zip Gun *or* Graphic Acceleration Projector for Thought Capture—Two modes: *possible languages* (represented here) and *concept poetry*. Frame for both modes set up below.
—

What is a diagram (or a page) that we can *read* it? How is it that we know that "that → this" means "this follows that," but we don't know what "this eieio that" means (cf. MacLow)? Could they mean the same thing? How do we take → or, for that matter, how do we take a poem? Always in the same way? That is, how rigid or "super-hard" is the arrow (cf. Wittgenstein)?

Before anything exists there is a poem. The problems of philosophy are utterances of the poem. Our concern should not be with the abstraction of Being but with the poetics that allow this abstraction to be our concern. The poem gives Being permission to organize our world. The poem permits Being to set up shop, permits Being to start the machines going.

Before the poem, there was already a poem. For there to be a poem there must already be a poem. An apparatus is activated for the poem to appear. The written poem is one such appearance. The appearance-apparatus is part of the poem.

The poem is your shifts in attention as you read / are instructed by the written poem. Focus/concentrate until it (the written poem) becomes unreadable: this "until" is the poem.

We are not instructed by the text; the text does not pre-exist us. The poem instructs the text, gives it permission (cf. Hennix). The poem is our attention; we give the text permission. The vexed distinction between the written poem and the real is the outcome of this permission. We find the putative real through the space of the poem. This finding re-finds our own acts of permission and attention.

In the beginning there is kinetics, speed, moving structures. A focus on metaphors of construction and construction of metaphors discovers narratives of the loss of this beginning, tells stories of the structure we are. Focus on movement leads to questions of forms of thought as forms of attention. Overall project: *PoetryLifeForms*. We must realize that abstraction in itself is not a problem but a way. No ideas but in abstraction, but finding the correct path to abstraction is the task (*right action*). *PoetryLifeForms* begins where abstraction and the end of abstraction are one (cf. Stein).

A concern with the self-understanding of technology. There is no distinction between magic and technology, beyond the discursive distinction between vocabularies used for self-understanding within each realm. There is no distinction between technology and its auto-generated discourse of self-understanding: its descriptions, theories, marketing brochures, warning labels. Technicity delineates all things of this epoch; the magic of language touches all things. For this reason: an alchemical poetics, where language corresponds to things. This correspondence is technicity, the apparatus that makes things live, including us: we survive in this way.

Jake Berry (Florence, AL): Most recent books include *Silence and the Hammer* (Ninth St. Laboratories, 2001), *Drafts of the Sorcery* (Potes & Poets, 1998) and the second volume of his long poem *Brambu Drezi* (Pantograph, 1998). Also, recent music CDs include *Roses on the Threshold* (Front Porch, 2000) and *Alabama Dust* (Front Porch, 1999) with Bare Knuckles, a duo with Wayne Sides.

Poetry is largely the art of possession, how to collaborate with a possessing other. The poem is the work of fluctuating self and other, an equal summons that simultaneously invokes and is the manifestation of that invocation. However, the "thing" invoked is no thing at all but that which lies beyond our notions of form and activity. Still, the whole process is utterly ordinary and natural. This is not quasi-mystical babbling but failed description of a poetry that refuses to describe.

Holley Blackwell (Jackson, MS): Publications include *Sati-Itaya* (Horseradish Press), "Stylus" (Millsaps College Magazine), "The Green Issue" (Publication of the Mississippi Green Party); Forthcoming from Horseradish press is *U.S.* with A. di Michele.

negation—it is my pity, a pretty pithy, an elongated non-verbal into verbal; outside, i am what they say that i am. the bones and skin liar. contradiction. at least two races with a demanded Zwilling (the past, present, and future attachment). My other is a mountain, seen, heard, expressed through every mirror shaken or.nor shattered. the flysheet and wheel is a six-sided and spiked corpuscle, spinning through my forehead. time over two; one-half commits the whole to itself. Studentenin in any caste, it is time, again, for words and the human, what is the advanced mode of language? The athletic aesthete joins its commital framework in my heart, the lowered brain, penetrating even tight pipelines, hidden from view. This model can stand outside, in a drizzle alone and take down proper notation. This model can defecate on the principles of the classroom, and drool hiddenly while walking with the click-clack of borrowed shoes. All, as for anybody else, is a burrow, so that there will be no skin showing and only fragmentation glowing. a purpose, an insult, a brain, a line and furrow, a blister and canopy for refugees too horrible to conceive and too beautiful to dispose. I would find discarded and nurtured remains of a past and build a perennial empire from the all-is-sand if there were the patience left in the world for a device like creation. God was time. This model could hesitate and begin again when the sun showed its face over ivys and riverbeds. I was born near a river but nobody cares about that, really. there was a hyper sunbeam between the 3 min. and 29 sec. lapse between us at our birth. I saw the squints in the eyes of worn-on humans before She followed. And this following is the word, the sound and statement of each fact of each moment's fact. This would I capture in paragraphs. and other trifling notation that makes each day pulse. the interruptions. are. . silence. (Gott ist zeit)

writing. I publish and will publish again. I write and will write always (even without the pen or the typewriter); there is a quality in language that may be found semiotically expressed in every venue of thought/vision/recourse, etc. the plaguing thing about writing, however, is the tension inherent in the imagination. an active "peak performance" imagination. coupled with the Eye is the difficulty in construction from raw data. Sometimes, scientists have it easy. Sometimes, artists have it easy—you can buy production or thought, if you will, in a kit (think about the paint-by-numbers scenario in a text). But it's rough. An intent of mine is Sati-Itaya, a jumbled batch of letters derived from another jumbled batch of letters from a Jain phrase meaning— CARE In WALKINg. the courting of oneself with an instrument; I think that you play the (x), true? neutrality in gender; repressed and dismantled everything; or, the union, as in the paintings of Alex Grey. I had a tape recorder with me today, I wanted to get your voice.

Dave Brinks (New Orleans, LA): Provocateur and guide terroristique of the American Spoken Language, is a central figure in the thriving New Orleans poetry world. He co-founded the weekly Madpoet Express open reading in 1996 and operates Trembling Pillow Press. His most recent project is the New Orleans School for the Imagination.

"The technical aspects of my writing are the same ones used by people who write on bathroom mirrors: when the face gets blurry, the poem appears." —Brinska

Joel Dailey (New Orleans, LA): A yankee by birth, has lived in New Orleans for the last twenty years. Recent publications include *Problem 35* (Acre Press, 2001), *Lower 48* (Lavender Ink, 1999), and *Not on the Cover* (Lot M, 2002). His works have appeared in hundreds of magazines since 1974.

Why I Wrong

As Dr. Johnson said "To a poet nothing is useless."
As Gertrude Stein said "Butter will melt."
As Pound sd "I need to see a troubador about a horse."
As Tammy Faye Bakker said "My face hurts."
As Jack Spicer said "Rabbits do not know what they are."
As Dr. Williams said "The bastards have taken over."

As Basil Bunting said "Cacaphony is at least as intricate an art as harmony."
As Yogi Berra said "You can observe a lot by watching."

Brett Evans (New Orleans, LA): Has new work in *Unarmed* and was included in Sun and
Moon's *Gertrude Stein Awards in Innovative Poetry* (1993–94). His books include *Tang Dynasty*
(Fell Swoop, 1996).

I started writing K-Does as English-language hieroglyphs on K-Doe's *Tomb of the Sun*,
passwords maybe to get me past the sphinx & to a drink at the bar. K-Doe's, see, is a palm of
Dew Drop Inn proportions, an R&B real mirage from the past projected into this our now, onto
my sphinx-colored dress. If I could only put these words onto the 2nd line umbrellas upside-
downing the ceiling, my glass . . .

K-Doe saved my life before he left the building.

Skip Fox (Lafayette, LA): Recent publications include *Fighting Kiwis* (Oasis, 1999), *Wallet*
(Bloody Twin, 1998), Kabul Under Siege (Bloody Twin, 1991), and poems in journals, including
*Fell Swoop, Croton Bug, o•blek, Talisman, House Organ, atelier, Texture, Hambone, New Orleans Review,
OASII: Broadside Series, Exquisite Corpse, lower limit speech, BadDog, Bullhead Anthology*

For Bill Lavender—Every time I write something concerning poetics it sounds, at best, flat or
dull in retrospect or I see how it doesn't advance the work itself, the doing it from word
stroke to line to how the "idea" whatever you call it, threads the marrow like a song of a
corpse, an active thing only in acting. When I'm writing I'm not thinking about writing I'm
writing. Or, since I'm thinking about anything when I'm writing I'm thinking about writing as
much and as little as anything other. (Though that is not actually the case.) Neither does it
have a presumed greater use than an other simply because it pretends to address the issue at
hand, wouldn't work any way, . . . it's not an issue but issuing. Sometimes a poetics is like a
diffident and troubled child sent out to help his father, not that it might be of use. For instance,
I once wrote of form as an occasion of possibilities, an occasion provisionally and fluidly bound
by circumstance in which we are allowed to participate when we give ourselves to an
understanding of the confluence that flows amid, between, and through a series of contiguous
states, ideas, experiences, phenomena, etc. The "antithetical center" H.D. calls it, from which
dolphins swim.
    Part of the thinking, here, includes the notion of form as a prescribed terrain, theirs *or*
ours, as impoverished. Then I remember that I have inhabited, or so it seems, such plains in
which I would write and think. Plans. So what do I know? That such a child might get in your
way. (Or it might not. I think the metaphor might be usefully extended just a bit: It depends
on the basic nature of the child, how rigified in adolescence, and it's dependent on how you
talk to him, or do you address him?)
    But other than the issue of form is it theory we want? Its place and how. Like a summer
morning when you were twelve. I'd break it open and see how it smells, return it to the pile
of the morning's presentments as the winter pile of presents under the tree when it was time
to eat: watch, wallet, sweaters and socks, maybe a book (what did they know of books? . . .
page turners, grazers of words). It's just one thing, like anything else and different of course,
but like form, far less than the sum of the aggregate, like the mass of the first four planets
minus Earth equals Earth, yet Jupiter alone is 318 Earth masses. How many Jupiters in the sun?
Such are numbers. And the first planet rising in the first dawn.
    But as I say, I now agree with what I wrote. So there are consistencies, which is to *seem*
over time *and* amid the flux, as there are rocks in current, rhythms, words and works that

might provide some cartography in the abyss ("Look into thy heart . . ."), in the way of the serious, unrelated to any measure but what they have said and done, are still doing. Williams's *Spring and All* still holds, as does most of "Projective Verse" and all of "Human Universe," especially its ending, dining on myth. Essays by Creeley and Duncan, Spicer. I could name others, but what would *that* do? Everyone finds them for themselves, or each for the self of each, finds them. Or doesn't. Naming is obsolescence. Like, it got old even on the First Morning. Etc. (Another interesting question might be how separate a poetics from living?)

Jessica Freeman (Baton Rouge, LA): Is salt-rising bread endive badminton racket tin roof her graphics & word Art widely published currently available   chapbook *New Orleans Dizzy Spit,* Anabasis Press via New Orleans booksellers Maple Street & Octavia & Beaucoup.

to cross party lines
to fondle flying buttresses
to breakfast in bed conjugate verb passe

to quiver lie abed live long day
to zydeco paper in shoe tarry rally troops
to moped past ancient ocher walls

  blush roses & peonies spit
  la cloche a sonne
  la cloche a sonne

Bob Grumman (Port Charlotte, FL): substitute teacher at Charlotte High; co-editor with Crag Hill of *Writing To Be Seen,* an anthology of visio-textual art (2001), most recent appearance of poems was in *5_Trope,* an online magazine.

Two of my poems here are purely visual, "Summer Rain" and "Reality." The former is an abstract expressionist attempt to capture something of the magnitude of summer's things, from its "merth" to its rain. "Reality" portrays the evolution of the word, "reality," through shapes I hope are aesthetically intriguing, to end, in an imprisoning box, as "definition."

I've also included three mathematical poems. The first, "Mathemaku No. 16" uses Emerson's "The Snowstorm" to claim that multiplying an actual winter by the spoken word for it (or by verbalization) especially by a poem like Emerson's, will result in something greater. But "winter," raised to the power of one, is (mathematically) not greater than plain "winter." I leave it to the reader to figure out why I nevertheless claim it to be poetically greater.

In "Mathemaku No. 17," I try for an agreeable haiku-like picture, playing with exponents to give movement to dolphins and sun and to reveal the "awe" that is in "song" (auditorily). In my six-part "Mathemaku for Beethoven," I again portray an evolution, this time from a problem's statement to its solution. The problem, a standard one in long division except that images take the place of numbers, begins with the information that we are going to divide the sky, or analyze it in some way. In the first step of this process, I establish a divisor, the color blue, and begin suggesting what the quotient, or answer, will be. In later steps, the quotient forms--as does the product of that quotient times the color blue. This product will be close to but less than "the sky," so allows me metaphorically to compare it to the sky. In the end, we learn (and it is mathematically certain!) that the sky is near-equal (somehow) to the color blue times explainability to the power of May (with pun intended). There is much more to it, including a remainder, that I unfortunately lack the space to discuss here.

The other three poems in my selection are cryptographic. The first of these simply depicts a boy writing a message in code. My hope is that a reader, in solving the poem's (very simple) code, will experience the joy of working with codes; but the coded material is intended also to speak metaphorically of the boy's writing his way into a secret world, of making/finding a world that is to the conventional one what an encrypted message is to a normal one. The other two cryptographic poems contain more sophisticated "cryptophors" (i.e., texts encrypted for some metaphorical purpose) that I'll leave to the reader to puzzle out.

Ken Harris (Charlottesville, VA): Bio note:
the ant
though scant
has too many legs to bother with pants

from a letter to John Bennett concerning his Sticky Forks:
    Sticky Forks hit me, apparently, in the psyche. I, bedded, after some time with *Forks*, dreamt several unidentified poems visually, that is as color fields, shapeless colored splotches displacing the textual\letteral bodies of the vowels while remaining arranged (mirrored) according to the vowel-sequence within the numerical-based structure of the individual poems. I should add the consonants remained where and as they were but for being blackened almost beyond recognition.
    Irrelevancy? Foible? every chance. But my guess is when a structurally procedural schema is combined with highly processual-improvisational hearings that do not revolve about cognitive intentionalities coerced from as by cultural connotations, then the resultant works, when attended to and experienced with, function like *some* organic psychoactives, that is as neurotransmitters.
    Of the endless radical experiences of synesthesia documented, many such-driven examples having graced pages of *LAFT, Juxta,* etc., Terence McKenna's description of the ayahuasca experience in the Amazon stands out, given the context, for two reasons: first, the chants, the long-tested ayahuascan musics of the highly conservative aboriginals, under the influence, became visually palpable; and, secondly, this experience was simultaneously transferable from one person to another and back again repeatedly.

Honorée Fanonne Jeffers (Talladega, AL): Work has appeared in several journals and anthologies, including *African American Review, Brilliant Corners: A Journal of Jazz and Literature, Callaloo, Dark Matter: A Century of Speculative Fiction from the African Diaspora* (Warner/Aspect 2000), *Identity Lessons: Contemporary Writing About Learning To Be American* (Viking 1998), *Massachusetts Review, Obsidian II, Obsidian III,* and *Poet Lore.* She is the author of *The Gospel of Barbecue* (The Kent State University Press, 2000), selected by Lucille Clifton as the winner of the 1999 Stan and Tom Wick Poetry Prize for a First Book. Honorée teaches English at Talladega College.

I consider myself primarily to be a blues poet, and though I don't always write literally about songs (or those songs aren't always blues songs), every poem I write is informed by the blues metaphor, by the three movements of the blues: locate, explore, resolve. I'm fascinated and bound not to just the notion of the blues itself but also the syncretic connections of the blues to region, race, gender, and spirituality. All this makes up who I am as a person and as a writer; all this is interwoven throughout the black experience.

Marla Jernigan (Atlanta, GA): Her work has appeared in the *New Orleans Review's* "An Other South" issue and is forthcoming in the Potes and Poets Anthology *Luddites, Start Your Engines!* edited by)ohn Lowther.

Poetics is sort of heart-broken pillow talk. It hides in analysis. A torch carried, a kiss-and-tell for whoever will listen. What you do when you can't or when it feels almost required. Show us, tell us something that we'll know you know the touch.

Fragility. At any moment interrupted, be lost. A listening. Not a memorial to or for. Not proof nor evidence. Summer snow.

Poems.

Blown into traffic, mistaken for trash, be lost. Place mats and envelopes on their backs, on napkins. Notebooks I lose and break computers. Never well at a desk. Hotel stationary and in bed. The sites finding poems most I forget. Where desires found me. Remind me. Too much though and/or they falter.

Strength their weakness, their weakness their . . .

Poems build if kisses. Dalliance in language. If places, then there to linger. Desires and the dice, satisfaction, might be, could, be lost. We don't come into it knowing. As Life. Taking chances. Hoping. At any moment.

At any moment could be lost. Ever-possible, interruption, receding climax. The waver as a foot cannot walk the straight line starts a poem. Could still be lost, immanent, sometimes drunk. No other line soon to dally.

Lines from past/future might collide. At any moment a hint, phrase that makes a flirtation. I feel _that_ touch _here._ Tongue as mind as tongue. Repeating _yes_ till it's breath. Poem. Flushed from it. Stupid smile.

Poem. As much as when I don't finish, never finish, that seeming just a trick, it ever says _from_ and is incomplete, all that there was. Never therefore, never thus. Some I think I know and some I think I'm finding out.

Joy Lahey (New Orleans, LA): Has published poetry in _New Orleans Review_ and other journals. Her book _Abandoned Premises_ was published by Lavender Ink in 1999.

Southern Cross/Ursa Major

*   *   *

*

*   *   *   *

*   *   *

On
other
viewless
wings of Poesie?
—a veritable flight
through a world of
words & connections
writer   and   reader
direct the enigmatic _craft_— select, imagine, experience the solitary boundaries and
meteoric play of language . . . if language is the night, it is the day— and the assembled red
horizon—
so can a poem be an infinite chart, varying from one heartwarming reading to the
next heartrending one
a chart of a flight's
wild risks and
tender rewards—
tracing the ever-

shifting, rolling
edge of emptiness
a silhouette of absence:
grief, desire, or boredom
in relief, against the exciting, rib-tickling
even portentous creations of joined words

Bill Lavender (New Orleans, LA): Poems and prose have appeared in numerous journals and magazines, including _Contemporary Literature, Poetics Today, New Orleans Review, Fell Swoop, Mesechabe, New Delta Review, Exquisite Corpse_, and _108_. Books include _Pentacl_ (Fell Swoop, 2001) _Guest Chain_ (Lavender Ink 1999) and _look the universe is dreaming_ (Potes and Poets, 2002). He is the proprietor of Lavender Ink press.

Discourse without recourse—to go across and not come back: this is writing. The obsession with interiority that has haunted poetry since the Romantics only exists inside the language, and language is as cold and impersonal as the ocean. Writing without recourse to the metaphors of interiority is collage, assembly of found materials, or a form of sculpture, hacking at a hunk of rock broken from a vein of ancient sedimentation, only the rocks are iterable. I like to think of this anthology as a workshop, a place where corners are mitered and components clamped together for gluing; we'll see how the glue holds, though the clamps themselves have a certain appeal, as frame or binding, and we might decide to simply leave them. Writing without recourse to transcendence; that is, it is what it is, answers a question, spoken or written or perhaps only indicated by a pause in the other's speaking, part of the conversation in a very crowded room.

Hank Lazer (Tuscaloosa, AL): Most recent books of poetry are _Days_ (Lavender Ink, 2002), _Simple Harmonic Motions_ (INK- A! Press, 2001), _As It Is_ (Diaeresis Chapbooks, 1999), _3 of 10_ (Chax Press, 1996), _Early Days of the Lang Dynasty_ (Meow Press, 1996), and _Doublespace: Poems, 1971–1989_ (Segue Books, 1992). With Charles Bernstein, he edits the Modern and Contemporary Poetics Series for The University of Alabama Press. His two-volume collection of critical writings on contemporary poetry, _Opposing Poetries,_ was published in 1996 by Northwestern University Press. Along with Jake Berry and Wayne Sides, Lazer is a founding member of The Alabama Poetry Ensemble. A Professor of English, Lazer is Assistant Vice President for The University of Alabama.

a sequence of our imagining, in sequence with our imagining, to know where & what & by contrast with. now, nearly a decade of looking, assembling our writing to see what resembling & assembly might be plausible. to learn who we are or might be. so many essences so carefully critiqued: who could still say region place person The South The Other at the margins or experimental without hearing the flapping wings of matched quotation marks or some nervous twitch of heady corrected synapses. yet one by one, in correspondence, by reading together, talking about it, in circulating manuscripts, and talking about one another's work— nothing so coherent as a "movement." i would though pull the car over to pick you up & recognize you as another rider; & you would do the same for me. knowing perhaps best what we are not, or, more clearly, the writing we will not do. ok, so we are here. but we refuse to package "here" as they have done. we will make it as it is now, & so compose, or partner with, the here & now, in each heartfelt sense of idiosyncratic embodiment of this other southern making, poem as residue where soul might reside, here & now where we choose to hunker down.

Jim Leftwich (Charlottesville, VA): Born in Charlottesville, attended college in North Carolina and lived for several years in California, returned to Charlottesville in '86, co-edited *Juxta* with Ken Harris during the 1990s, currently editor of *xtant.*

Useless Writing

Skills are acquired behaviors, similar to acquired tastes. They are learned behaviors valued by the dominant culture to the extent that it can use them. Different areas of the dominant culture value different skills. Skill is developed originally, jump-started if you will, through training, then honed, refined, through experience, through practice, the practice of the particular skill. One sets out to learn a skill, seeks out an expert in the field, and is trained by rote and through information until one has acquired the desired skill. It is the same whether one wishes to repair an automobile engine or write a sonnet, program a computer or paint a portrait. There is a hierarchy at work here, and those who reside at the highest levels do so due to their possession of a specialized knowledge and their mastery of its requisite activities: the arcana and its secret gestures: the gnosis and its rites. Almost all of us can learn almost any skill if we desire to do so. All that is required is the desire and the work, the desire and the willingness to put in the time and put forth the effort to acquire the skill. All the skills that are taught, and the ways in which they are taught, are structurally necessary to the culture that teaches them, else they would not be taught. We should think of this usefulness as meaning only one thing: useful means useful to the dominant culture, always and only. That which is deemed useful is such only insofar as it reinforces the fundamental structure of the culture. The power relations that are structurally in place must remain structurally in place. Change is not only allowed, it is required, but only in the details of the larger pattern; the larger pattern of necessity must remain intact.

What happens if one desires to practice useless skills, skills that are not useful in maintaining the structure of the culture? First of all, one will not be able to acquire these skills in the usual manner. There will be no teachers provided by the culture; no training will be available. One's desire will of necessity need be nearly an obsession. The work, the time and effort required, may seem disproportionate to the desire. One will likely decide to pursue some other skill, to alter one's desire, to attune one's desire to those regarded as useful by the culture.

What happens if one persists in the pursuit of useless skills? It is unlikely that an entirely unforeseen activity will be invented, so one will work in the shadows of an already established tradition. But, at least at the outset, one will work alone, without guides or guidelines. The wheel will likely be reinvented accidentally and often. (Reinventing the wheel is useful in the pursuit of useless skills.) But the wheel is not a part of the desire, so it will be discarded—discarded not as useless, but as useful, therefore inappropriate to the pursuit. One trains by sorting and wandering, sifting, brooding, drifting, gathering and discarding, always discarding. This is a nomadic pursuit, not necessarily directionless or circuitous, but always everything but the steady step along a straight and narrow path. This is the crooked path, and its passage is along the low road.

This autodidact will learn to do things that others have no desire to do, that others are not allowed to do, that others are not able to think of doing. This is obvious from the outside looking in, but only acknowledged by the dominant culture in moods of elitist condescension. The normative reaction of the dominant culture will be derision or a haughty indifference. Structural superiority, however, permits itself the privilege of praising from a position of ignorance. This is a method that attempts to appropriate the useless. A cursory glance at recent cultural history in America alone reveals several instances of this. There is only one way around this: if one is truly committed to the practice of useless skills, one must be constantly on guard against one's own tendencies towards usefulness. (3.12.01)

John Lowther (Atlanta, GA): Unacknowledged and unrightful heir to Castle Lowther in Scotland, John Lowther is the locus of blame for the magazine *108* and the press 3rdness. Called Loungechair by his friends. Slurs. Implicated in the Atlanta Poets Group but maintains deniability. Quit writing to improvize for a year. Loves wiggling his koolaid pupillometry (the price of fixity is unintelligibility after all). Favorite TV show: *Buffy the Vampire Slayer*. Once wrote a poem about a hose and mirror. Keeps his eyes pealed. Talks too much. Put a ferocious whoopin' on Bill Lavender in a Texas ChainLink Death Match. Vegetarian. *You-get-the-idea* poetics. Knows that hats are the new shoes and suspects that Dana is right, that shoes are the new jewelry. Likes Olde English 800. As J. Luther Jondross he stars in many APG Poetry Adventure novels. Is suspicious of your poetics. Says "all language is poetry" and wrote a play about it and talked up a manifesto about it and scraped off the excess to have a sort of painting about it too. Holds to the zzacian dictum "haphazard & deliberate" in most things. Sometimes signs Jennifer Lopez, John Lydon, Jerry Lewis, Jack Lord. Wrote .1. Wrote The Wreadings. Wrote Slurs and Antics (forthcoming from Potes & Poets). Spoke (then wrote) LONG DAY. Paints newspapers and reads trash. Improvizes sonnets too. Spells improvize with a Z. Motto du jour: "Luddites start your engines." p.s. spelled idea rrong.

Dana Lisa Lustig (Atlanta, GA): "Got south" by way of Interstate 95. She originally hails from Queens, New York, but for the past five or so years has lived in Atlanta, where open-toed-shoe season tends to run from mid-April through late October. Her work has been published in *Mirage 4 Period(ical)*, *Ixnay*, *108:98* and *Gestalten*. Additional work is forthcoming in *Facture*.

Camille Martin (New Orleans, LA): Collections of poetry include *sesame kiosk* (Potes and Poets, 2001), *rogue embryo* (Lavender Ink, 1999), *magnus loop* (Chax Press, 1999), and *Plastic Heaven* (Fell Swoop, 1996). She founded and co-curates the Lit City Poetry Reading Series.

from *experience and language as reciprocal* . . . *recognizing to a matter of degree /of unfast night/ experience awakened:* invent and receive . . . performance /recovered/ that recognizes multiple matters of degrees, an inclusive inventing, embracing also its emptiness— a matter and a transparency, roiling gently . . . not /only/ language in the service of experience— an alchemy of experience into language, act of descriptive translation . . . capturing the present concludes it into an idea of the past, a convention of history . . . rather an unfast, a slow detached feast pausing for stretches into the quick of perception and collapsing the hierarchy of tenses . . . what Robin Blaser, writing of Jack Spicer, says "involves a reversal of language into experience, which is not a dialexis between ourselves or a discourse true only to itself, but a broken and reforming language which composes a 'real'" . . . language as experience, which starts the recovery of lost perception . . . its illegibility expands the instant, shatters it into a plural feasible, breaks the poverty of camps (imagination, personality) troubled by experience and language loosened to blur into one another or self/self/other easily slipping into one another (yet these also being discrete and being both and none) to publicly intimate a truce acknowledging their violent and painful origin, proclaiming the emptiness of origins, the legible futility of the original . . . Leslie Scalapino's recovery of a public realm in which convention is not transparent but which consists of bodies in motion shaping speech, speech as bodies in motion; a public world recognized as phenomenological, and just as void of inherent meaning and existence as any other category (Nagarjuna) . . . already the gesture of bringing the recognition of the emptiness of the nominal or conventional into being is subject to this acknowledgment, soon misremembers/dismembers itself . . . breaks /in order to/ re-form then to break again in a different place . . . the murder of one shape suggests a plagiarized and embryonic occasion, unknowing and unraveling redemption . . . night suspended, a puzzle prevails . . . a shadow of its message when public desire resembles errant center leveling the several times . . . intended encounters with ragged witnesses in the town square /merely/ dormant . . . perspective breathes, and is always around the corner from the calm structure of night, to which entrance is suspended . . . /real/ events glide and morph /and/ here one finds the spell of the lingering particular /vividly/ remembered into subtle variations . . . outside ourselves isn't what we feel it to be . . . we as other to ourselves, to a language creating rebel, a something encountering something else /outside/ in the public or outside a group, however amorphously spoken of . . . believing that one thinks deeply, the depth composed of the layering of what is taken for granted as the "real" in private as well as in public . . . muscles/synapses of private/public bodies shape activity (community) and discourse . . . the "composition of the real" takes place on the surface of what is nominally interior or exterior . . . acknowledgment /of depth's conventionality/ laced with despair is hierarchical, nostalgic for ideal states and measured self . . . virginity was never like this . . . but anyway, one doesn't mind saying that one "loves the night" while sensing the impertinence of the history of darkness.

Jerry McGuire (Lafayette, LA): Director of Creative Writing at the University of Louisiana at Lafayette. His first book of poems, *The Flagpole Dance*, was published by Lynx House Press in 1991, and his second, *Vulgar Exhibitions*, by Eastern Washington University Press in 2001, and his second, *Vulgar Exhibitions,* by Eastern Washington University Press in 2001. He has just completed a third manuscript, *The Nicknames,* whose title poem won first prize in the 2000 *Sow's Ear Poetry Review* Competition. He also won the 2001 Publishing Online POL Poetry Contest. Much of his work is poetry, drama, and experimental fiction done in collaboration with musicians, dancers, and visual artists and designed for specific performance environments.

Things not only change, they proliferate. Thus if they get more confusing they also project an ever-increasing range of possibilities, and any artist who pegs him/herself to a "school" or "movement" has missed the point, or a point. Williams wrote about "what is found there," but it's missed more than found, because it isn't resident but transient. "Poetry" isn't a B&B reserved for a special class of genius, though it's treated as such more broadly than my stomach can bear. It isn't a lace-curtain B&B, a rustic B&B, a whites-only B&B, an ethnic-theme B&B, or a psychedelic B&B. It's much more a cardboard box under a bridge where you can hole up with other castaways, and frankly that suits me fine. While visiting, you may babble, rant, clown, comment sensibly on the cruel world, go nostalgic over past glories, celebrate banality or extremity. You may get sick of all these and invent a secret language. None of these is as interesting as the buzz of the aggregate, whether considered technically, aesthetically, psychologically, sociologically, anthropologically, or politically. And no language interests me at all if it's all buzz, if it doesn't have an occasional brick in it. Put that in your cardboard box.

Thomas Meyer (Highlands, NC): Although not a native, Thomas Meyer has lived his entire adult life on a hillside in the mountains of western North Carolina where he has written poems and assisted Jonathan Williams in the publications of the Jargon Society. His most recent book is *At Dusk Iridescent (A Gathering of Poems, 1972–1997)*.

Poetry celebrates not only presence but the multiplicity of presence and the infinite possibilities of *there*. The poem has the power of location, it is a place—an actual (not metaphorical) spatial event of language that begins in the mouth and lungs and moves outward into time, the mind, the body. There it starts, flirts, catches the imagination with abstraction and the ear with concrete patterns, shifts and comes back changing words into things, things into words.

And I might add, as well, a commentary written to accompany hexagram 48 of the *I Ching*:

Deep, inexhaustible, centered source of nourishment and meaning. It receives from and gives back to the individual's experience. What is essential, abundant, unchanging in the human condition. Take care of life's fundamentals. Do not deplete resources. A natural source cared for by man. Mutual concern. Recovery at the bottom, the source returned to upon exhaustion. Personal nurturing to benefit others. The inherent underlying nature of all change. The effort of many is necessary. Use an understanding based on human nature.

A. di Michele (Jackson, MS): Dekonstijl: DesignsEnviromentsSituationsTexts; Jett Design-Build (woodworker/construction); Mississippi Humanities Council (evaluator); New Orleans School for the Imagination (instructor). Recent publications: *The Minarets of Alabama* (Trembling Pillow, 1999), *Black Market Pneuma* (Lavender Ink, 1999), *Flaxen Sprawl* (Semiquasi Press, 2000), *Sentient Mulch* (with K. Chapman, Cowcumber Press, 2001), *Hoof Swarm Among Bridhe Glyphs* (with Amy Trussell, Surregional Press, 2001), *Green Tara Sutra Blues* (Mississippi Proto-Green Party, 2001), *U. S. & 78* (with Holley Blackwell, Horseradish Press, 2001).

THE EXTINCTION OF ABOUT
the problem for the anthropologist is that he does not know how to interpret his experience
hans peter duerr

i wanted to know the exact dimensions of hell
kim gordon

I. INTRA-TRAILS
towards a left-hand "poetics"   /////////////////////////   away from   transcending
(prepositions)   p-o-e-t-i-c-s,   <<poetics>>   (a propos)   this is | the extinction
of about   :of the tension between: documentation and performance   expression
and   impression   experimental and experiential   ozymandias and wormhole
vernacular and mantric   verbal and glyphic | meanderthal   polyamnesia   cognizant
disintegration of   the western (accumulated) "self"   uaohuaohuaohuaoh
uxuaohuxuaohuxao   bio-modular signature of   auto-primeval "sense"   self as embassy
of   subconscious, as go-between   or outpost for de-colonizing   the text   (mojo
hand, graffito gripping the high-five air)   meso-sino axis tracked in   geo-goetic tundra
fevers: crossroads   :about the extinction of: the left-hand path is increasingly less and
less   concerned with academia's role in this   project. and less concerned about being less
concerned with academe power points.   more interested in "channeling" or   being a
conduit :not for "entities"   but rather voids, margins,   de-conceptualized notions of "self"
returning the newly caramelized, primal   "self" to the colonized ruins of   "language" |
"poetry"   self   here   then   as sweatlodge of the everyday,   between the vulgar
tongue and   dreaming-in-tongues: i crouch instead.   the old problem of the   function
of the text-field   being a problem   (absorbed, mulched)   may hoodoo bake the
hagiographers
II. BLACKWORMHOLES & JAGUARSUNSPOTS
when the anthropologists arrive, the gods leave the island
—haitian proverb
there's a hell of a universe next door let's go
—ee cummings
comments/feedback: polyamnesia@hotmail.com

Mark Prejsnar (Atlanta, GA): A native of Stockbridge, Massachusetts, he has lived in many parts of the U.S. and Brazil, residing in Atlanta for the last eight years. He works as a library professional and edits the poetry magazine, *Misc. Proj.*, which has recently launched its second series. He also runs BirdJag Press. His long poem, *Burning Flags* (Atlanta: 3rdness, 1999), appeared as a chapbook. His work has appeared in numerous print and web magazines. Mark is a founding member of the Atlanta Poets Group, the main forum for innovative poetry in northern Georgia over the last four years.

Speaking Live poetry balances on an edge, an edge it carries forward with it; words leaning forward into the future, off balance: unstable
in some ways, there's too much velocity to poetry for generalizations to grab at it
i can only speak for my own practice
for me poetry moves thru 3 movements—when words enkindle in the middle of heartache; when they escape thru the smoke while the prison burns; and when they move outward, finally making their own agenda, expanding social space
this dynamic is intently political; but it can't carry politix forward; the only way to do that is to build a socialist movement, which is another level of praxis; the politix remains encoded in the fire and in the escape from the fire; and in the villages that the words will try to build; the political drives poetry but is not driven by it; the movement outward reorganizes who we are; it's possible that only poetry, only words, can do this; (other media sacrifice too many of the incongruities and grievings, the smashed circuits needed for flight)
out of all this comes glint and sparkle—a riotous life—agreement inhering in words; they buzz all around society and zoom in on it like a lens
(i strongly support contemporary multimedia projects, by the way . . . the effort to "move poetry off the page," as was recently said up in NYC during the Poetry Plastique event; the Atlanta Poets' Groups, with which i've been active for some years, is a prime locus for such work—Atlanta is clearly a hotbed of these newer syntheses; i will almost certainly be more involved with them in the future myself; my stress here reflects the fact that such experiments do sometimes seem to misunderstand how much intensity and unfinished work still resides *in the words*)
the dynamic outward (if i manage it) is probably most alive in the pieces i write for two or more voices—performance pieces not included here; the nature of poetry is to struggle to engulf all uses of language that can be wrenched away from commodification; all utterance that can be lifted into uselessness; this claim is linked to the urgency with which i feel that poetry must begin to understand itself as polyphonic.

Randy Prunty (Atlanta, GA): Recently published in *New Orleans Review, Brown Box, The Chapbook of the Deep South Writers Conference* (1999 John Z. Bennet poetry award winner), *combo, 108, gestalten, mirage #4/period(ical), tripwire* and online at *readme* and *poetpoetzine*. Has a chapbook: *van gogh talks* from 3rdness.

everything that is not the case. the banjo out of its case your internet just in case. you a cast of characters tripping process and product.
how much consciousness to walk across a field?
"enuf to keep the field from bursting into flame."
making carbon out of gas. systems out of smaller systems. it takes discipline to walk across. walking is a simple complex of systems or a poem. a poem marks a possible path tried its remainder an unstable conflux.
sometimes i like examples and sometimes i like cases. why?
example: fillets
case: that pink belly
taps strains operates and plays itself out. come out to play? as opposed to what?
collecting fields and those that case them. vegetables in gardens where they're supposed to be. under common'd things hidden in familiarity.

everything not in the field. everything not fielded. you help my poem. many pages fled across the field. helping you reshepherd them reversing every path.

a collection of theories has a group leader openness basic rules boundaries. the poem writes itself the poem reads itself the poem rewrites itself the poem writes another poem. a group poem wants to live forever designs pockets with practice.

Alex Rawls (New Orleans, LA): Most recent book is *What's Your Sign* (Lavender Ink, 2001).

All of the words (except those used by A. di Michele) and most of the phrases have already been written, so the myth of originality is one we have to outgrow along with Santa and the tooth fairy. In a post-originality world, it seems like the most honest poem is aware of the past and all the written words that came before it. For me, that involves appropriating text to create something that is first an interesting thing, but also something that reflects on the sources and concept of writing. My most recent poems employ MS Word to create new texts from existing texts, calling into question my role in the process, and by extension, the notion of what an author is and what a poem is.

David Thomas Roberts (Midridge, MO): Composer-pianist, writer and visual artist David Thomas Roberts was born in Moss Point, Mississippi, in 1955. He pioneered and named the eclectic piano genre Terra Verde and established himself as a leading composer of New Ragtime with such works as *Roberto Clemente* and *Through the Bottomlands*. His poetry has appeared in many small press journals around the U.S., and his mixed-media paintings have been featured in the British magazine of visionary art, *Raw Vision*. He now lives in the poorest and most remote section of the Missouri Ozarks.

I call myself a *terrain wrangler*, a commandeer of the land's visionary potential, a topographical rowdy bent upon revelation-through-landscape.

Kalamu ya Salaam (New Orleans, LA): Is founder of Nommo Literary Society, a Black writers' workshop; co-founder of Runagate Multimedia; leader of the WordBand, a poetry performance ensemble; and moderator of e-Drum, a listserv of more than 1,500 Black writers and ethnically diverse supporters of literature. His latest book is *360° Revolution of Black Poets,* edited with Kwame Alexander. Salaam's latest spoken word CD is *My Story, My Song*. He is a 1999 senior literature fellow of the Fine Arts Work Center in Provincetown, Massachusetts. *The Magic of Juju: Appreciation of the Black Arts Movement* is forthcoming from Third World Press. Salaam can be reached at kalamu@aol.com.

James Sanders (Atlanta, GA): Is some part of the Atlanta Poetry Group.

Love Connection: A Manifesto

Basically when I'm writing a poem I try to be Chuck Woolery on *Love Connection* (but without the hair, which is the color of a heart at the bottom of a swamp). The contestants are the words, or you can think of it as the words being one contestant and your audience as the other contestant (there are two axes). After all (this parallel even works within the game show itself) while Chuck is earnestly trying to facilitate the love connection between the contestants (the contestants can be thought of as [1] the contestants and [2] the audience, and Chuck attempts to love connect them both) he's also interested in the audiences, not to mention busy maintaining an adequate level of nonchalance (which is important to the other audience, the TV audience). In any case, as a poet you try to be a "host" (being the host is like being the space in a quadrilateral* balancing two contestants and two audiences [one immediate and one mediate]*—and the sides of the quadrilateral are the poem and its about bringing the words together in front of audiences [although generally all you care about are the contestants and the immediate audience]) but not the host of Wheel of Fortune (which Chuck Woolery hosted prior to Pat Sajak) where the host is basically a narrator and the contestants are competitors in a zero sum game. The "contestants" (words, audience, etc.) in *Love Connection* are creative participants rather than competitive contestants.

How do you create a love connection? Obviously, you don't. You just show up every day (and sure, you have to have the job, but who knows exactly how that happens) and it either happens or it doesn't and Chuck really doesn't care whether it does (well he might, but ultimately he doesn't [it's the nonchalance]); Chuck realizes that he can't do anything directly (the contestants are active) but he listens and tries to recognize and refract with the goal of love connection in mind (among other things, one of the other things being entertaining the audiences and himself), and hopefully the contestants go home together.

* Insert diagram.

** The studio audience in *Love Connection* plays an active role in determining the outcome of the game unlike most other game shows (of course there's *Price is Right* but its certainly different in *Price is Right* where the audience member steps out of the chorus and where the audience as chorus acts only as a guide): the audience in *Love Connection* can be a guide in that it reacts like most audiences do to entertainment but it also has the limited power to select which contestants can go on a date with each other (at least within the game [as far as that goes]) because it provides the default option in case the contestant wants another chance if he/she fails to make a love connection the first time (although the studio audience certainly can't prevent anyone from going out with anyone else except with *Love Connection's* money).

Christy Sheffield Sanford (Gainesville, FL): Has received state, regional and national grants including a National Endowment for the Arts Fellowship in Poetry. She is the author of seven books, including *The H's: The Spasm of a Requiem, The Italian Smoking Piece, Only the Nude Can Redeem the Landscape,* and others. Hundreds of her individual pieces have appeared in small press literary magazines, such as *Exquisite Corpse, Central Park, Fiction International,* and *Mississippi Mud.* For fifteen years she pioneered "Genre Fusion" primarily working with fiction and poetry but also with biography and nonfiction. For the last six years, she has been defining Web-Specific Art-Writing. Her online work is indexed at http://fdt.net/~christys.

On "Rachel's Recovery (Fucking with the Angels)"

This epic death scene loosely follows the life and illness of the nineteenth-century French tragedienne, Rachel. In this turbulent passage through space-time, a key thematic focus is the tension freedom and the need for others engenders. The subject of "recovery" in the title is less related to physical illness than to biographic and historic questions, such as how and why legendary figures are presented as they are.

The work was influenced by readings in nineteenth-century French literature. During this period, women's rights were treated less plaintively and more assertively than previously and can be seen in novels by George Sand and Germaine de Staël and in stories about women bent on freedom such as Dumas' *La Dame aux Camélias* and Merimée's *Carmen.* Baudelaire's poems, such as "The Beautiful Dorothea," inspired a few phrases and his feel for the ocean and the voyage inspired wave-like rhythms.

Poetic expressions and fictional narratives are weighted in importance to further a fusion of fiction and poetry. Sets of enlarged phrases and words, mostly nouns of varying degrees of abstraction, are intended to resonate against the narrative, which surrounds them. In physics, resonance refers to a vibrating body's ability to reinforce the vibrations of another body on the same frequency. This metaphorically reflects my attempt to energize the work internally.

Lorenzo Thomas (Houston, TX): Editor of *Sing the Sun Up: Creative Writing Ideas from African American Literature* (Teachers & Writers, 1998) and author of several collections of poems. He teaches at the University of Houston. His critical study, *Extraordinary Measures: Afrocentric Modernism and 20th-Century American Poetry* was published by The University of Alabama Press.

Poems can be riddles or trumpets; as clever as a spider's web or as obvious as elephants.

In our time, here, we need poems that comment boldly on the society we live in. This does not mean, however, that such poems must necessarily be strident.

As a poet, I am heir to several traditions, not the least of which is the Blues—a form that is immediate and timeless, built upon a standardized stanza that remains capable of infinite personalized variation. You can listen to the records of the 1940s and 50s—to Elmore James or Weldon "Juke Boy" Bonner—and hear how every player invented his own sound for the electric guitar, much as each singer developed his or her own signature approach to the lyric that, whispered or shouted, is always within the range of everyday conversation. Except that it is a conversation made magic by the poetry in it.

But I am also not afraid to employ the techniques of surrealism or the "breath unit."

I will be pleased if some reader finds in my poems a note of solace, a syllable of wit, a breath of truth. These poems, true enough, are essays in self-discovery; but I hope that they might also assist others along the path.

Stephanie Williams (New Orleans, LA): A professional book publicist, and is actively involved in the Publisher's Association of the South and the New Orleans Gulf South Booksellers' Association. Her work has appeared in such publications as Naropa University's *Bombay Gin, PersePhonic,* and *Mungo vs Ranger.* She has performed her work at venues across the country and is currently working on a poet's opera of New Orleans, a collection of short fiction, and a collection of poetry.

A Brief Statement of Auto-Poesis:
From the world singing itself into being, to investigations of line and play, to each word for its own self, and the way drunkards walk on garbage-strewn streets, the composition of a poem, of poetry is interpellation—all (language, symbol, image) is called into being at the service of the poet, who is at the same time being made of will, or chance. Each thing brings into the poem and changes those things outside, and so are the things outside also changed. What is outside? What separate? Of what? From what? As a paradigm, poetry implies by its existence that there is speech, song, movement outside poetry, before and in ignorance of a reader of a specific text who may skip words or lines, may speak in a dialect that creates unintended rhythm, who repeats, stammers, stutters, goes on and on. A reader who becomes, for a time, in that world into which she is sung, a poem arising now, or a part of an ancient genetic song, erasing itself, a palimpsest, forever gone, momentarily changed. So there is time, and the effect of it on the body and form of both the poem and the poet. And all that "out there" out there. Light and where it falls, the sound of cool water, and fondness, burning.

Andy Young (New Orleans, LA): Her chapbook, *mine,* was published by Lavender Ink in April 2000. She received a 2001 fellowship from the Louisiana Division of the Arts and was the 1999 winner of the Marble Faun Award, given by the Faulkner Society. Her poems have appeared in such publications as *Exquisite Corpse, mind the gap, New Laurel Review,* and Dublin's *The Stinging Fly.* She is a creative writing instructor at the New Orleans Center for Creative Arts/Riverfront and at the New Orleans School for the Imagination.

I wish I could speak in italics, that the voice that came from my throat could represent that strange, leaning font that has been creeping into my well-behaved, "regular" lines of late. I think it would sound lilting, metallic, and like it came from a wet cave. So far, I have only been able to give it rein on the page, though I have not given up hope. The italic voice is bigger than me. It feels other. I try to tune into it and hear what it says so that I may represent it accurately. It is the voice of the night, the voice of my echo. I grew up in the mountains of southern West Virginia, and it lives in the hills there. I live, now, in New Orleans, and it rises from the musty cracks of the sidewalks and from the residue of souls that have passed through its decay. This voice feels like a whisper whooshing through my blood. It compels me to seek the music of words to contain it.

Seth Young (Marietta, GA): Is the Production Editor for *Facture*. He has written and lived in various places throughout the South.

Grilled Catfish

2 catfish fillets (thin)
2 lemons (big)
1 tsp. blackened fish seasoning
1 tsp. Creole seasoning
1 tsp. Greek seasoning

To have grilled catfish you must first know how to make a boat with tin foil: simply fold over a 1' x 1' strip of tin foil and mold outer edges into a quarter-inch hull with your fingers. Then, lay catfish filets in bottom of boat, visceral up, as if in life swimming opposite directions. Cut lemons and squeeze juice on filets. (Should be extra juice in bottom of boat when you are done.) Sprinkle Creole, Greek, and blackened fish seasoning evenly on filets. Place boat on hot grill and let fish cook until they are tender to the fork. (Juice in bottom of boat is nearly gone by now.) Garnish with lemon wedges and parsley if desired. Side suggestions: steamed new potatoes and corn on cob (grilled half-shucked in foil), and rolls. Serve with a white wine, iced tea, or mineral water.